The West Cornwall Railway

Truro to Penzance

by
S.C. Jenkins & R.C. Langley

THE OAKWOOD PRESS

© Oakwood Press, S.C. Jenkins & R.C. Langley 2002

First published in 2002 in conjunction with a major exhibition entitled '150 Years of the Railway to Penzance' held at the Penlee House Gallery & Museum, Penzance.

British Library Cataloguing in Publication Data
A Record for this book is available from the British Library
ISBN 0 85361 589 6

Typeset by Oakwood Graphics.
Repro by Ford Graphics, Ringwood, Hants.
Printed by Cambrian Printers, Aberystwyth, Ceredigion.

The Penzance station's throat and view towards Marazion in August 1948.
P.J. Garland Collection

Title page: The West Cornwall Railway seal includes representations of the ancient arms, or heraldic devices, of Penzance, Truro, Falmouth and Helston. The seal dates from 1846, the optimistic 'promotional' stage of the railway's history - as built, there was no good reason for including Falmouth or Helston in the design though, it has to be said, there were no more enthusiastic celebrations of the opening of the railway than those at Helston. *Penlee House Collection*

Front cover: A 'Duke' class 4-4-0 is seen at Penzance in this *c.*1905 postcard view of Penzance station. 'Cornish Riviera Express' stock can be clearly seen in the foreground.
John Alsop Collection

Rear cover, top: The Railway Clearing House map showing lines in west Cornwall. The GWR bus routes are also marked.
Rear cover, bottom: A contemporary postcard view of Redruth, looking west towards Penzance. Carn Brea is prominent in the background. *John Alsop Collection*

Published by The Oakwood Press (Usk), P.O. Box 13, Usk, Mon., NP15 1YS.
E-mail: oakwood-press@dial.pipex.com
Website: www.oakwood-press.dial.pipex.com

Contents

	Introduction	4
Chapter One	The Hayle Railway	5
Chapter Two	An Important Undertaking - The West Cornwall Railway	22
Chapter Three	Operating the West Cornwall Railway	45
Chapter Four	Loss of Independence - The Associated Companies and Great Western Railway Take Control	62
Chapter Five	Subsequent History of the West Cornwall Line	99
Chapter Six	The Stations and Route - Truro to Carn Brea	145
Chapter Seven	The Stations and Route - Camborne to Penzance	177
Chapter Eight	Penzance and the Railway	221
Chapter Nine	Into the Millennium	233
	Acknowledgements	236
	Bibliography and Further Reading	237
	Index	239

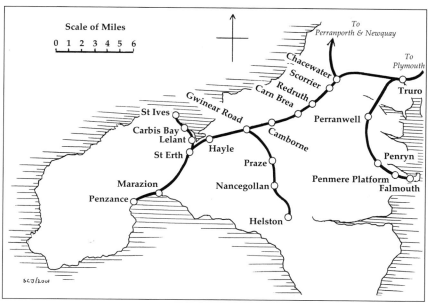

Introduction

In 1968, G.H. Anthony wrote an Oakwood Press book entitled *The Hayle, West Cornwall and Helston Railways* which was - as its name implied - a combined history of three distinct railways in West Cornwall. In this publication (Oakwood Library No. 21) Mr Anthony provided a fine introduction to the West Cornwall Railway, the reading and re-reading of which has given immense pleasure over the years, as well as prompting further research.

G.H. Anthony's book focused primarily upon the earlier periods of railway history in West Cornwall and, for this reason, a number of important developments were omitted, including the rebuilding of stations towards the end of the 19th century, the growth of tourist traffic, the introduction of Great Western Railway (GWR) road motor services, and the development of train services.

The present volume is an entirely new work, based upon primary sources. The authors have focused on the West Cornwall Railway Company and the lines it bequeathed to the Associated Companies and the Great Western Railway, at the same time aiming to fill in the gaps in G.H. Anthony's account. The Penlee House Museum & Gallery in Penzance is holding an exhibition in 2002 to celebrate the 150th anniversary of the opening of the West Cornwall line and it is appropriate that this book should be published to coincide with the exhibition.

This new history of the West Cornwall Railway (WCR) adopts a broadly chronological framework. Chapter One deals with the pioneering Hayle Railway and Chapters Two and Three with the history and operation of the West Cornwall Railway, from its incorporation in 1846 until its loss of independence in 1866. The next two chapters cover the subsequent history of the West Cornwall Railway main line during the GWR and British Railways periods, and these are followed by a detailed examination of the stations and route of the line. Chapter Eight is an introductory study of the impact of the railway on Penzance and the surrounding district. The concluding chapter entitled 'Into the Millennium', looks towards the future and, at the same time, attempts to place the story of the West Cornwall Railway into a wider historical context.

The text has been supported by numerous photographs, and also track plans prepared by Mike Jolly, to whom the authors owe a particular debt.

A cautionary note - over the years the route between Truro and Penzance was 'improved' at various places and times and distances quoted must be related to the historical context in which they are given.

It is hoped that this new history will be of interest to railway enthusiasts, model makers, local historians, holidaymakers and other visitors to West Cornwall; *The West Cornwall Railway* should also form a useful companion volume to the Oakwood Press history of *The Helston Branch* (1992) - which contains much additional detail and photographs relating to the Helston Railway and its junction with the West Cornwall main line at Gwinear Road.

Stanley C. Jenkins & Roger Langley
2002

Chapter One

The Hayle Railway

Situated in an isolated position, at the western extremity of the south-west peninsula, Cornwall has always been regarded as a somewhat remote and mysterious area. This was especially true before the Industrial Revolution and the development of rail transport; in those far off days, the largely Celtic inhabitants of Cornwall were imagined to be semi-primitive barbarians who devoted much of the time to their favourite activities of smuggling and ship-wrecking.

Few travellers from 'up-country' ever ventured beyond the River Tamar, and those that did were not impressed by the desolate moors and savage coastlines of this far-western county. 'Cornwall', wrote one Tudor visitor, 'is a pore and very barren countrey of all maner of thing except tyn and fysshe'!

In reality, Cornwall was the surviving remnant of the ancient Celtic kingdom of Dumnonia which, in pre-Roman times, had encompassed much of the West Country peninsula. The Roman occupation had very little impact on Cornwall, but in 710, during the Anglo-Saxon period, King Ine of Wessex fought against Geraint of Dumnonia and in 722 penetrated as far west as the River Hayle. The indigenous people of Cornwall nevertheless continued to enjoy a large measure of independence until the 9th century, when Egbert of Wessex defeated a mixed force of Celts and Vikings at the Battle of Hingston Down in 835.

The Anglo-Saxon conquest of Cornwall was finally completed during the reign of Aethelstan, King of Wessex, and by the time of the Norman Conquest Cornwall had been assimilated into Wessex. It was, by then, regarded as an English county - although it was in fact the remaining portion of Dumnonia, rather than a West Saxon 'shire' like Devon or Dorset. Moreover, Cornwall retained many distinctive Celtic features; its villages, for example, tended to be scattered clusters of farmsteads and hamlets, rather than nucleated settlements such as those found in supposedly 'Saxon' areas of England.

Pre-Railway Transport

The Romans had taken little interest in the exploitation of Cornwall's mineral resources - ample supplies of tin being readily available in Iberia. Perhaps for this reason, the main Roman road network does not appear to have extended beyond *Isca* (Exeter). The Medieval rulers of England generally made at least some attempt to keep the Roman roads in a reasonable state of repair, but as such roads had never existed in the far West, wheeled transport remained virtually non-existent in Cornwall until the 18th century.

There were, it is true, two recognised land routes into Cornwall, one of which passed through Okehampton and Launceston while the other, more southerly route, involved an often hazardous river crossing at Cremyll Ferry near Plymouth. Neither of these routes would have been suitable for wheeled traffic, and most long distance journeys were taken on foot or horseback. Heavy goods, such as loads of Cornish tin, were typically sent 'up country' on pack horses, ponies or mules. Pack saddles were sometimes used, but hay, corn, timber or similar consignments were piled up on special wooden saddles; tin was carried by teams of perhaps 80 mules, two sacks being carried by each animal.

As roads, as we know them, simply did not exist in the far South-West in pre-industrial times, land transport could sometimes be a highly-dangerous activity. Indeed, when Celia Fiennes, the intrepid 17th century topographer, ventured into Cornwall she narrowly escaped serious injury when her horse stumbled into a huge, water-filled pot hole. The rough track upon which she was travelling was, she recalled:

> A deep clay road . . . which, by the rain the night before had made it very dirty and full of water in many places. In the road there are many holes and sloughs wherever there is clay ground, and when, by the rain they are filled with water, it is very difficult to shun danger. Here, my horse was quite down in one of these holes filled with water, but with the good hand of God's Providence, which has always been with me, ever a present help in time of need, I, giving him a good strap, he flounced up again, though he had gotten quite down, his head and all, yet he did retrieve his feet, and got clear of the place with me on his back.

The local road system started to improve during the 18th century, the first turnpike in Cornwall being built between Falmouth, Truro and Grampound during the 1750s. In 1759, an Act was passed 'For Making a Road, or Repairing a Road, from Launceston to Camelford, Wadebridge, St Columb and Truro', and in the next few years many other Cornish roads were progressively improved. There were, on the other hand, very few wheeled vehicles, and in the 1760s the brother of Sir Humphry Davy recalled that when his mother was a girl 'there was only one cart in the town of Penzance, and . . . if a carriage appeared in the streets it attracted universal attention'.

Water transport offered a partial alternative to the hazardous road conditions which had prevailed in Cornwall for so many years, and in this context it is interesting to recall that small vessels were able to travel upstream on incoming tides to places such as Truro or Lostwithiel, or to smaller ports such as Gweek near Helston or Devoran on Restronguet Creek. In this way, the benefits of coastal transport could be extended inland to places sited at some distance from the sea. On the other hand, many population centres or mining areas were situated at some distance from navigable rivers or tidal creeks and, in such circumstances, water transport was clearly of very little use.

Canals seemed to offer an ideal solution to the limitations of river transport in Cornwall, and in the 18th century ambitious landowners and entrepreneurs planned a variety of canal schemes. In 1796, for instance, it was suggested that a waterway might be dug between the Hayle River at St Erth and the Helford River near Gweek, thereby creating a useful link between the north and south coasts of Cornwall. The proposed canal would have been about 14 miles long, with inclined planes at St Erth, Bosence, Drym, Nancegollan, Trannack, Mellangoose and Gweek. A route was surveyed by Robert Fulton (1765-1815), the American engineer, who estimated that the 'Helston Canal' would cost £32,000.

The large number of inclined planes that would have been required underlines the fact that Cornish topography was not really suitable for ambitious canal schemes, and it perhaps comes as no surprise that the Hayle to Helford canal scheme was never implemented. Five years later there were proposals for a 7 mile 50 chain canal from Hayle to Carwinin Bridge, near Camborne. The surrounding terrain was such that this scheme would have involved an inclined plane at Angarrack; alternatively, boats could have been conveyed uphill via a flight of locks, but in either case the civil engineering required would have been considerable.

Coastal transport was obviously of immense significance in all periods of Cornish history, and in addition to the many natural havens around the indented Cornish coastline, man-made harbours such as Portreath became increasingly important during the heyday of Cornish mining. There remained, however, the problem of transporting tin or copper ore between the mines - most of which were sited at some distance inland - and the nearest convenient ports. As Cornwall was considered unsuitable for canal building, the transport needs of the local mining industry were ultimately satisfied by the provision of tramways and railways.

The Industrial Revolution in Cornwall

Cornwall is now regarded primarily as a holiday area, but it is also an important mining region. Rich deposits of tin, copper and (more recently) china clay have traditionally formed the basis of Cornish mining activities, and these extractive industries have always required good transport facilities on land and by sea. Tramways or wagonways had been employed in mines since the Tudor period, wooden rails being used to provide a guided path for colliery wagons or tubs. Iron rails were later introduced in place of the earlier wooden rails, the usual form of permanent way on colliery railways being formed of 'T'-shaped rails resting on stone blocks.

At the same time as the Industrial Revolution gathered momentum during the 18th century, the Cornish mines exhausted seams near the surface and went deeper. As a consequence they needed large numbers of steam pumping engines to prevent the workings from flooding. The first practical steam pumping engine, was invented by Thomas Newcomen (1663-1729) of Dartmouth, and is said to have been built near Dudley in 1712. This worked on the vacuum principle, whereby steam was introduced into the cylinder and then condensed by a jet of cold water; the partial vacuum thus produced caused the piston to descend, and by this action a pump was raised by means of an overhead beam. Newcomen's engines were simple but effective, although at the same time they consumed large amounts of coal. In later years, James Watt (1736-1819), William Murdoch (1754-1839) and other inventors introduced improvements such as two-stroke pistons, centrifugal governors, safety valves and other innovations, as a result of which the steam engine was perfected as a power source and a potential form of motive power.

In the latter context, it is interesting to recall that the very first locomotives were developed in Cornwall. In 1784, William Murdoch constructed a working model and tested it at Redruth while, in 1796, Richard Trevithick (1771-1833), the son of a Cornish mine manager, built a similar mobile steam engine. Trevithick's locomotive made its first really successful run at Camborne in 1801, but as the roads of the period were so bad, he decided to run his engine on rails, and in this way the world's first railway locomotive was created.

In 1804, a Trevithick locomotive demonstrated its hauling capabilities on the Penydarren tramroad in South Wales, while another Trevithick engine was taken to Tyneside, where it was seen by the young George Stephenson. Famously, in 1808, Trevithick's locomotive *Catch-me-who-can* was displayed on a circular test track in north-west London, passengers being allowed to ride behind the engine for one shilling per ride!

Early Railway Development in Cornwall

The conditions needed for pioneering railway developments were present in abundance in early 19th century Cornwall. The local tin and copper mines were at their peak in terms of production and investment, and the mines were already served by short lengths of primitive tram lines. Capital for further investment was readily available, and Cornwall was replete with capable engineers and surveyors with the ability to plan and construct longer, more ambitious lines. Although the earliest tramways would initially be worked by horses, the level of expertise was such that, within a very few years, Cornish lines would be worked by steam locomotives - thereby becoming railways in the modern sense of the term.

Inevitably, Cornish landowners, mine owners and entrepreneurs were active railway promoters, some of the earliest lines in the country having been built in Cornwall. It was realised that the existing system of transporting ore to the coast by trains of pack horses was totally inadequate in relation to the output of tin and copper during the early 19th century, while primitive transport of this kind made it difficult to import large amounts of coal for the pumping engines. Accordingly, on 25th October, 1809, construction of Cornwall's first railway was started at Portreath Harbour, when the prominent mineowner Lord de Dunstanville laid the first rail of the Poldice Tramroad.

The Poldice to Portreath tram line was built as a transport link between the copper mines around Scorrier and St Day, and the harbour at Portreath - which had itself been constructed in the 18th century as an outlet for local copper ore. The first section of the line was probably in use by 1810, and the tramway was in full use by 1812. It was worked entirely by horses, and its permanent way was formed of 'L'-shaped cast-iron rails resting on square granite sleepers. A contemporary description states that 'the wheels of the carriages run on cast iron, which facilitates in an extraordinary manner the progress of the vehicles and greatly lessens the force of animal exertion'.

The Poldice Tramroad yielded reasonable returns to its adventurers, though declining with the fortunes of the mines from, for example, £600 shared in 1831 to £150 in 1842. Needless to say, there were also tangible benefits to the mine owners, often the selfsame adventurers.

In 1819, a Prospectus was issued for construction of a tramway from Hayle to Helston and, in the early 1820s, the pioneer railway promoter William James (1771-1837) surveyed a number of possible lines in the Cornish mining areas. In the event, these schemes were abortive, but they served to focus attention on the concept of improved transport links between the mining districts and convenient ports such as Hayle and Portreath.

On 17th June, 1824 the Redruth & Chasewater Railway [*sic*] was sanctioned by Parliament with powers for the construction of a mineral line from the Gwennap mines to Narabo Quays, near Devoran on Restronguet Creek. The line was officially opened on 30th January, 1826, when some of the promoters rode by gravity from Wheal Buller Mine to Devoran, the return journey being made behind a horse. This 4 ft gauge line was laid with wrought-iron rails resting on stone blocks, which left a smooth central path for the horses employed to haul the ore wagons. Traffic soon reached 60,000 tons per annum, and by the 1830s the Redruth & Chasewater Railway was making profits of £3,000 a year.

Another line promoted at this time was the 2 ft 6 in. gauge Pentewan Railway, which was built to convey china clay from clay pits around St Austell to the nearby harbour at Pentewan, a distance of four miles. The short tramway, opened in 1829, was worked by a combination of horses and gravity. At a later date, both the Redruth & Chasewater Railway and the Pentewan line adopted locomotive haulage, though in the short term they remained simple, horse-worked tramways.

The Bodmin & Wadebridge Railway was Cornwall's very first steam-worked railway. It was incorporated on 23rd May, 1832, with a capital of £22,500. The first section was opened between Wadebridge and Bodmin on 4th July, 1834, and the line was completed throughout to Wenford Bridge on 30th September. This small system encompassed 22 miles of entirely self-contained track, there being no connection to any other lines. The Bodmin & Wadebridge Railway was, nevertheless, a flourishing concern, which formed a useful transport link between the navigable River Camel and Wenford Bridge; there were also two short branches to Bodmin and Ruthern Bridge.

The line carried sand and manure from Wadebridge to the nearby farmlands, while in the opposite direction a profitable traffic in mineral exports soon developed. Coal was also conveyed to Bodmin and other places *en route*, the price of coal having fallen from 25 shillings to 15 shillings a ton following the opening of the railway. This pioneering Cornish railway was initially worked by a small 0-6-0 engine known as *Camel*, though a second locomotive named *Elephant* was obtained in 1836. Passengers were carried on the 'main line' between Wadebridge and Bodmin, with occasional excursions on the Wenford Bridge branch, which was otherwise a goods-only line.

Formation of the Hayle Railway

The obvious success of the Redruth & Chasewater Railway had led to demands for the promotion of further lines, one of which was the Hayle Railway from Hayle to Redruth. The Hayle Railway Company was incorporated by Act of Parliament on 27th June, 1834, with powers for the construction of a railway commencing at Hayle Foundry in the parish of St Erth, and terminating at Tresavean in the parish of Gwennap, in the County of Cornwall. The authorised capital was £64,000, with a further £16,000 by mortgage.

Hayle was, at that time, an important mining port and industrial centre at the mouth of the Hayle River. Two famous Cornish firms were already well-established in the area. One of these owned the smelting works at Copperhouse, in the parish of Phillack, while the other operated the Hayle Foundry in the parish of St Erth. Established around 1780, the Hayle Foundry was one of the largest of its kind in south-western England, and its mighty pumping engines were employed in mines and water works throughout the British Isles and indeed all over the World.

There was incessant rivalry between Harvey & Co. and the neighbouring Copperhouse Company. Both of these undertakings built mine engines, marine power plants and other equipment on a large scale, while Harvey's were also ship builders, timber merchants and general traders. Harvey's and the Copperhouse Company were also the joint proprietors of Hayle Harbour, and both companies were keenly interested in the provision of a rail link from this flourishing port to the booming mining districts around Redruth, Camborne and Gwennap.

As first authorised in 1834, the Hayle Railway included branch lines to Tresavean, Helston, Roskear, Wheal Crofty and the Sandhills at Hayle, but on 4th July, 1836 the company obtained a new Act, permitting deviations of the original route, and a branch from Pool to Portreath in place of the line to Helston.

In engineering terms, the authorised route from Hayle to Redruth presented a particular problem for the early railway engineers. It was thought at that time that locomotives would be unable to cope with significant gradients, and the first railways were therefore planned on canal principles with long, level stretches interspersed with inclined planes. In the case of the Hayle line, the route started at sea level at Hayle, and then climbed to its summit level on an inclined plane at Steamer's Hill, near Angarrack. Nearing Camborne, a second incline at Penponds would carry the railway up towards Pool and Redruth.

Other inclines would be required on the Portreath branch at Portreath, and on the Tresavean branch near its junction with the main line at Pool. It was intended that these four inclined planes would be rope-worked, the inclines at Angarrack and Portreath being worked by stationary engines, while those at Penponds and Redruth would be operated on the counter-balance principle. Apart from the four inclines, the other notable engineering feature would be an interesting drawbridge over a navigable channel at Hayle, which would enable the railway to reach the Hayle Foundry without impeding navigation.

The railway builders made very good progress, and the Hayle Railway main line was substantially complete between Hayle and 'Pool', which later became

Carn Brea, by 1837. Good progress had also been made on the important branch line from Pool to Portreath, and it was therefore decided that the line would be brought into operation between Hayle, Pool and Portreath, before the main line was completed through to its eastern terminus at Redruth.

At this juncture, a minor problem arose when the Directors, who were understandably keen to see the line in operation, suggested that the railway might be opened in the first instance to a temporary western terminus at Copperhouse. This would allow sufficient time for the installation of the lifting bridge at Hayle, which was a relatively complex structure that needed considerable attention and adjustment before it could be brought into use. Unfortunately, Henry Harvey, the owner of the Hayle Foundry, objected to this course of action on the grounds that it would harm his business and place the rival Copperhouse Company in an advantageous position.

The Hayle Railway Act had stipulated that the line should be 'completed before opening', and Mr Harvey insisted that this clause should be obeyed to the letter. There was, in consequence, no question of the railway being opened from a temporary terminus, and the troublesome drawbridge was therefore installed without further delay. This task having been accomplished, the railway was opened from Hayle to 'Pool' (Carn Brea), and on to Portreath, on Saturday 23rd December, 1837.

The Opening of the Line

The opening was celebrated in comparatively modest style by a locomotive bringing a train of coal wagons from Hayle to Carn Brea, and then proceeding along the branch line to Portreath in order to collect another train. The engine gave a good performance and, to underline the historic nature of the occasion, 'there was a firing of guns and a display of colours for the occasion'.

A few days later, on 29th December, 1837, *The Royal Cornwall Gazette* described the opening as follows:

> On Saturday last the locomotive engine intended for the Hayle line brought up a train of coal wagons from Hayle to the Carn Brea mines; and immediately after proceeded to Portreath and took a similar train from that place to the aforesaid mines, doing its work admirably.
>
> Great praise is due to the company's agents for their indefatigable exertions in the execution of this important undertaking; for although there is still a great deal of work to accomplish, yet the most sanguine could scarcely have anticipated that the engine would have travelled such a large portion of the line - more particularly the whole of the Portreath line - at so early a period.

The wording of this extract would suggest that the Hayle line was only partly finished at the time of its opening, and although it is reasonable to assume that the main line from Hayle to Pool was substantially complete, the situation *vis-à-vis* the Portreath branch was clearly rather different. On the other hand, it seems likely that the Sandhills branch, giving access to Hayle Wharves, would have been brought into use at an early date, together with the short mineral branches to Roskear and North Crofty. The last-mentioned lines provided a link to the 'Carn Brea mines', which were mentioned specifically in the opening report published in *The Royal Cornwall Gazette*.

Work was, meanwhile, proceeding apace on the remaining part of the main line between Portreath Junction and Redruth, and this section was ready for opening by the following Spring. The route was officially opened on Thursday 31st May, 1838, on which day the Hayle Railway main line was completed throughout between Hayle and Redruth. It is interesting to note that the official opening of the Hayle Railway coincided with the inauguration of the initial section of the Great Western Railway main line between Paddington and Maidenhead.

It had originally been anticipated that the public opening would take place on 4th June, 1838, but as this was Whit Monday the Directors decided that there would be so many high-spirited spectators that 'accidents might occur', and the opening was therefore postponed until 11th June. The branch from Redruth Junction to Tresavean was opened just 12 days later and thus, by the middle of 1838, the 17¼ mile Hayle Railway system was completed.

Although the Hayle Railway was essentially a localised mineral line that was built primarily to serve the various mines and industrial concerns around Hayle and Redruth, the new line was more advanced than the Redruth & Chasewater Railway in that it was worked by locomotives from its inception. Indeed, *Cornubia* - the very first engine to run on the Hayle Railway - was actually built at Hayle for use on the line in 1838. (Further details of *Cornubia* and the other Hayle Railway locomotives will be given in a subsequent chapter.)

The new line was single track throughout, except for short sections of double track on the inclines. Starting at Hayle, the railway ran along the side of Copperhouse Creek, and ascended the 1 in 10 Angarrack Incline. Beyond, the route proceeded generally eastwards to Penponds, where the second incline ascended at 1 in 22 towards Camborne. Continuing east-north-eastwards, the line ran via Pool (later Carn Brea) to its eastern terminus at Redruth. Branches ran north-westwards from Pool to Portreath, and south-eastwards from Redruth Junction to Tresavean, while shorter mineral lines served Hayle wharves, North Crofty and Roskear.

The distance from Hayle to Redruth was 9 miles 44 chains, while the branch from Redruth Junction to Tresavean had a length of 2 miles 55 chains. The Portreath branch, which diverged from the main line at Portreath Junction, to the east of Pool, was 3 miles 6 chains in length, whereas the Hayle branch was only 25 chains long. The other branch lines to Roskear and North Crofty had lengths of 77 chains and 48 chains respectively - the total length of the Hayle Railway main line and its branches being 17 miles 15 chains. The permanent way was formed of 'T'-shaped rails resting on stone blocks, and the entire system was built to a gauge of 4 ft 8½ inches.

The western end of the line below the Angarrack Incline was initially worked by horses - although *Cornubia* had presumably been hauled up the incline when it left Hayle for the first time and made its way to the part of the line that would be worked by locomotive power. In 1843, it was decided that locomotives could be regularly worked over the Angarrack Incline - the rope being used to provide assistance on the ascent, and a means of restraint on the way down.

The Introduction of Passenger Services

The 1834 Hayle Railway Act of Incorporation had provided for the carriage of passengers, but as first opened in 1836 the Hayle line was a goods-only route; passengers were undoubtedly carried on an unofficial basis, but there were no scheduled passenger services. However, the very existence of the new railway led to demands that some provision should be made for the carriage of fare paying passengers and, in response to these demands, a passenger service was introduced on Monday 22nd May, 1843. The Great Day was celebrated in appropriate style, 'amid much public rejoicing, in which the bands of the neighbourhood took part'.

On 26th May, 1843, *The West Briton* newspaper printed the following account of the Opening Day festivities:

HAYLE RAILWAY - On Monday last, this line of railway was opened for the conveyance of passengers and, as no charge was made for that day, the carriages were literally crammed with persons of both sexes, who were anxious to enjoy the luxury of a gratuitous ride. We are glad to learn that although the train went three times over the line during the day, no accident of any consequence occurred.

On that same day, *The Royal Cornwall Gazette* published a useful eye-witness account of this historic occasion, with much interesting detail relating to the operation of the Hayle line. Some of this information is worth quoting:

OPENING OF THE HAYLE AND REDRUTH RAILWAY FOR PASSENGER TRAFFIC - On Monday last, this important line, the benefits of which have hitherto been exclusively confined to the carriage of ore and coal for the mines in the neighbourhood, became for the first time available as a conveyance for passengers through the populous districts with which it communicates . . . The principal benefits arising from this arrangement are the increased facilities it affords of communication between the important districts of Truro, Falmouth, Hayle and Penzance, between which the mail and stage coaches have hitherto been the only conveyances.

To persons sailing by the Hayle steamers, it will be found extremely convenient, the difficulty of the journey to Hayle having been in many cases the chief objection to that route to London.

It having been announced that passengers would be conveyed gratis on the day of opening there was, as might be imagined, no lack of persons desirous of a free passage . . . The first train left Redruth at nine in the morning and was, we need not say, crammed full. Indeed, there could not have been far short of 200 persons crowded upon the wagons and carriages, and very many were disappointed. For the comfort even of the fortunate ones little can be said: those on the trucks being clustered like bees, and the carriages resembling the hold of a slave ship. All however seemed pleased, so great is the charm of gratuitous amusement.

This consignment had hardly left the yard, when the Truro Omnibus, which in order to meet this train had anticipated its usual hour of departure by an hour and a half, arrived at the gate, and loud were the complaints of its disappointed inmates at finding themselves too late.

At this point, *The Royal Cornwall Gazette* pointed out that, although the Hayle Railway had been open for several years, it was little known outside of the

A 1937 view of the Redruth terminus of the Hayle Railway which, from completion of the West Cornwall main line in 1852, became a goods yard. Though 85 years have passed since passengers used the station the train shed, to the left, and goods depot are still recognisable as such. The siding to the left was the only line here converted to mixed gauge and led under a shearlegs, where minor repairs such as wheel changes could be undertaken.

Great Western Society/Reed Collection

The Hayle station of the old Hayle Railway was finally demolished in December 1948, at which time it was claimed to be the second oldest station building on the mainland. This view dates from 1938.   *Great Western Society/Reed Collection*

immediate locality. For this reason, the paper included the following description of the line, as it appeared on the Opening Day:

After leaving the station at Redruth, which is situated just out of the town on the Camborne road, the train proceeded through a short but steep cutting, emerging from which, it came out upon the great embankment under Carn Brea, the most difficult and expensive part of the whole road. The views here are of much interest, the ancient hill rising above it on one side, and the open country to the north of Redruth spread out on the other. A succession of comparatively shallow cuttings leads to the central depot or station of the company, near Wheal Fanny Mine, and from which the Portreath Junction branches off.

After a short stay for coals and water, the train was again in motion, and skirting Cook's Kitchen Mine, of the peculiar workings of which a fine view was afforded, crossed the main road at Camborne, where passengers were put down; from thence for some distance the line proceeds along high ground, commanding fine views of the country around Camborne, until it arrives at the Pen Pond Incline, the descent of which, however, compared at least with the other on the same line, is slight. The weight of the descending train was on this incline counterbalanced by that of another which ascended on the other line.

Leaving this, after passing over an embankment which crosses a wild looking valley near Roseworthy, the train arrived at the great Angarrack Incline, and which indeed deserves the appellation of frightful. At the summit of this a stationary engine is placed, and the carriages being made fast to a stout rope, were slowly let down, so slowly indeed, that anyone disliking the ride down would have time to walk beside it. Arrived at the bottom, the engine was again started, and after running for a mile and a half over a low swampy bottom, came to Copper House.

At Hayle Bridge, the engine and train parted company, and the remaining part of the journey was performed by horses. Although some parts of the road were passed at very great speed, in one or two places not far short of 30 miles an hour, yet the journeys during the day averaged more than an hour and a quarter, which is attributable to the immense crowd of passengers, and the caution consequently required, especially at the inclined plane where half were left down at once. The estimated usual time is three quarters of an hour.

After a short stay at Hayle, the train returned to Redruth, making two subsequent journeys in the course of the day. The weather, with the exception of one or two partial showers, was fair, and the day seemed to be observed as a holiday along the whole line. We have not heard of any accident. The motion, even at the greatest speed, was perfectly easy, a very satisfactory proof of the goodness and stability of the line.

As far as passenger rolling stock was concerned, *The Royal Cornwall Gazette* recorded that the new passenger service had been made possible due to the enterprise 'of an individual at Hayle', who had 'at his own expense fitted up two convenient railway carriages'. Each of these vehicles could accommodate from 20 to 30 people, and they were described as 'omnibusses'. On the opening day, three additional wagons were coupled-up behind the 'omnibusses' to provide sufficient vehicles for the large number of first-day travellers. The 'individual at Hayle' mentioned in this extract was Will Crotch, a Hayle innkeeper.

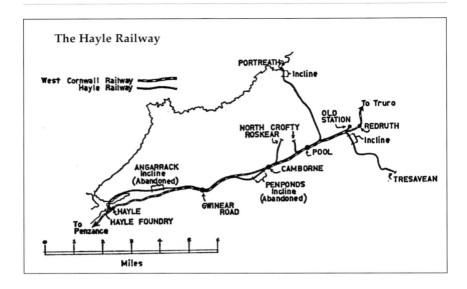

The Hayle Railway

The Line in Operation

It had originally been intended that there would be two daily trains in each direction between Hayle and Redruth, with a running time of around 45 minutes. By July 1844, however, there were three passenger trains in each direction, the times of departure from Redruth being 9.00 am, 12 noon and 5.00 pm, while the balancing northbound services departed from Hayle at 10.00 am, 1.00 pm and 6.00 pm respectively. The journey time was one hour for the 9 mile 44 chain journey - this leisurely timing being due, at least in part, to the need for stops at the top and bottom of the intermediate inclines at Penponds and Angarrack.

The Hayle Railway did not serve Penzance directly, but a service of horse-drawn omnibuses was arranged between Hayle station and Penzance, and between Redruth station and Truro. By this means it was possible to travel through from Truro to Penzance, the fares from Truro being 3s. 3d. for first class, 2s. 3d. for second class, and 2s. for third class travellers. As far as can be ascertained, the 'stations' or recognised stopping places were at Hayle, Copperhouse, Angarrack, Gwinear, Penponds, Camborne, Pool and Redruth. There were no stations on the branch lines, which carried freight traffic only.

Relatively complex track layouts were provided at Pool, and at terminal stations such as Hayle, Redruth and Portreath. As usual on early lines, there were large numbers of spurs and sidings, many of which were reached via wagon turntables. This type of infrastructure was designed for use with large numbers of relatively small wagons, which were frequently attached or detached with the aid of horses or human muscle power. Stables, workshops and maintenance shops were also provided, all of these structures being simple, vernacular style structures reflecting local building practices.

Little is known of the day-to-day working of the Hayle Railway, though it would appear that the first trains to carry passengers were 'mixed' formations that conveyed both passenger vehicles and goods wagons. The line was worked as simply as possible on the 'time interval' system, all pointwork being worked manually. There were no fixed signals, all movements being controlled by hand signals or oral commands.

Mixed trains were apparently run with the passenger vehicles marshalled at the rear and, on approaching Hayle Quays, it became the practice for the passenger stock to be detached while the train was in motion. By this means, they had sufficient momentum to reach the passenger terminus, while the locomotive continued ahead with the freight rolling stock. As might be expected, this mode of operation resulted in several minor accidents, the first of which took place just four months after the introduction of passenger services. On 8th September, 1843 *The West Briton* reported that:

> The passenger coaches had, as usual, been cast off for the terminus before the train reached the branch to the North Quay. The passenger carriages followed the train by the given impetus. The train became derailed before reaching the junction as the rails had been taken up for repairs and not fixed down again, the trucks with the ore were all smashed. The passenger coaches which were following ran into the wreckage, but only a few passengers were bruised, and only slightly.

As a result of this mishap, several people wrote to the paper about the dangerous methods of working employed on the Hayle Railway at that time. One correspondent stated that not only were the passenger carriages detached from moving trains but it was also normal practice for horses to be harnessed to the passenger vehicles while they were still in motion! There were also complaints about people jumping into and out of the moving trains as they approached Hayle station. Although there was no doubt an element of risk in these operations, the prevalence of such seemingly dangerous methods of working suggests that the speed of trains on the Hayle Railway must have been very slow.

As might be expected, the steep inclines at Angarrack and Penponds on the main line, and at Tresavean and Portreath on the branches, were the scenes of numerous minor accidents - most of which involved goods vehicles. On 12th January, 1838, for instance, *The Royal Cornwall Gazette* described an accident that had recently taken place on the Angarrack Incline:

> On Monday last, as the train was returning to Hayle, an accident . . . took place. In descending the incline at Angarrack the conductors did not pay sufficient attention to the drags; a run took place in consequence, and a train of three wagons ran down with tremendous velocity. At the bottom they came into contact with another wagon which had previously been let down . . . the concussion was so great that one of the conductors is said to have been thrown out of one wagon into the other, which was propelled to Hayle, upwards of a mile off, at the rate of at least an hundred miles an hour (!)

Similar incidents occurred during incline working through failures of the couplings or ineffective braking, an accident of this kind being described as follows in *The West Briton*:

A few days since, a very trifling accident occurred at the incline plane leading up from Portreath when two or three of the coal carriages, which had been drawn half-way up the plane, in consequence of the breaking of the hook by which the chain held them ran back with frightful velocity, but with no damage other than the breaking of a shaft of a coal cart.

A further reference to the railway in operation was recounted by the Cornish historian A.K. Hamilton Jenkin (1900-80) in his book *Cornish Seafarers* (1932). Based on oral evidence collected by the equally-famous Cornish scholar R.J. Noall, A.K. Hamilton Jenkin relates the tale of a notorious smuggler called Trevaskis, who persuaded an innocent and unsuspecting miller to store a large consignment of illegal goods on his property. Unfortunately, the smuggled goods were discovered by a perspicacious exciseman, who demanded a large bribe in order to remain silent about the miller's involvement. However, having discovered that the real villain was Trevaskis, the exciseman arrested the culprit.

Having refused to pay a bribe, Trevaskis was told that he would be taken to the assizes, and the smuggler and the triumphant exciseman accordingly set off from West Cornwall *en route* to Bodmin:

At Hayle, the couple boarded the train at the little station which may still be seen in Foundry Square, beneath the arches of the more modern railway line. Passing along under Clifton Terrace and through the grounds of the present Penmare House, the train at length reached the foot of 'Steamer's Hill', near Angarrack, where a stationary engine at that time pulled the trucks up a steep incline to a point near the present Gwinear Road station.

On this occasion, however, the train had not got more than half-way up the incline when the wire rope attached to the front carriage parted. Back rushed the trucks gathering terrible speed, till finally, reaching the bottom, they crashed into a bank and overturned. Strange to relate, few of the passengers were seriously hurt, and only one was killed, that one being the exciseman! With no one who could now act as a witness against him, Trevaskis took his own release, and returned home, amid universal triumph, to his own village.

The story, however, ends on a tragic note. The miller's wife, hearing of Trevaskis's escape, never ceased to reproach her husband for his weakness and folly in having bribed the exciseman, and at length the worry of this preyed on the old man's mind so much that one morning he was found hanging dead from a beam in his own mill.

The Portreath Branch

In retrospect, the Hayle Railway was something of an anachronism by the 1840s. Although it had been worked mainly by locomotives from its inception, the inclined planes belonged to an earlier era of railway operation, and their presence meant that the line from Hayle to Redruth could not easily function as part of a main line link between West Cornwall and the outside world. There were, as a result, suggestions that the Hayle Railway should be completely reconstructed and realigned as a conventional main line route and, as we shall see, this task was finally accomplished in the following decade.

Paradoxically, the goods-only branches to Portreath, Tresavean and elsewhere were nevertheless retained in being for many years - their relatively primitive engineering being perfectly adequate in relation to the carriage of goods traffic. Moreover, these mineral lines and sidings continued to generate heavy traffic and, as such, they remained a valuable adjunct to the main line network in West Cornwall. It would therefore be fitting to conclude this chapter by looking more closely at some of the Hayle Railway's industrial branches and sidings.

Leaving the Hayle Railway main line on the east side of Pool station, the Portreath branch ran generally northwards to Illogan, and thence north-westwards in the direction of Portreath. Nearing its destination, the line turned northwards once again for the final 1 in 7 descent down the incline to Portreath Harbour. The branch was 3 miles 6 chains in length, and single track throughout - apart from the Portreath incline, which was a 26 chain length of double track. Having reached Portreath harbour, the line branched out into several sidings, one of which served a lime kiln, while others gave access to the quays.

The Portreath incline was worked by a stationary engine with two winding drums, one of which coiled, while the other uncoiled the rope. Methods of working the incline may have varied slightly over the years; in the days of the Hayle Railway, it appears that two or three wagons were drawn up or let down the incline at one time, although in GWR days only one vehicle was allowed up or down at any one time. As the rope on this incline was not continuous, the two lines must have been bi-directional, insofar as when a wagon was hauled up the incline, the end of the rope reached the top; it was then ready for attachment to the next descending wagon.

Contemporary references to the Hayle Railway inclines mention the use of a 'rope' to haul vehicles up and down, the obvious inference being that actual ropes were employed. In view of the convenient proximity of rope walks in maritime centres such as Falmouth, it seems likely that hemp ropes were indeed used, and this may explain the comparatively frequent references to the 'rope' breaking in operation. In later years, progress in metal technology and production meant that more reliable steel wire ropes could be employed, and these were certainly used on the Portreath and Tresavean inclines during the 20th century.

Portreath itself was primarily a man-made harbour. In Medieval times, there had been little shelter for any mariners brave or foolhardy enough to use the cove, but in the 18th century a small harbour was established to serve the nearby copper mines. The resulting port facilities were originally known as

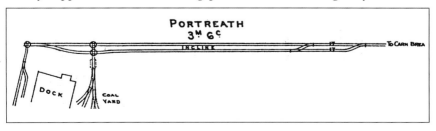

THE INCLINE, PORTREATH.

The Hayle Railway prospered through its mineral traffic, much of which used Portreath harbour. The branch was worked by locomotives as far as the incline heading. On the pier, horsepower reigned supreme. In this undated photograph the winding house can be seen at the top of the incline.

R.C. Langley Collection

Bassets' Cove after the Bassets of Tehidy, who had been responsible for the exploitation of the mineral resources on their land. Various harbour works were constructed, including wharves and a pier or breakwater, though the harbour remained narrow and dangerous - especially during northerly gales when Portreath was exposed to the full force of the Atlantic.

Despite its obvious imperfections, Portreath was a flourishing port, large amounts of copper ore being exported to South Wales, while in the opposite direction incoming cargoes of Welsh coal arrived regularly to serve the needs of the pumping engines at nearby mines. In the early 19th century, before the construction of the Hayle Railway, there had been an attempt to promote a large scale fishing industry at Portreath, new pilchard cellars and other facilities being constructed around 1802.

In its heyday, from about 1840 onwards, Portreath was a place of bustling activity, with traffic arriving and departing on both the Hayle Railway and the earlier Poldice Tramway. The quays would be lined with sailing vessels, with up to a dozen schooners, brigantines or similar craft arriving on every tide. The little port went into decline from about 1870, following the decline in Cornish copper mining, though as late as 8th May, 1873, *The West Briton* noted that, on the previous Sunday, 'upwards of twenty vessels, three of which were steamers, were in the docks at Portreath laden with coals'.

The Tresavean Branch

With a length of 2 miles 55 chains, the Tresavean branch was slightly shorter than the neighbouring Portreath line. This goods-only route diverged from the Hayle Railway main line at Redruth Junction, and immediately doubled at the foot of the half-mile Tresavean (or 'Redruth') Incline. Like the Penponds Incline, the Tresavean Incline worked on the counter-balance principle, the weight of descending vehicles being used to raise ascending wagons by means of a continuous rope that ran between the rails. At the top of the incline, the rope passed from one line to the other in a figure of eight arrangement, incorporating spreading and crown pulleys.

When trains worked over the Tresavean branch, they were stopped at the bottom of the incline so that the engine could be detached. The locomotive then climbed the 1 in 15 incline under its own power and, on reaching the upper level, placed loaded wagons at the top of the incline. These vehicles could thereby form a balancing load for ascending coal wagons - which were hauled up the incline by the weight of the descending traffic. Seven or eight minutes were allowed for this operation, the maximum permitted load being 84 tons, or the equivalent of four loaded goods wagons.

At one point the Tresavean branch ran more or less parallel to the Redruth & Chasewater Railway, but there was no provision for the exchange of traffic and, indeed this would have been difficult in view of the difference in gauge between the two lines. The Tresavean line served several mines and industrial premises, including Wheal Buller, the Cornish Tin Smelting Company and the Redruth Tin Smelting Company.

Chapter Two

An Important Undertaking -
The West Cornwall Railway

Plans are Laid

At the ceremonial opening in Penzance of the rail connection to Truro, on 25th August, 1852, the line was described as 'an important undertaking'. This was a modestly phrased welcome to the most momentous event in the town's history, the forging of the westernmost link in a chain that would soon extend to the rest of mainland Britain and, though it could hardly have been foreseen at the time, to Europe and continental Asia.

The civic leaders of Penzance had long been conscious of the town's isolation at the western tip of Cornwall and saw as their first priority the development of its harbour. In 1839 a public meeting to consider the construction of a new breakwater was followed up by a 20 page open letter to the Mayor from Mr Seymour Tremenheere, a local worthy and barrister of the Inner Temple. His townsmen had considered the narrow objective of improving the harbour, whereas Tremenheere linked the proposed breakwater with the concept of a 'central' rail connection to the Bristol & Exeter Railway, at Exeter. He argued that together the rail link and new breakwater would make Penzance an attractive destination for sailing merchantmen. Rather than risk being becalmed in Mount's Bay, or having to round the treacherous Lizard peninsula, they would be able to discharge their cargo at the improved harbour, for onward carriage by rail.

Alternative schemes had already been advanced for carrying a line forward from Exeter through Devon and Cornwall. The London and South Western Railway supported a narrow gauge (4 ft 8½ in.) 'Devon and Cornwall Central Railway', via Okehampton, terminating at Falmouth. This was the option favoured by Mr Tremenheere, but with Penzance as the railway's ultimate destination. The Great Western Railway put its weight behind two complementary broad gauge (7 ft 0¼ in.) schemes. These were the 'South Devon Railway' following a coastal route from Exeter to Plymouth, and the 'Cornwall Railway' taking the line on from there to Falmouth. The threat to Penzance of relegation to a branch line under either scheme was sufficient to prompt formation of 'The West Cornwall Railway' in 1844. Backed by local interests, the objective of the West Cornwall was to link Penzance with Truro.

The proposed West Cornwall main line from Penzance to Truro was to be 25 miles long, with branches to Falmouth, Penryn and St Ives. By incorporating the Hayle Railway within their scheme, the promoters hoped to achieve economy in first cost and operation, while at the same time benefiting from an assured income flow. Atmospheric traction was to be employed on the hillier section of the new line, between Redruth and Truro, and rope-worked inclines on the Hayle Railway section were to be retained, at Angarrack and Penponds. The whole undertaking was to be leased to and managed by the Hayle Railway.

A Bill was introduced in the 1845 session of Parliament and, following a second reading 'on the nod', fell to be examined by a House of Commons Select Committee on 5th May, 1845. The Committee's brief was to determine whether there was a good commercial case for the proposed railway and, if so, that its route and construction were based on sound engineering principles and practice. In addition, but no less importantly, the Committee sought assurance that finance was secured to see the scheme through. The Committee also heard petitions from those who believed their livelihoods or property were threatened, or were promoting rival schemes. If the Committee was satisfied the Bill would be published and, given fair passage through Parliament, be enacted. Despite the West Cornwall's status as a minor undertaking the Committee's proceedings lasted many days and are recorded in a volume of over one thousand hand-written pages.

The opening testimonies in support of the commercial case for the railway were based on a census of a fortnight's traffic on the roads between Penzance, Hayle, Marazion, Camborne, Redruth, Truro and Falmouth, multiplied by 26 to give an annual rate. Seemingly unscientific now, the logic behind this calculation was nevertheless quite acceptable to the Committee. The figures presented for the year's traffic between Penzance and Hayle (a distance of eight miles) were as follows:

Mode of Travel	Tons/Heads/ Passengers	Cost (whole journey) per ton	Passengers Inside	Outside
Market Cart	6,136 T			
Stage Wagons	52 T	4s. 8d.		
Private Wagons	3,848 T			
Carts with sand	1,820 T	3s. 6d.		
Cattle	2,678 H			
Coach (2 horse)	7,280 P		2s.	1s. 6d.
Omnibus (2 horse)	49,010 P		1s.	6d.
Omnibus (1 horse)	4,550 P		1s.	6d.
Vans (2 horse)	4,680 P			6d.
Vans (1 horse)	7,488 P			6d.
Post Chaises	1,352 P			
Private carriages	2,652 P			
Cars and gigs	4,680 P			

Journey times from Penzance to Hayle ranged from 1 hour, for a 2-horse coach or omnibus, to 2 hours for a van. To put the passenger fares into perspective, a contemporary fisherman and his family would have considered themselves fortunate if they had a weekly income of just £1.

In support of the statistical evidence, businessmen journeyed to London to represent the industries that would use the new railway. These included tin and copper mining, fishing, market gardening and tanning among others. In addition the Committee had ample evidence of Hayle Railway traffic in statutory returns, the most recent of which cited 66,221 tons of minerals and 57,135 passengers carried in the year to 31st March, 1845.

The commercial case having been made, the Committee considered technical matters. Although Isambard Kingdom Brunel (1806-1859) had been engaged as consulting engineer it fell to Captain William Scarth Moorsom (1804-1863), a civil engineer, to put the case for construction and running of the railway.

Captain Moorsom was sharply questioned about the suitability of atmospheric traction for the Redruth-Truro section of the line. It had the advantage of being virtually unaffected by hillier terrain, removing the need for expensive tunnelling and embankments, and promised swift and silent travel into the bargain. Atmospheric traction had already been proposed for the South Devon and Cornwall railways but to see it in action Captain Moorsom had to journey to Ireland, to the recently opened, 1½ mile long, Kingstown & Dalkey section of the Dublin & Kingstown line. On the basis of his observations there, Captain Moorsom assured the Committee he was perfectly satisfied the system was suited to the West Cornwall's needs. When asked about the possible speed of travel, he replied that 60 mph was well within the system's capabilities but that 30 mph was more likely to be the operating speed. Doubtless he had heard that 60 mph had been attained on the Irish line, albeit in a highly irregular manner.

Despite Captain Moorsom's assurances the Committee was not entirely satisfied about the necessity for atmospheric traction on the West Cornwall and, when pressed further, he agreed that locomotive traction would also be feasible between Redruth and Truro. As well he might, for he had surveyed the Birmingham & Gloucester Railway whose Lickey Incline was far more formidable than any between Redruth and Truro and was worked by adhesion alone.

The evidence suggests Brunel was behind the inclusion of atmospheric traction in the West Cornwall scheme and one of Captain Moorsom's references to Brunel's views must have been hard for the Committee to digest. When asked 'Do you think that the engineer [Brunel] upon such a question would talk nonsense?' Captain Moorsom replied 'When a man is asked a nonsensical question by those who don't understand the matter he may give nonsensical answers'!

Considerable time was devoted by the Committee to the vexed question of the track gauge to be adopted on the West Cornwall - broad, narrow or mixed. The Hayle Railway was narrow gauge and Captain Moorsom, who admitted to having had no experience of mixed gauge, argued for narrow gauge as a means of saving cost. He added, in a reply of far-reaching implications, 'there would be no difficulty in converting to broad gauge at a cost of some £500 per mile'. As the Gauge Commission was then sitting Moorsom may well have been 'hedging his bets', a brave course to take when the railway proposals for Cornwall were strongly supported by the broad gauge interests of the Great Western Railway.

The route to be followed by the West Cornwall main line was closely scrutinised by the Committee and vigorously, but ineffectually, opposed by competing carriers and owners of some estates it would pass close by, or through. Others in opposition questioned the severity of some of the curves on the line and there was much discussion on this issue - apparently stimulated by a fear of the effects of centrifugal force on the trains or their passengers. The objectors received little comfort from the Committee, as there were few engineering features on the main line to cause concern.

The cost of construction of the main line from Penzance to Truro was estimated by Captain Moorsom to be £180,000. This figure did not include the value of shares to be issued to the proprietors of the old Hayle Railway, whose Hayle to Redruth line contributed a significant mileage to the project. The Committee was soon satisfied that the West Cornwall would be well funded. The first Directors had secured promises to take up £400,000 of share capital, on which deposits of £40,000 had already been received. In addition, the Bill provided that the company could borrow up to £165,000, once half of the capital had been paid up.

After considering the evidence put before it, the Committee threw out the proposed Bill on the grounds that the line would not adequately serve western Cornwall. The strength of the promoters' commercial case, allied to their efforts to keep down costs had combined to bring about their downfall. A journey from Penzance to Truro on their proposed line would have involved locomotive haulage, rope-worked inclines and atmospheric traction - an enticing prospect for a 21st century railway preservation society and tourist industry, but not fulfilling the needs of the 19th century!

Undaunted, the proposers tried again. The West Cornwall Board was strengthened by the addition of Charles Russell, Chairman of the Great Western Railway, and Isambard Kingdom Brunel was requested to survey a more fitting main line, avoiding the inclines at Angarrack and Penponds. A new Bill, with his revisions, was presented in the 1846 Session of Parliament, progressed through the Parliamentary procedures and fell to be examined by a House of Commons Select Committee on 27th July, 1846.

A strong commercial case having already been made at the previous application, the 1846 Committee concentrated on the technical substance of the new proposal, particularly the new route between Truro and Penzance. Early on it was established that it was one of Brunel's assistants, 'Johnson', who had actually surveyed the line. This was probably W. Johnson, described in 1846 as 'an elderly but very competent surveyor who had already done good work for Brunel on the Sardinian Railway'. Probing further, the Committee discovered that Brunel had been in Italy, engaged on the Genoa-Turin line, when the West Cornwall survey was being undertaken and he was eventually forced to admit that he had spent just two hours in West Cornwall. Not a whit abashed, Brunel asserted that it was perfectly possible to cover the ground between Penzance and Truro in that time.

Opposition to the West Cornwall Bill was once again led by landowners and competing carriers, and with as little impact as before. However, the promise of a more persuasive argument came from the promoters of the 'Cornwall and Devon Central Railway'. They asked to be heard as 'their proposal was greatly superior in every point' but the Committee rejected their request on the grounds that, as no Bill for such a railway as theirs was before Parliament, they had no *locus standi*.

Having had a favourable report on the West Cornwall proposal from the Railway Department of the Board of Trade, and being satisfied with the results of its own examination, the Committee allowed the new Bill to go forward, though with some amendments. Viscount Morpeth, the Committee Chairman, reported that the Committee had struck out the Falmouth branch and two small branches to Truro River and Penryn, which were common to the Cornwall

Railway. They also rejected the proposed St Ives branch for which, they decided, no adequate case had been made. The only branch line retained in the Bill was from Redruth to Ponsonooth, to connect with the Cornwall Railway. The amended Bill, with additional conditions concerning the gauge to be adopted, received the Royal Assent on 3rd August, 1846 (9 & 10 Vict. cap. 336).

The main line surveyed by Johnson, and confirmed in the Act, was to run from Carvedras, in the parish of Kenwyn, Truro, to the East Cliff, at Penzance. It would cross 19 parishes in its 22 miles and, in the Committee's words, encounter 'no peculiar engineering difficulty'. The Penzance station bounds were defined in the Act as 'nothing beyond or westward of a line drawn from a red mark on the cliff wall 150ft east of cellars and premises occupied by Thomas Stephens to another red mark 200ft from the first'. This seems a somewhat impermanent means of determining boundaries.

Under the Act, the gauge adopted was to be the same as the Great Western Railway (7 ft 0¼ in.) but the company was also obliged to lay down additional rails to accommodate narrow gauge, if required. The West Cornwall was also instructed to apply in the following session of Parliament to construct a branch to Norwayman's Wharf, opposite Hayle, and provide there a public wharf at least 2,000 ft in length, for passenger and goods traffic. This appears to have been a late insertion in the Bill, as it was not mentioned in the Select Committee Report. The branch and wharf were built but to no great purpose. Opposition from Harvey's, of Hayle, who argued against competition from the railway to their established service to Bristol, resulted in the railway being prevented from trading at Norwayman's Wharf, by a Commons Committee decision in 1847.

The Hayle Railway proprietors made certain that a heavy price would be paid for their support of the West Cornwall, causing a provision to be inserted in the Act fixing charges for passengers and goods on the Hayle Railway sections of the West Cornwall line at no more than the *minimum* levels already in force. This was an onerous provision. By custom or contract, the Hayle Railway had carried 21 hundredweight of ore for every ton for which they charged freight to the mine owners - who were, in many cases, shareholders in the railway – and this provision was to cause friction between the railway and its less privileged customers, and depress the company's financial results for the lifetime of the West Cornwall Railway.

The capital of the West Cornwall was fixed at £500,000 (25,000 shares of £20 each). This was equivalent to the calculated cost of the main line, £270,000, the Cornwall Railway connection, £80,000, and stations and contingency provision, £150,000. As in the Bill, borrowing was permitted up to £165,000 after all shares had been subscribed and half paid up. Ten directors were named in the Act, five of whom - Edwin Ley, James Oliver Mason, Frederick Ricketts, Edmund Turner and Louis Vigurs - had interests in Cornwall. Charles Russell was also on the first Board.

A False Start

The West Cornwall contracted to take over the Hayle Railway at a cost of 4,000 shares of £20 each, fully paid, plus the assumption of debts and liabilities amounting to £47,960. Following possession of the Hayle Railway, on 3rd November, 1846, the West Cornwall attempted to raise capital to complete the main line. This was easier said than done, for the expected positive return from the old Hayle Railway operations failed to materialise and losses were incurred in the first year under new management. This required strong Board action to correct and an investigation undertaken by Captain Moorsom uncovered several problem areas one of which, the heavy fixed cost of operating the four inclined planes, was a major and unavoidable drain on the company. However, potential savings were identified and Captain Moorsom announced that 'remedies would be implemented without any loss of efficiency on the company's part', a phrase that has a familiar ring to modern ears.

The medicine worked and a return to modest profits was achieved. This was some relief to a Board struggling to raise capital to lay the main line. Sufficient capital had been applied for but worsened economic conditions made it increasingly difficult for some subscribers to honour their commitments. Each case was considered on its own merits, a defaulter of means taken to court to be made to pay up and a man of straw losing any monies he had paid over and his shares re-issued, invariably at a discount. The process, in both cases, was long and expensive for the company and did nothing for its reputation in the money market.

The court route didn't always produce the desired result. For example Mr Mowatt, a Member of Parliament, agreed to take up 5,017 shares at a discount of £5 each but failed to pay his calls in 1848. As Mowatt was a wealthy man and his was a major shareholding (which would have produced over £75,000 for the company - close on £4,000,000 in 2001 terms), the Board decided to pursue him with the utmost vigour. Three years later the Board was still pursuing Mowatt through the courts and then, acting on advice that he might fend them off for a further three years, it settled with him for a reduced allocation of shares.

Meanwhile patience was wearing thin in Penzance. On 12th June, 1849, a Prospectus was circulated by 'some gentlemen more especially connected with west Cornwall (but in no way connected with the existing company)' who sought efficient communication between Penzance and Truro. As a first step, they proposed the completion of the section of the line between Penzance and Hayle. This, with the former Hayle Railway line, would give passage through to Redruth. The proposal was costed by William Brunton, the West Cornwall Engineer, at £50,000. Eleven signatories to the Prospectus, including Seymour Tremenheere and a local Member of Parliament, E.W.W. Pendarves, agreed to subscribe for 717 shares at a discount of £6 per share, provided a call of £4 per share was made on the previously issued capital. With monies already to hand, this would finance construction of the line from Penzance to Hayle, a distance of eight miles.

Faced with the Penzance Prospectus, and underfunding of the original proposal following defaults such as Mowatt's, the Board called in Brunel to advise on less costly alternatives to the original plans, and excluding the branch to Falmouth. On 17th August, 1848, Captain Moorsom, now Chairman of the West Cornwall, was able to report Brunel's findings to the shareholders. Including earth works and bridges sufficient for a double line between Penzance and Truro, the cost of a single line throughout was estimated by Brunel to be £292,628. This was thought to be within the company's funding capabilities yet, one year later, contracts had still not been entered into while the Board dithered over the 'precise cost' of buying the land and building the broad gauge line envisaged in the 1846 Act.

The people of Penzance and the West Cornwall shareholders became increasingly dissatisfied with the lack of progress and, as a result of their pressure on the Board and its new Chairman H.O. Wills, of Bristol, a new Bill was submitted to Parliament in 1850 to permit the company to lay the main line to the less expensive gauge of 4 ft 8½ in. This Bill was enacted on 14th August, 1850 (13 & 14 Vict. cap. 98), but at the expense of a proviso that the works should be sufficient to lay broad gauge track if demanded at six months' notice by a connecting railway (a mirror image of the gauge clauses in the 1846 Act). The 1850 Act also prescribed the setting up of a lodge or station at every level crossing of a road, permitted minor deviations from the original plan and approved the laying of further branches to mines in the area.

The Main Line

With finance in place a contractor, Ritson, was engaged in February, 1851, to construct the line and other works between Hayle and Penzance Pier, at a cost of £29,100. Ritson also agreed to construct deviations by-passing the inclined planes at Angarrack and Penponds which, the Board believed, would pay for themselves through a general improvement in efficiency and cost savings resulting from abandonment of the stationary engine at Angarrack.

A time limit for the purchase of land for the railway had been written into the Act of 1846 and was due to expire in August 1852. The Board, still nervous about the cost of land, engaged Brunel to see if there were any further economies to be made at Penponds and Angarrack. This stratagem to defer the 1846 Act deadline failed in its purpose when Brunel advised that there were no more economies in prospect. The Board then had no choice but to proceed with the purchase of all the land needed for the line.

Construction of the line then went ahead and the Board arranged for a half-yearly meeting of shareholders to take place in Penzance on 27th August, 1851, confident the Penzance to Hayle section would be complete by then. Unfortunately their confidence was misplaced. Always receptive to modern ideas, Brunel had recommended that Barlow rails should be used on the West Cornwall. In 1849 William H. Barlow (1812-1902), Engineer to the Midland Railway, patented rails of saddleback profile, varying in weight from 90 to 112 lbs. per yard, which were laid directly into ballast, without sleepers or other support, and tied at intervals to maintain gauge. The cause of Ritson's delay lay in Wales, where teething troubles beset the machines rolling rails to the Barlow design. Brunel visited the contractors in Wales to ascertain what was going wrong and, perhaps as a result of his intervention, a few miles of rail were soon ready for shipment. In a report to the Board Brunel sought to justify his choice of rail:

> The advantages which have been found to attend the use of Mr Barlow's system of permanent way are considerable, and it appears particularly well adapted to our case, the economy both in first cost and in subsequent maintenance when compared with the cost of rails of equal strength is considerable, and it has also the advantage that should the completion of the Cornwall Railway involve the alteration of gauge, this can be effected almost without expense, at all events so trifling a cost that it is not worth considering.

First Captain Moorsom and now Brunel made light of the cost of conversion to broad gauge, the eventual cause of the West Cornwall's loss of independence.

At the August meeting the Chairman turned the setback to the West Cornwall's advantage, commenting in his report that, as Ritson had not yet finished work on the deviations at Angarrack and Penponds, it was as well the line from Penzance to Hayle had not been completed! Weathering the setback, he ended on an upbeat note with news that 'an agreement had been completed with the Town Council of Penzance for a large plot of ground on the present pier as a site for the proposed terminus . . . at a rent charge of £200 per annum' and that a contract had been entered into with Ritson for construction of the Redruth to Truro section of the line, at a cost of £31,300.

The Corporation of Penzance, meanwhile, was pressing ahead with its plans to improve the harbour. A notice in *The London Gazette*, on 31st December, 1851, announced that it was to extend the South pier from the entrance to the harbour to the proposed West Cornwall terminus. Part of the finance for this project came from conversion of the £200 perpetual rent charge to the West Cornwall into a capital sum of £4,000. Completion of the extension, in 1855, gave Penzance a large, sheltered harbour though not yet a floating harbour, or a harbour of refuge.

As Ritson pressed on with the line from Penzance and the deviations at Angarrack and Penponds the impact of the railway construction work on the area must have been considerable. By the 19th March, 1851, Ritson was employing 513 men and 78 horses at Penzance and Hayle and 12 days later the numbers had swollen to 660 men and 86 horses. Most of the men were navvies by trade, moving from contract to contract, but doubtless some men (and horses!) were recruited locally. In the winter of 1851/52 bad weather at sea forced Ritson to engage steamers to bring rails from Wales but, despite such setbacks, the Directors believed the entire line from Penzance to Truro would be completed by the Summer of 1852.

On 25th February, 1852, an engine was seen testing the track at Penzance and the following day an engine and tender, with three or four carriages, arrived from Hayle. On 27th February an inspection of the whole line was carried out by the Directors, who left Redruth at 10.30 am in a train headed by the 0-4-2 tender engine *Penzance*. *The Penzance Gazette* announced that the line between Penzance and Redruth was complete and 'anticipations have been raised high as to the probably increasing prosperity and importance of the borough when its railway communication with the metropolis and with the rest of the empire

Above: The *Illustrated London News* report of the opening of the West Cornwall Railway main line from Truro to Penzance, in 1852, was accompanied by this etching. A comparison between this and the earliest mixed gauge view on page 82 shows that the artist was pretty accurate in his depiction of the buildings and the general scene but less certain when it came to the track plan and train.

Penlee House Gallery & Museum, Penzance

Right: The organising committee for the opening celebrations went to considerable lengths to ensure that no tickets fell into 'undesirable' hands. Supervision by two of the town's leading citizens also ensured an appropriate leavening of jollity by decorum at the dinner tables.

Penlee House Gallery & Museum, Penzance/Tom Richards

NOTICE.

All persons having **Dinner Tickets** will bring a **Plate, Knife and Fork, and Pint Cup.**

The **Dinner** will consist of **Roast and Boiled Beef, Pudding, Bread, and Beer,** and those who intend to dine will assemble on the **Western Green,** at *Two o'Clock,* there to await the arrival of the **Procession** from the **Town Hall,** and then proceed to the **Dinner Tables,** which will be presided over by the **Rev. HENRY BATTEN** and **EDWARD BOLITHO, Esq.**

No one to be admitted without a Ticket.

F. T. VIBERT, PRINTER, &c., PENZANCE.

OPENING OF THE "WEST CORNWALL" RAILWAY,

Wednesday, August 25th, 1852.

DINNER TICKET.

No. 288.

Collier Hon. Sec.

becomes complete'. A week later the Government Inspector, Captain Laffan, examined the line. His report is dated 10th March, 1852 and, as the railway was part old and part new, he prefaced his remarks with a brief explanation:

> The West Cornwall Railway now leaves Penzance, passes through Marazion, St Erth and Hayle, and about 3 miles from Hayle joins the rails of the old [Hayle Railway] line; a mile and a half further on it again leaves the old line, and at the Camborne station it once again joins it and the old line alone goes on to the old Redruth terminus.

Captain Laffan reported favourably on the new work but strongly criticised the old Hayle Railway line even though it was not within his remit, having carried passengers for some years:

> . . . as I happened to travel over it I directed my attention to the state of the permanent way and found it to be in a very defective state. I would earnestly press upon the attention of the directors the necessity of relaying this portion of the line with the least possible delay.

Notwithstanding Captain Laffan's reservations, the entire Penzance to Redruth section of the West Cornwall was opened without delay. The first timetable, published in *The Penzance Gazette* of 10th March, advised that on weekdays there were to be three trains each way, one in the morning and two in the afternoon, and on Sundays one morning and one afternoon train each way. With intermediate stops at Marazion Road, St Ives Road, Hayle, Angarrack and Camborne, the 16½ mile journey from Penzance to Redruth was timed to take precisely one hour. The fares for the full journey were - first class 3s., second class 2s. and third class 1s. 4d. Return tickets were available only for the day on which they were issued and added, for example, 1s. 6d. to the single first class fare. The timetable gave notice that there were omnibus connections with trains at Redruth, for Truro, and at unspecified stations, for Penryn and Falmouth.

Though trains were now running on the West Cornwall line, it was decided that an official opening should await completion of the section of the line from Redruth to Truro. Construction of the Redruth-Truro line proceeded apace and in August 1852 Captain Laffan returned to examine the line. His report of 18th August, to the Lords of the Committee of Privy Council for Trade, was brief and approving, though some gradients he found to be in excess of those specified under the Act. He recommended that the railway continued single engine working over the whole line and made no further reference to the Hayle Railway lines, where replacement of the old trackwork (as he had suggested) was almost completed.

The opening passenger service between Penzance and Truro was three weekday passenger trains in each direction, taking 1¾ hours for the 25 miles, with an additional train leaving Carn Brea for Truro at 6.35 am and returning at 10.30 am. The first timetable shows no Sunday service, presumably an oversight.

The date fixed for the official opening in Penzance of the West Cornwall Railway was 25th August, 1852 and a fortnight earlier a meeting was held in the

Town Hall to determine what celebrations should take place. The first decision taken was to declare the opening day of the railway to be a public holiday! From this encouraging start flowed plans for a procession, a Public Dinner for the labouring classes, a Public Tea for the children of the town, and their mothers, and a Grand Dinner at the Town Hall for the Mayoral party, Chairman and Directors of the Railway and other distinguished guests. The festive programme was set out in *The Cornish Telegraph* on 11th August. The procession was to be formed in strict order -

The boys from the various schools
The members of the Philanthropic Society
The members of the Young Tradesmen's Society
The Odd Fellows of Penzance and neighbourhood (with splendid banners and regalia)
The members of the Union Benevolent Society
The Free Masons in full Masonic Costume
The Magistrates, Aldermen, Councillors and
 Gentlemen of Penzance and neighbourhood
The Pilots and Shipwrights of the Port (the latter carrying the tools of their trade)

- and assemble at the Town Hall at 12 o'clock. Processing to the station, they were to await there the train from Truro bearing the Mayor of Penzance and the Chairman and Directors of the West Cornwall Railway. The procession would reform and move up the town's main thoroughfare, Market Jew Street, to the Guildhall, where an Address was to be read by the Town Clerk.

After the Address, and an appropriate response from the Chairman of the West Cornwall, the Mayoral party and procession would adjourn at the Western Promenade, and the railway party would attend a half-yearly shareholders' meeting at the Union Hotel, Chapel Street. They would all meet again for luncheon, at Ball's Hotel.

The midday dinner for the labouring classes and the tea for the mothers and children (to prevent accidents, none under six years of age to attend) were to be held on the Western Green and all partaking were advised to bring appropriate cutlery and crockery. In the event of wet weather, the dinner and tea would be held in the Corn Exchange and Pork Market. The day was to be rounded off by a firework display on the New Pier, at 8 pm.

The newspaper notice concluded with an appeal to the townsfolk: 'Happy smiles and cheerful countenances are to be the order of the day, and it is hoped that all will unite in carrying out the foregoing with credit and honour to the town'.

On a down-to-earth note, a Committee of 10 prominent citizens, headed by the Mayor, was appointed to solicit subscriptions to pay for the day's celebrations.

The 25th August dawned and promised showers but the 'soft' rain that fell did not dampen the celebrations. The order of procession had expanded since the advance notice and the marchers were headed by a trumpeter and accompanied by bands from Truro, St Just, Ludgvan, Helston, Towednack and Penzance. Nor did the notice hint of the many multi-coloured banners, wands, flags and ribbons that would be carried by the marchers, or the floral arches and decorations that lined their route.

The Mayor's party left on time for Truro, at 8.30 am, but their return journey was delayed for an hour at Camborne by a 'monster train' of three engines hauling 32 carriages of folk heading for the celebrations. It was not until 2.30 pm, therefore, that gunfire from the Revenue cutter *Sylvia* (dressed overall) signalled the Mayoral party's arrival from Truro. The procession was then formed and, to loud cheering from the assembled multitudes, made its way to the Guildhall for the reading by the Town Clerk of the town's 'Address to the Chairman and Directors of the West Cornwall Railway'. The opening words of the Address set out the hopes and expectations Penzance had of the railway –

> Gentlemen - we, the inhabitants of Penzance and the vicinity beg, on this joyful occasion, to offer our congratulations to you on the completion of your important undertaking - important, inasmuch as it is the introduction to a line of railway throughout Cornwall - the first successful effort for breaking down the barrier which has, for so long a time, separated this county from the eastern parts of England - the establishment of facilities (the wondrous results of modern science) for bringing the stranger to our beautiful scenery and salubrious climate, as well as conveying the productions of our soil, our seas, and our mines, to all parts of Britain.

Being first was important to Penzance. *The Cornish Telegraph* observed:

> Already our neighbours at Falmouth have taken the alarm, as will be seen by a glance at our report of the Cornwall Railway meeting; they are fully alive to the importance of a railway; and with the jealousy with which commerce too often regards its neighbours buckles itself up for a contest with a rival port.

Buoyed by a good beginning, the programme went off as planned. The labouring men had their lunch - 'an ample spread of excellent beef and bread, washed down with a pint of Sir John Barleycorn, to each man' - and at Ball's Hotel the Mayor and 120 guests had a splendid luncheon, with many congratulatory speeches. The mothers and children had their tea and in the evening various celebratory dinners were held in the town. The festivities ended with fireworks, and dancing at the Prince's Hall until the small hours of the following morning. To mark the occasion in a more permanent form the Corporation commissioned a fountain to be erected 'on the site of the upper portion of the fish market at the eastern end of the Guildhall', approximately where the statue to Humphry Davy now stands at the top of Market Jew Street. The granite for the fountain came from Lamorna and the entire cost, met out of the rates, was £39 1s. 3d. The Corporation then forgot about its fountain and some years elapsed before it could be seen in operation, and even then not where originally planned and with no indication on it as to why it had been commissioned!

Soon after the opening of the main line between Truro and Penzance, the West Cornwall applied to extend the railway south-eastwards from its terminus at Truro Road (Higher Town) to a new station beside the Truro River, at Garras Wharf, in the Newham district of Truro. A broadly similar proposal had been included in the 1846 Bill and rejected by Parliament at the Committee stage. The Truro Road terminus was on a hill, on the outskirts of Truro, and lacked a commercial *raison d'etre* until a link could be made with the Cornwall Railway.

Garras Wharf, on the other hand, was closer to the residential and commercial centre of Truro and, having access to the sea, promised a considerable increase in trade. As the Newham line would cross the Cornwall Railway line from Truro to Falmouth, the West Cornwall application also included proposals for effecting the crossing, as well as for eventual connection at Truro with the Cornwall Railway. The scheme needed Parliamentary approval and a Bill was prepared for submission in the 1853 Session.

Truro Town Council opposed the Bill on the grounds that, by taking its lines on to Garras Wharf, the West Cornwall would deny public access from across the river to the foreshore and the Wharf. The Council invoked the aid of the Duchy of Cornwall and the Admiralty. They were much disconcerted, however, when it transpired that the local landowner, Lord Vivian, had recently purchased the foreshore from the Crown, for £1,000, and proposed to finance the building of the wharf to rent to the West Cornwall. Further consternation was caused when it was erroneously reported to the Council that the West Cornwall would take its line to Penryn if the opposition to its proposal continued. The Council's case was lost but its members were anxious to protect themselves from attack by their own burgesses and they caused a 15-page statement to be published in 1853, justifying their argument with the West Cornwall. After the fashion of its title, 'The Corporation of Truro and The West Cornwall Railway and Baron Vivian's Estate Acts' the paper is a tortuous read.

The West Cornwall Bill passed safely through Parliament and an Act 'To enable the West Cornwall Railway Company to make certain new Railways' received the Royal Assent on 15th August, 1853. The Act (16 & 17 Vict. cap. 187) authorised the construction of an 'Extension Railway' to Newham and a 'Junction Railway' between Penwithers and the neighbouring station of the Cornwall Railway (not then in existence). Some widening of the main line, and a new branch at Hayle, were also authorised under the Act.

The Newham extension would enable West Cornwall trains to proceed beyond the existing terminus at Higher Town to a station on the south side of the Town's centre. The Truro Junction line would extend north-eastwards from the Newham extension to reach the Cornwall Railway at a location described as 'Ostler Field'. Three years were allowed for the compulsory purchase of the land for the new lines and five years for completion of the works.

Further sections of the Act dealt with the gauge of the authorised lines and provided that, if the Cornwall Railway gave notice it wished to run broad gauge trains down to Newham, management of those lines would be vested in a joint operating committee of three West Cornwall and three Cornwall Railway Directors. This provision was never invoked and the Newham line remained narrow gauge (4 ft 8 ½ in.) throughout its life.

As prescribed under its enabling Act of 1846, the Cornwall Railway's broad gauge line would continue from Truro through to Falmouth and cross the projected Newham line on the level, at Penwithers. Clauses were therefore included in the 1853 Act to protect the prior rights of the Cornwall Railway, stipulating that it would not be lawful for the West Cornwall Railway, or any person using their railway to:

. . . cross the said Cornwall Railway, with any engines or carriages, excepting at such times, and at such speed, and under such Bylaws and Regulations, as the Cornwall Railway Company shall from time to time determine.

The penalty for infringement of this provision was a fine of £30. The 1853 Act also stipulated that 'any signals, lodges, gates, sidings or other works' needed at the level crossing would have to be constructed and maintained at the expense of the West Cornwall and to the full satisfaction of the Cornwall Railway Engineer.

To move its proposal forward, the West Cornwall empowered Brunel to negotiate terms with Lord Vivian but the latter wanted more than the railway was willing to pay. As a result of the stalled negotiations the Newham extension eventually ended 15 feet short of Garras Wharf, still close to the town and with good river access.

The Newham extension was two miles and 33 chains in length and was opened on 16th April, 1855. The main line from Penzance to Newham was single track throughout, with crossing points at three stations - Hayle, Camborne and Redruth. The stations served by the West Cornwall are shown below, with distances in miles and chains from Penzance.

Station	Position	Notes
Penzance	-	
Marazion Road	1 m. 75 ch.	Renamed Marazion 1st October, 1896.
St Ives Road	5 m. 52 ch.	Renamed St Erth 1st June, 1877.
Hayle	7 m. 19 ch.	
Angarrack	8 m. 50 ch.	Closed 16th February, 1852.
Gwinear Road	10 m. 50 ch.	
Camborne	13 m. 12 ch.	
Pool	14 m. 60 ch.	Renamed Carn Brea 1st November, 1875.
Redruth	16 m. 61 ch.	
Scorrier Gate	18 m. 63 ch.	Renamed Scorrier, March 1856, Scorrier Gate 1st June, 1859 and Scorrier on 1st October, 1896.
Chacewater	20 m. 50 ch.	Published timetables indicate that Chacewater station was opened between 14th December, 1853 and 12th April, 1854. All the other stations were opened when the relevant section of line was brought into use.
Truro Road	25 m. 22 ch.	Truro Road was the official name of the station at Higher Town, Truro. Closed 16th April, 1855.
Truro (Newham)	27 m. 55 ch.	Opened 16th April, 1855.

There were no stations on the mineral lines but that is not to say passengers were not carried on them! A newspaper advertisement of 29th July, 1859 gave notice of a teetotal excursions from Penzance, Camborne and Truro to Lovely Cottage, a level crossing on the Portreath branch near to Tehidy House, home of the influential Basset family, where the revellers where bound. Nor was this the first occasion on which such excursions were offered, though the Portreath line was never apparently sanctioned for passenger trains.

In architectural terms the completed West Cornwall line was a typical Great Western style route. There were 'Brunelian' train and goods sheds at Penzance and Newham stations, and buildings at many of the intermediate stations also

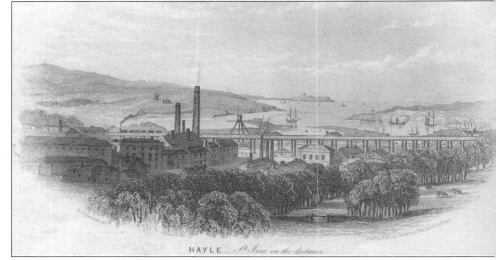

A Besley print, *circa* 1852, of Hayle viaduct. A train has just passed over Harvey's works, heading for Penzance. An idyllic scene that belies Hayle's place as one of the foundations of the Industrial Revolution.   *Cornish Studies Library*

An early view of Redruth viaduct, before masonry piers were added in 1866.
                                                        Royal Institution of Cornwall

bore the hallmarks of Brunel's designs. At Hayle, Redruth and Marazion, for example, the station buildings were small, wooden structures with low-pitched roofs and projecting canopies. Goods sheds, where provided, were rectangular buildings with central platforms and separate entrances for road and rail vehicles. The buildings were similar to those found on contemporary Great Western lines, including the South Wales Railway and the Oxford, Worcester and Wolverhampton line. All owed much to Brunel's advocacy of standardisation.

There was only one tunnel on the main line, a brief affair 47 yds long at Redruth station, but there were nine viaducts, as shown below (distances again measured from Penzance):

Name	Position	Length	Max Height	Type
Penzance	0 m. 40 ch.	347 yds	12 ft	Trestle
Hayle	7 m. 11 ch.	277 yds	34 ft	Trestle
Guildford	8 m. 25 ch.	28 yds	51 ft	Fan
Angarrack	8 m. 78 ch.	266 yds	100 ft	Fan
Penponds	12 m. 01 ch.	291 yds	45 ft	Trestle
Redruth	16 m. 51 ch.	163 yds	61 ft	Fan
Blackwater	20 m. 62 ch.	132 yds	68 ft	Fan
Chacewater	21 m. 04 ch.	99 yds	52 ft	Fan
Penwithers	24 m. 47 ch.	124 yds	54 ft	Fan

The viaducts were of timber construction, designed by Brunel and claimed to combine cheapness of first cost with ease of maintenance. There was ample evidence to support the first claim, the viaduct at Angarrack being reported to have cost just £4,000 to build, compared to estimated costs of an embankment, £18,000, or a stone viaduct, £30,000. It was also true that minor repairs could be undertaken without any interruption to traffic on the viaduct, but for more extensive repairs the maintenance teams required complete occupation of the viaducts. As the viaducts aged, and traffic increased in weight, repair costs became a major burden.

There were two standard viaduct designs on the West Cornwall, 'Fans' to span the deeper valleys between Penzance and Truro and 'Trestles', of simpler construction, elsewhere. They are illustrated in photographs on page 36 and 44. There was a deviation from the standard 'Fan' design at Hayle, where the viaduct straddled Harvey's foundry and masonry piers were later used, to avoid the risk of fire.

The Angarrack viaduct was beheld locally with a mixture of awe and apprehension, the Chairman of the West Cornwall referring to it as a 'fearfully dreaded part of the works'. A fellow Director also thought fit to express widely held fears:

I have great confidence in Mr Brunel as an engineer, though I confess some of his bridges appear rather frightful. The height of some of them and their narrowness! But I have no doubt he can satisfy us and the public at large that they are safe.

The main line could boast few level stretches and from Newham there were gradients of 1 in 60 and 1 in 88 as the line climbed up to Penwithers Junction. The next station, Chacewater, was situated on a brief stretch of falling gradient but the line then climbed to 1 in 60 on the approaches to Scorrier. From Scorrier there were long downward stretches of 1 in 60 punctuated by brief but sharp ascents, including a 1 in 72 section as Gwinear Road was approached. The line then dropped down to Hayle on a series of gradients, 1 in 169, 1 in 59 and 1 in 74. The 1 in 74 falling gradient continued for about a mile beyond Hayle, after which St Erth was entered on a 1 in 88 rising grade. Thereafter the line was virtually level as it continued westwards, to Marazion and Penzance.

The section of the main line from Newham to Redruth was all new construction but from there to Trenowin, about three-quarters of a mile west of Gwinear Road station, the bed of the old Hayle Railway was used. From Trenowin to Hayle, two and a quarter miles, and Hayle to Penzance, eight miles, was all new construction.

At Redruth, the terminus of the old Hayle Railway remained in use as a goods yard, reached on a short branch joining the new main line just westward of the West Cornwall station. The Hayle Railway branches to Portreath and Tresavean, and the sidings at Hayle Wharves, North Crofty and Roskear remained *in situ*, the Hayle Wharves branch and sidings being accessed from a new spur line, at the west end of the West Cornwall station.

Years of Quiet Progress

The years following the opening of the West Cornwall main line saw a steady development of services and facilities on the railway, despite an almost constant shortage of funds. Shareholders' hopes of some return on their investments were whetted by a maiden dividend, before the main line was laid, but were doomed to disappointment time and time again. In retrospect, it seems clear the speculators' original expectations were over-optimistic. It was a failing that attended many railway promotions of the day.

In the year ended 30th June, 1848, the last before the main line was opened, 69,026 passengers were carried, yielding receipts of £1,713, or just under 6d. per journey. In the first full year after the opening of the main line 299,804 passengers were carried yielding £13,189, approximately 10½d. per journey. The improvement in the journey rate was less than satisfactory, bearing in mind that the new main line lengthened the track miles from 12 to 25, and was attributed to a disproportionate increase in the number of 'Parliamentary' passengers carried. Earnings from the carriage of goods were £12,615 in the year to 30th June, 1848 and just £16,408 in the first main line year. The bulk of goods traffic in both years was between destinations previously served by the Hayle Railway and the additional costs of working the West Cornwall extensions ensured a lean financial background to the Railway's opening years.

Believing there was little opportunity for passenger takings to increase significantly until the Cornwall Railway reached Truro, the West Cornwall Directors sought to expand the goods carrying business. In September 1852, the shareholders were asked to approve the making of branches from the Tresavean line of the old Hayle Railway to Wheal Buller and the neighbouring Bassett mines, at an estimated cost of £750. For that outlay the Directors predicted an annual yield of £1,000, from the carriage of 2,500 tons of copper ore and 1,000 tons of coal. This was to be the only branch extension of any significance undertaken by the West Cornwall. Copper mining, mainstay of the Hayle Railway and source of much of the West Cornwall's income, was entering a period of recession.

Precarious finances were dealt another early blow on 27th December, 1852, just five months after the main line was opened, when a portion of the sea wall and 180 ft of the western end of the viaduct at Penzance were destroyed by a severe gale. In his Engineer's Report to the Directors on 17th February, 1853, Brunel was at pains to imply that the collapse of his viaduct was not solely due to the bad weather - 'There are strong reasons for believing that a great part of the damage was caused by the washing ashore and against our works, of a large timber framing from the [Penzance Corporation's] works of the harbour'. The rebuilding and strengthening of the viaduct he estimated to cost £600 and there is no indication that the Corporation of Penzance was prevailed upon to contribute towards that cost. Despite the vulnerability of the viaduct in its exposed seaward position, Brunel did not think it necessary to alter the line taken by the railway.

In 1855, the management of the railway came under severe pressure from shareholders who saw the prospect of a dividend becoming increasingly remote. The depression in the mining industry had also affected the railway and threw into sharp relief the favourable terms given to the copper companies and protected under the 1846 Act. In a characteristic response to poor results a Committee of Shareholders was appointed to examine the Board's decisions and management.

The Committee's report was not made public but, in reality, there was not a great deal it or the Directors could do to remedy the West Cornwall's plight. Aside from unprofitable freight contracts the company was handicapped by its small size, the average distance goods were carried being just seven miles. As was pointed out to the shareholders, the cost of providing that service was proportionately far more than on a railway having a 70 or 170 mile main line. Even so, the West Cornwall's return compared favourably with other railways of similar size. The Board was not complacent, however, and some economies were made. The Directors agreed to waive their remuneration, until the company became more profitable, and the Secretary, Traffic and Locomotive Superintendent offices were relocated from London to 5 Penrose Terrace, Penzance.

These economies had hardly been implemented when serious problems emerged on the main line, which had been laid with Barlow rails on Brunel's recommendation. Maintenance of the line's 25 miles was contracted-out to Ritson, in 1853, for a period of seven years at a cost of £2,180 per annum, but the contract did not cover the replacement of rails. As more and more rails proved unable to stand up to the traffic, the replacement costs escalated and in 1857 Brunel had to be called in to examine the main line. He concluded that three factors contributed to the line's sorry state. Firstly, Barlow rails demanded a greater amount of ballast than had been laid under them by the West Cornwall. Secondly, some of the iron used in the rails making was of inferior quality and, thirdly, the rails were secured with too few rivets. On his recommendation, a rolling programme of track renewal with fished rails was set in motion, commencing with the busiest section of line, between Hayle and Redruth. These rails were said to be of Brunel's own design but what is certain is that they were secured by six rivets rather than four, as before. The

Engraving by William Willis *c.* 1860, which shows the original Penzance railway terminus and the harbour beyond. The coming of the railway in 1852 effectively put Penzance on the map. A road was later constructed from the docks, across Ross Bridge and along the waterfront to connect with the station. Recently a large section of the harbour was filled in to create a car park.

Cornish Studies Library

No. 5 Penrose Terrace, Penzance, was for a time the head offfice of the West Cornwall Railway. This view was taken in 2001. *R.C. Langley*

renewals got off to a flying start, the additional works costing the company £2,214 in 1857, but thereafter the pace of renewal slowed. Would it be uncharitable to remark that Brunel had visited the West Cornwall as recently as 1855 and pronounced himself 'perfectly satisfied with the state in which he found the road'?

Putting behind them the disappointing results of the first years of operation, the West Cornwall looked forward to linking up with the Cornwall Railway, at Truro, and thus the rest of England. Completion of the line from Plymouth had been much delayed by recurring financial problems but backing from the Associated Companies (the Great Western, Bristol & Exeter and South Devon railways) enabled completion by 1857 of the southern sections of the line, to Truro. This prompted some West Cornwall shareholders to suggest the time had come to forge the link at Truro with the Cornwall Railway but the Directors rejected the idea as unremunerative, on the grounds that there was little hope of increased traffic until the bridge over the Tamar was completed. Nevertheless, in anticipation of this event the Cornwall and West Cornwall Boards reached agreement for the railways to share the Truro station built by the Cornwall Railway and opened on 4th May, 1859. A week later the rail link for the West Cornwall was completed and its passenger trains commenced using the joint station. Only the first down and last up trains continued to use the station at Newham.

The West Cornwall Directors were confident that the new arrangement at Truro would greatly benefit the company but the passenger receipts still proved disappointing. Also there were complaints from travellers wondering why they should continue to suffer the inconvenience of having to change trains at Truro, due to the differing gauges. More serious, perhaps, were the problems of missed connections at Truro, on downward journeys. Although the late running of Cornwall trains was a primary cause the West Cornwall was also culpable. An instruction had been given to drivers and guards that a train due to depart from Truro for Penzance was not to await a connecting train from Plymouth unless that had at least reached Grampound Road. As the intervals between the West Cornwall departures from Truro to Penzance ranged from three to three and a half hours, to miss a connection caused considerable inconvenience. The Board promised to look into the matter but the suggestion by a shareholder that more time should be allowed at Truro for the connection earned the unsympathetic response 'that would only result in the Cornwall train being even later'!

At numerous half-yearly meetings it was declared that the West Cornwall had an excellent relationship with the Cornwall Railway and, from time to time, they had Board members in common. (The Cornwall Railway was run by a Committee of 10, of whom six were from the Associated Companies.) However, the threat of having to convert to broad gauge, at six months' notice, was a constant cause of concern to the West Cornwall Board and shareholders, and in the meantime there were lesser, but still vexatious problems associated with the break of gauge. These included the sharing of additional trans-shipment costs at Truro between the two railways:

I am sure [reported the Chairman at a shareholders' meeting] the West Cornwall as well as the Cornwall Railway will admit the break of gauge at Truro is a very serious inconvenience to the development of goods traffic. The Cornwall Railway is advised one way as to the legal responsibilities [for sharing costs] and the West Cornwall is advised another. We have had a good deal of communication on the subject.

In addition to the difficulties at Truro, an otherwise welcome increase in traffic to the rest of England strained the facilities at some West Cornwall stations to breaking point:

> No one can go to any roadside station without perceiving that the increase of parcels and goods traffic since the opening of the Cornwall Railway is such that the stations - especially the smaller ones - are generally blocked with goods and parcels, and the passengers have to stand outside. [*Cornish Telegraph*, 28th August, 1861]

Immediate attention was given to the problem at Redruth where Colonel Yolland, called in to inspect an unauthorised and wholly inadequate extension to the platform, pointed out, pragmatically, that the cost of one accident there would exceed the cost of any improvement.

The Board took steps to finance much additional work, including the cost of laying broad gauge, obtaining Parliamentary approval for the issue of £35,000 Preference Shares, under an Act passed in 1861. By 31st December, 1862, £28,000 of these shares had been issued and some work went ahead, including a re-arrangement of facilities at Truro station, to accommodate the new Falmouth branch, and completion of the trackwork at Penwithers Junction, where the West Cornwall and Cornwall Railway lines crossed. There 'an extensive system of signal machinery' was erected and approved by the Government Inspecting Officer. Plans were also approved for the replacement of timber in the viaducts by masonry and for additional rolling stock. An incidental advantage of issuing Preference Shares was that the Board was able to redeem expensive loans, increasing the profit available for distribution to ordinary shareholders.

The pattern of traffic on the West Cornwall was revealed in the course of a rating appeal in March, 1864, when it was stated that between Penzance and Hayle the average annual gross yield was £800 a mile, from Hayle to Redruth £2,000 a mile and from Redruth to Truro £1,100 a mile. These statistics confirmed what had been clear for some time - and not only to the West Cornwall Directors - for, in the same year, sponsors independent of the established railways submitted a Bill to lay a broad gauge line from Redruth to a junction with the Cornwall Railway. Such a railway would cream off the West Cornwall mineral traffic, as coal and ore formerly shipped to and from Hayle and Portreath would instead be railed direct between Redruth and South Wales. The proposed line would also have pre-empted any similar intentions the Cornwall Railway might have had and, predictably, both the West Cornwall and Cornwall railways opposed the Bill.

Opposition to the Bill proved fruitless, but the West Cornwall secured a proviso in the Act that the new line should be mixed gauge. This was with an eye to linking up with a proposed narrow gauge Launceston, Bodmin and Wadebridge Junction Railway Company. This confection of the London and South Western Railway sought powers to extend to Truro and was confirmed by an Act of Parliament in 1864. Had their line been built the West Cornwall would have gained narrow gauge access to London and the rest of the country, and freedom from dependence on the Cornwall Railway.

Events now gathered speed. To protect its interests, in 1864 the Cornwall Railway gave the statutory six months' notice to the West Cornwall requiring it to lay broad gauge and the West Cornwall, having no option but to comply with the notice, commenced laying 11 ft sleepers to accommodate broad gauge rails. At its September meeting, the West Cornwall Chairman advised shareholders that the laying of broad gauge would cost £40,000 but, though pressed several times to do so, he would not open up the topic for discussion. The mood of the meeting was firmly in favour of a narrow gauge link.

The Minute Books of the West Cornwall company have been destroyed, else they might have given some hint of behind the scenes activity of a feverish nature! The next 'straw in the wind' came in November, 1864, when the West Cornwall promoted an amendment Act giving the company the power to enter into arrangements with other railways. These were named as:

> The Great Western Railway Company, the Bristol & Exeter Railway Company, the South Devon Railway Company, the Cornwall Railway Company, the Launceston and South Devon Railway Company, the Okehampton Railway Company, the London and South Western Railway Company, the Launceston Bodmin and Wadebridge Junction Railway Company and the Bodmin and Wadebridge Railway Company and any Company to be incorporated in the next Session of Parliament for making a railway on the narrow gauge to Truro.

or combinations of the foregoing both as to companies and gauge. This Act, if passed, would also give the West Cornwall Railway power to lease or sell its undertaking.

The Board had cannily left all their options open but the broad gauge interests had the upper hand, being already at Truro, and, it must have come as no surprise when it was reported, on 22nd March, 1865, that arrangements had been made in their favour. This did not deter the promoters of the narrow gauge railway and a meeting was held in Penzance, in April, to explain the advantages that would accrue from a connection with the 'Cornwall Central Railway'. However, the less direct broad gauge route held sway and gained a monopoly of the trade between western Cornwall and the rest of England for many years. Not until modern times was Seymour Tremenheere's 'central' dream of 1839 fulfilled - and then by the A30 trunk road!

There are few relics visible now of the independent years of the West Cornwall Railway Company but one such is on Penzance station - the entrance to the coke store that was burrowed under the Eastern Promenade in 1852/3. Permission was granted for this 'warehouse' at a rent of 2s. 6d. per annum payable to Penzance Corporation.   *R.C. Langley*

The gigantic train on Hayle viaduct has hitherto been described as a teetotal excursion, of 1852. However, the matching outlines of the three locomotives are those of early South Devon Railway broad gauge engines. The leading carriages also appear to be broad gauge. Lastly, the two telegraph lines crossing the wooden viaduct were not in place until early 1854. No doubt there was a teetotal excursion in 1852 but this was not it.

Chapter Three

Operating the West Cornwall Railway

Until 1852 the West Cornwall Railway continued where the Hayle Railway left off, serving the mines around Camborne and Redruth, the ports of Portreath and Hayle, and maintaining the combined road and rail service between Penzance and Truro. Under the combined service a horse omnibus was taken from Penzance to Hayle, where the traveller joined a train to Redruth, the final leg of the journey, to Truro, being by horse omnibus. Fares for the single journey ranged from 2s., for third class passengers, to 3s. 3d. for those able to afford first class travel. In 1849, coach proprietors sought to cut out the rail section, offering a faster but more expensive service.

Traffic

When the main line was opened between Penzance and Truro in August, 1852, a policy of cheap pricing was adopted by the railway. The coaches and omnibuses were no longer able to compete and there was a surge in the numbers of rail passengers carried. A further increase was registered when the West Cornwall linked up with the Cornwall Railway, in 1859. The statistics below are drawn from official returns and include passenger traffic for 1864, the last full year of an independent West Cornwall Railway.

Passenger Traffic

	Number				Value	
Year	First	Second	Parl.	Total	Total	Per journey
					£	d.
1849	8,857	4,165	49,163	62,185	1,521	5.87
1851	12,357	6,904	77,086	96,347	2,361	5.88
1853	17,080	50,494	232,230	299,804	13,189	10.56
1860	23,854	68,372	323,681	415,907	17,126	9.88
1864	26,490	176,672	157,250	360,412	18,150	12.09

The switch in numbers between the Parliamentary and second classes, from 1860 to 1864, was secured during 1863 by the simple expedient of reducing the number of trains having third class carriages! This the railway could afford to do, having eliminated competition from the roads. The collapse of copper mining was largely responsible for the reduction in the number of passengers carried after 1860.

Freight Traffic

	Value	Minerals	Merchandise	Livestock
	£	Tons	Tons	Numbers
1849	12,443			
1851	12,523			
1853	16,408			
1860	21,046	83,044	30,215	3,687
1864	24,722	84,814	46,542	4,143

The freight statistics are incomplete and, taken on their own, misleading. For example, other sources show that a fall in the carriage of copper ore from 27,142 tons in the half year to 30th June, 1851, to 4,665 tons in the corresponding period in 1864 was compensated for by a dramatic increase in the carriage of coal, largely for domestic use, from 15,169 tons to 37,400 tons. Between the same half-years there was also a significant rise in the remunerative carriage of general merchandise, from 2,483 tons to 22,464 tons.

Passenger Services

The Hayle Railway had operated a weekday service of three passenger trains each way between Hayle and Redruth and this level of service was continued when the line was extended to Penzance. There was also a Sunday service of one morning and one afternoon train each way. The journey time between Penzance and Redruth was one hour - a not very exhilarating average speed of 16½ miles per hour - and the single fares ranged from 3s. (first class) down to 1s. 4d. (third class). Return tickets were only available for the day of issue and cost 4s. 6d. (first class) and 2s. (third class). There was an intermediate second class. A 'one passenger engine in steam' policy is suggested by the timings of the departures from Penzance and Redruth.

When the main line was opened to Truro the weekday service between Penzance and Truro was increased to four trains each way. There was an additional early morning service leaving Camborne for Truro at 6.30 am, presumably for train positioning. The Sunday service was two trains each way between Penzance and Truro, plus an early train leaving Carn Brea at 7.30 am for Truro, matched by a 10.00 pm departure from Truro, arriving at Carn Brea at 10.40 pm. Trains crossed at Camborne or Hayle stations and the timings for the 20 mile journey were as leisurely as before. One innovation greatly welcomed by the residents of St Just-in-Penwith was an omnibus service connecting with the morning departures and afternoon arrivals at Penzance.

With the completion of the Cornwall Railway between Truro and Plymouth, in 1859, services to and from Paddington, Bristol, Exeter and Plymouth were included in the published timetables. First and second class passengers departing from Penzance at 6.10 am and travelling on West Cornwall, Cornwall, South Devon, Bristol & Exeter and Great Western lines would reach Paddington by 6.00 pm. Theirs was an arduous journey but it was at least accomplished within the day. Third class passengers could also travel to the capital from Penzance but they had to leave Penzance at 4.37 pm to connect with an overnight train from Plymouth, which would deposit them at Paddington at 4.45 am the next morning. The third class single fare was 22s., about equal to a week's earnings for most folk. First class passengers were allowed 112 lb. in weight of luggage, second class 60 lb. and third class 55 lb.

In June, 1865, the combined timetable for the GWR and 'other railways in connection' shows six trains each way on weekdays between Penzance and Truro. Three up and two down trains between Penzance and Paddington were for first and second class passengers, with a typical journey time of 12 hours up and 11 hours 15 minutes, down. Third class passengers were still not encouraged. The timings were rather more sprightly north of the Tamar and there was a veritable litany of stations to be called at in Cornwall.

Infrastructure

Up until March 1852, the West Cornwall was virtually the Hayle Railway writ large and the infrastructure was attuned predominantly to mineral traffic. As Captain Laffan's report inferred, track maintenance on the old sections of the permanent way left much to be desired but the Penzance to Hayle and Redruth to Truro sections of the main line started off with the advantage of being newly laid. Unfortunately for the Directors, this advantage did not last long due to the adoption of Barlow track, on Brunel's recommendation. Almost from the outset the West Cornwall had forced upon it a programme of track replacement and renewal.

Renewal was undertaken slowly and in a thrifty manner. Uprooted rails not planed and put back provided a steady source of replacements for less stressed mineral branches or sidings. They might even be used on the Penzance to Hayle section of the main line. Where Barlow track was replaced the substitute was Vignoles fished rail, which was also to prove not entirely satisfactory, and there were frequent reports of engines leaving the rails and track being relaid.

Aside from track renewal there were regular calls on the company's meagre resources for expansion and renewal of the locomotive and rolling stock fleets (dealt with in the following section) and not a great deal was left for other demands. It was a constant struggle for the Directors to keep pace with the requirements of the local services, let alone the increase in demands from 1859 on, when the Cornwall Railway linked the West Cornwall to the rest of mainland Britain.

Up until 1859 there was relatively little expenditure by the Board on infrastructure, aside from track and general repairs. In 1852, a coke warehouse for locomotive fuel was constructed (or, more accurately, burrowed) in Penzance, under the Eastern Promenade. Also in 1852, a plot of land on Albert Pier was taken for 'building purposes', probably for a goods shed. Two years later the company laid rails on the pier for two cranes, to be operated by the Corporation and a contribution was made to the cost of extending the Promenade on Eastern Cliff, above the station.

The improved goods handling facilities at Penzance proved unable to cope with the expansion of traffic and, in 1861, the goods shed was doubled in size and a new siding was added between the station and Penzance viaduct. The following year the goods shed was again extended and in 1863 a modest extension was added to the station's single platform. The last development at Penzance by the West Cornwall was in 1864 when it laid a siding on Albert Pier, complete with a goods platform and 5 ton crane.

Elsewhere, there were modest outlays. Passenger facilities were improved at Redruth, Marazion Road, St Ives Road and Camborne, in 1861 and 1862. A new goods platform was provided at Marazion Road in 1861 and new sidings, with cranage, were added in 1862 and 1864 to cope with a dramatic increase in the carriage of market-garden produce. Sidings were also added at Hayle and Camborne, in 1863. Facilities at the company's workshops at Carn Brea were constantly being improved, as the railway undertook more of the construction and maintenance of its locomotives and rolling stock.

Mention has already been made of the coke store at Penzance. In 1850, tests were made to compare the costs of coal and coke fuels for the locomotives. Coke was a cleaner fuel and early locomotives were required by law to consume their own smoke. However, improvements in firebox design made coal a possible alternative and both fuels could easily be obtained from South Wales. The test results came out in favour of coke and the West Cornwall set about securing a supply of 100 tons per month. The search took over three years. The first solution favoured by the West Cornwall was to erect coking ovens at Hayle, where coal from South Wales would be converted, but it proved impossible to find a suitable site. Harvey's, of Hayle, then offered to supply the railway's needs but their price exceeded that obtainable from South Wales. Eventually a compromise was reached and a five year contract was entered into with Harvey's, to supply all the railway's needs save that, if the railway brought in engineering supplies by ship, any remaining space in the holds could be taken up by coke.

Locomotives

As did many small railways, the Hayle Railway engaged a contractor to provide suitable motive power, in this case J. Chanter, a man of many parts. According to evidence given before the House of Commons Committee, Chanter used six engines on the Hayle lines, but the number had shrunken by one by the time the West Cornwall came on the scene. The contract with Chanter was not to the West Cornwall's liking and they sought to curtail it. Inevitably the lawyers were called in and Brunel and one James Easton were appointed as arbitrators to determine the compensation to be awarded.

The arbitrators valued Chanter's contract at £5,500, subject to a deduction of £2,000 for two engines, *Coryndon* and *Chanter*, already paid for by the Hayle Railway. This award, dated 23rd September, 1847, was reduced at some stage by £100, possibly by the Court, to whom the award was referred on 10th November, 1847. In the West Cornwall accounts for the half-year to 31st December, 1850, there is a statement showing how the net award, of £3,400, was apportioned. Chanter handed over three locomotives valued at £1,100: *Cornubia* £350, *Carn Brea* £500, *Pendarves* £250. He also received compensation of £1,340 for giving up control and £960 for 'additional stock'. The £2,000 cost of *Coryndon* and *Chanter*, the locomotives supplied by the Hayle Railway, would have been included as part of the settlement between the West Cornwall and Hayle railways.

The origin of *Coryndon* is puzzling. In 1840 a 2-2-2 tender engine of that name was supplied to the London & Croydon Railway by 'Messrs Chanter & Co'. This was one of a batch of six, built by the Dundee firm of Peter Borrie & Co., with Chanter's patented drafting and coal feeding arrangement. His idea was not a success and *Coryndon* had to be rebuilt before it entered service with the Croydon Railway, in 1844. This *Coryndon* ended its working life as a stationary engine at

Redhill, before being scrapped, in 1865. The other five engines were put up for sale at 'a considerably reduced price' by Borrie on the 8th February, 1841. The subsequent history of only one of these locomotives is known and it is possible that it was one of the remaining four that saw service on the Hayle Railway. In July 1850, a West Cornwall minute described *Coryndon* as 'having been in use for over 10 years', which makes it about the same age as the Croydon engine. Perhaps the name had a sentimental significance for Chanter - despite the name's resemblance to Croydon, there is no connection between the two.

From the details in the arbitrators award it seems possible that *Chanter* was another of the four Borrie engines. At least it is likely that *Coryndon* and *Chanter* came from the same stable. In January 1851, *Chanter* entered Carn Brea for general repairs and, three months later, *Coryndon* was also reported as being laid up. *Coryndon* alone re-emerged from the workshops and it may well be that the best parts of the two engines were put together. Having dispensed with his services, the West Cornwall would quite likely wish to abandon the *Chanter* name.

Cornubia was built for the Hayle Railway by Sandys, Carne and Vivian, of Hayle, at their Copperhouse Foundry. This, the first locomotive built in Cornwall, was described by a contemporary writer as 'in all respects a splendid machine, capable of 40 miles per hour, satisfactory in working and possessing simplicity and beauty of design'. Unfortunately, the aesthetic approach of the writer did not extend to a more precise description of the engine.

The origins of *Carn Brea* and *Pendarves*, are unknown. Possible sources are Sandys Carne or Borrie (two more of the 'reduced price' engines). Carn Brea is a hill castle near Camborne and Pendarves was the name of a prominent local family connected with the railway - which might suggest a local builder of the two engines.

By 1851 all the West Cornwall locomotives were long in the tooth but some replacements were in hand. *Penzance*, a new 0-4-2 tank engine, was in course of erection at Carn Brea, from parts supplied by Stothert & Slaughter, of Bristol, and a similar engine, *Camborne* was on order from the same source. To ensure both were up-to-date in all respects the Carn Brea locomotive foreman was sent to view construction at the Great Western works at Swindon and the London & North Western works at Crewe.

Camborne had a 14 ft wheelbase and 5 ft coupled wheels, the driving wheels flangeless to enable the engine to negotiate the sharper curves on the branch lines. Weighing 22 tons 2 cwt empty and 28 tons 15 cwt full and with a considerable proportion of that weight carried by the trailing wheels, *Camborne* suffered a number of derailments and was later modifed to set its driving wheels 2 ft 1 in. further back. This resulted in some improvement to its running. *Penzance* of basically similar design, seemed not to be so prone to derailment.

The opening of the main line from Penzance to Truro in 1852 forced the purchase of three more engines. The first of these, *Ironsides*, was bought second-hand. This engine was described in *The Railway Magazine* of February 1899 as having the driver at one end and the fireman at the other. This was a feature of engines with return flue boilers, as built by Timothy Hackworth and W. & A. Kitchings for hauling coal trains on the Stockton & Darlington Railway. Early modifications to *Ironsides* by the West Cornwall locomotive engineer, William Brunton, were reported to have improved its performance considerably, but it was never heard of again.

West Cornwall Railway Locomotives

Name	WCR No.	Wheel arr't	Maker †	WCR Service #	WCR Usage §
Ex Hayle-Railway					
Pendarves				1846-52	
Carn Brea 1				1846-53	
Cornubia			SCV	1846-52	
Coryndon 1				1846-51	
Chanter					
/Coryndon 2				1846-60	
West Cornwall Railway					
Penzance 1		0-4-2T	SS/WCR	1851-60	
Camborne	1	0-4-2T	SS/WCR	1852-65	
Ironsides				1852	
Redruth 1	2	2-4-0	RS	1852-65	
Truro	3	2-4-0	RS	1852-65	Passenger
Hayle	4	0-4-2T	SS/WCR	1853-65	Passenger
Penwith	5	2-4-0	SS	1853-65	Passenger
Carn Brea 2	6	0-4-2	SS	1853-65	Coal
Mounts Bay	7	2-4-0	RS	1853-65	Goods
St Ives	8	2-4-0	RS	1855-65	Passenger
Falmouth	9	2-4-0	RS	1855-65	Goods
Penzance 2	10	2-4-0	RS	1860-65	Passenger
Helston	11	2-4-0	RS	1860-65	Passenger
Redruth 2*	12	0-6-0	SG/WCR	1865-65	Coal
St Just	13	0-6-0	RS	1865-65	Coal

Notes

* Redruth 2 is the only locomotive for which a West Cornwall number is known. The other numbers are suggested by the writers.

† Makers - SCV - Sandys, Carne and Vivian (Hayle), SS - Stothert & Slaughter (Bristol), SG - Slaughter, Gruning (Bristol), successors to Stothert & Slaughter, RS - R. Stephenson & Co. (Newcastle).

There are no precise records of the dates on which locomotives were withdrawn from service, or scrapped, and no record of any having been sold.

§ From a return by Henry Appleby, West Cornwall locomotive engineer, for quarter ended 30th September, 1864.

It was possibly through connections of William Brunton's father, William Brunton senior, that *Ironsides* was purchased. He was a pioneer engineer in the North of England and a friend of Richard Trevithick and George Stephenson. At Butterley, Brunton senior designed and built what was possibly the most eccentric steam locomotive ever. This was his 'walking machine', propelled by legs and likened to a man pushing a weight forward. The legs 'walked' alternately and each step moved the engine on 12 ft. The engine achieved notoriety when its boiler exploded, killing 13 men, the first such fatality in railway history. William senior moved down to Cornwall to live with his son, in whose home he died in 1851. His patented calciner was to be found at many mines in the Duchy.

The long wheelbase 0-4-2 tank engines were not entirely suited to passenger work and the other two purchases of 1852 were R. Stephenson & Co. 2-4-0 'long boiler' tender engines, *Redruth* and *Truro*. The records of the Stephenson company do not show these two engines as new sales to the West Cornwall and it is probable they were bought second-hand. They had a better weight distribution and lighter axle-load than their tank engine predecessors and these were telling points at a time when the Barlow track was giving trouble. Against that, the running of passenger trains between Penzance and Newham required the turning of the engine at each end, if tender-first running was to be avoided, and the turntables at Penzance and Newham were too small to take both engine and tender. Turning those separately would have been a tedious exercise but the West Cornwall was not alone in having to resort to such a practice.

The West Cornwall had eight engines at the end of 1852 but the ex-Hayle Railway engine, *Carn Brea*, was out of service. Seven serviceable engines were insufficient for the railway's growing needs and a further four engines were purchased in 1853, three from Stothert & Slaughter and one from R. Stephenson & Co. The Stothert & Slaughter engines were a mixed bag, suggesting that the West Cornwall took what was available, as a matter of urgency. They comprised an 0-4-2 tank engine, *Hayle*, an 0-4-2 tender engine, which inherited the name *Carn Brea* from its predecessor, and a 2-4-0 tender engine, *Penwith*. At least one of these engines, *Hayle*, was assembled at Carn Brea.

From R. Stephenson & Co. came *Mounts Bay*. This was the first of five new long-boilered 2-4-0 tender engines from that source, the others being acquired in 1855 - *St Ives* and *Falmouth* - and 1860 - *Helston* and *Penzance* (assuming the name of the Stothert *Penzance*, which was scrapped in 1860, after a comparatively short working life). The build records for the 1855 and 1860 Stephenson engines show they had virtually identical specifications including:

Boiler	Length	13 ft 0 in.
	Diameter	3 ft 8 in.
	Tubes	123
	Heating surface	978 sq. ft
Cylinder diameter		15 in.
Stroke		24 in.
Driving wheel diameter		5 ft 0¾ in.
Leading wheel diameter		3 ft 4½ in.
Wheelbase		11 ft 10¼ in.
Tender	Gallons	1,000
	Wheels - Number	4
	Diameter	3 ft 5½ in.

A Stephenson 2-4-0 long-boiler engine of the Stockton & Darlington Railway and virtually identical to the West Cornwall Railway's Stephenson engines (of which no photographs have been traced). Comparison with the watercolour of *Helston* shows great similarity between Reed's evocation and the locomotive in this photograph.   *R.C. Langley Collection*

The West Cornwall Railway locomotive *Helston*, as depicted in a watercolour by the late P.J.T. Reed. *Helston* was one of four Stephenson long-boiler engines surplus to the Associated Companies' requirements transferred to the Llynvi & Ogmore Railway in 1868. In Llynvi hands she was converted into a tank engine. *Helston* had a brief life - delivered to the WCR in 1860 and withdrawn by the Great Western Railway in 1875.   *Great Western Society/Reed Collection*

Having thus far remained faithful to 2-4-0 and 0-4-2 configurations, in 1865 the West Cornwall purchased two 0-6-0 tender engines *Redruth* and *St Just*.

Photographs of *Redruth* show it both as a West Cornwall narrow gauge tender engine and as an 0-6-0 broad gauge tank engine, in which guise it was used from 1871 on South Devon lines. The parts for *Redruth* were purchased from Slaughter, Gruning (successors to Stothert & Slaughter) and assembled at Carn Brea. Mounted on 4 ft 10½ in. wheels, with cylinders of 17¾ in. diameter and 24 in. stroke, and a 9 ft 7 in.-long boiler, *Redruth* was a compact and powerful engine, well suited to its work of hauling coal trains. The second 0-6-0 tender engine, *St Just*, was ordered from R. Stephenson & Co. and of that company's 'long boiler' type. Apart from its wheel arrangement it was similar in size and design to the West Cornwall's 2-4-0 tender engines from the same source.

The West Cornwall had 11 locomotives on 1st January, 1866, the date the railway was taken over by the Associated Companies. Nine were valued at £14,622 by the West Cornwall's locomotive engineer, Henry Appleby, as follows:

Maker	Type	Name	Value
Stephenson	2-4-0 tender	*Truro*	£1,012
		Mounts Bay	£1,235
		St Ives	£1,495
		Falmouth	£1,450
		Penzance	£1,900
		Helston	£1,930
	0-6-0 tender	*St Just*	£2,250
Stothert & Slaughter	2-4-0 tender	*Penwith*	£1,150
Slaughter, Gruning	0-6-0 tender	*Redruth*	£2,200

Carn Brea and *Hayle* were also transferred to the Associated Companies but, being in bad condition, were considered of no value. Matthew Kirtley of the Midland Railway, was appointed adjudicator by the railways and he awarded the West Cornwall £14,501 for its locomotives, a close match to Henry Appleby's estimate.

In view of the condition of *Carn Brea* and *Hayle*, and the continuing growth in traffic, the West Cornwall had ordered three further engines in 1865, shortly before the railway was taken over. One was a new 0-6-0 tank engine designed by Henry Appleby, to be supplied by Vulcan Foundry at a contract price of £2,600. The other two were second-hand 0-6-0 tender engines held by Messrs Hunt and Sacre, who had recently purchased them from the London & North Western Railway. These three orders were ratified by the Associated Companies and the engines are described in the next chapter.

It might be wondered why the West Cornwall sent its locomotive foreman to Crewe in 1851 to see modern engines under construction and, in 1865, was seeking to buy former London & North Western engines. The connection, the writers believe, lay in the fact that Francis Trevithick, formerly locomotive superintendent of the London & North Western, had retired with his family to a large house at Chyandour Cliff, overlooking Penzance station. In 1861 he gave his occupation as 'land steward', but he was probably more heavily engaged on a two volume biography of his father, Richard. It must have been tempting for Francis to pop into the West Cornwall offices, which were only 100 yards away, and doubtless his advice would have been sought, from time to time.

Redruth in its original form (1865-1871), as an 0-6-0 4 ft 8½ in. gauge tender engine. The top-hatted gentleman may be the West Cornwall locomotive engineer, Henry Appleby. Redruth was assembled at Carn Brea from parts supplied by Stothert & Slaughter, of Bristol. Note the WCR number '12' allocated to this engine and its livery - in creation order, of course. And who was the small boy, in pride of place on the footplate?

Royal Institution of Cornwall

Rolling Stock

The Hayle Railway was built with a specific clientele in mind, the mines around Camborne and Redruth. That, and the four rope-worked inclines, severe curves on the mine branches and the use of horse power for shunting, at places such as Portreath and Hayle harbours, restricted the size and type of wagon it used.

The photograph on page 56, which is undated but pre-dates the introduction of broad gauge in 1867, shows a typical West Cornwall goods train in the siding at Redruth station. The number of one wagon shows quite clearly between its buffers - 121 - indicating it is an example of the commonest type of wagon used on the railway and built at Carn Brea. It has a wooden body on an iron chassis, probably bought in, and a four ton payload. The very 'square' appearance is accounted for by a length of only 10 ft compared to a width of 7 ft 4 in. The wheelbase is 4 ft 9 in. and the wheels of 3 ft diameter. With only 1 ft 9 in. between the fore and aft wheel rims, a train of these wagons must have appeared more appropriate to a mine tramway than a main line.

The West Cornwall took over 119 wagons and vans from the Hayle Railway and, over the following years, these were scrapped or rebuilt and new stock added. The table below indicates the numbers allocated to the different types of goods wagons and vans built, or acquired, by the West Cornwall. It is not known how many of these survived into Associated Companies' ownership, in 1866, but 223 saw service some 10 years later with the Great Western:

Carn Brea built	No.	Description	WCR Numbers
1855-9	236	Mineral wagons (4 ton)	Range 1-77, 79-237
1855	2	Low side goods	1,2
1855	3	Goods break [sic] vans	1,2,391
1856	15	Covered goods (6 ton)	401-403, 428-439
1859	24	Base wagons (6 ton)	404-427
1861-6	41	Timber trucks (6 ton)	350-390
1863-4	6	Goods brake vans	392-397
1865	1	Mineral wagon (6 ft wheelbase, 4 ton)	78
Bought in			
1864	32	Coal wagons	301-332

The two low side goods wagons were rebuilt by the West Cornwall from carriage trucks and three of the goods brake vans had seen service as third class carriages. The 32 coal wagons were purchased from the Oldbury Carriage Company and all passed into Great Western ownership.

The first West Cornwall record of passenger vehicles in service is in a Minute of 31st July, 1850 - two composite, two third class, two open third class and one 'sheep'. This Minute pre-dated the opening of the main Penzance-Truro line and the details correspond closely with the carriages taken over from the Hayle Railway. But what was a 'sheep'? At the next Board meeting it was stated that an additional two composites and three third class carriages would be needed to service the main line, yet the next carriage built was another 'sheep'.

Redruth station in West Cornwall Railway days, before the Associated Companies added the broad gauge. Believed to have been taken by Edward Hawke, an amateur photographer of Gwennap, this is the only known photograph that can positively be identified to the independent years of the WCR. Between the platforms are original (1852) Barlow rails while the lines crossing the nine-trestle viaduct beyond are laid on longitudinal baulks. The almost 'square' proportions of the WCR goods rolling stock are readily apparent. One man only appears to be at work and the station is deserted, though the semaphore signal is set for an up train. A ladder rests against the end of the station waiting room, beside a pole carrying the line's two telegraph wires - which themselves date this photograph to post-1854.

Royal Institution of Cornwall

By October, 1851, a carriage building programme was underway at Carn Brea. A first class carriage was then nearly complete, one second class carriage lacked only the wheels, two third class open carriages were half-built and a composite frame had been assembled. No more sheep! Though this and subsequent minutes over the next few years refer to the building of carriages at Carn Brea, plans of West Cornwall carriages dating from 1852 show bodies by Messrs Brown Marshall & Co., of Birmingham. In those plans the first class carriage was carried on four wheels, the others six.

The composite carriages had four passenger compartments, two first class, two second class and one compartment for luggage. Second class carriages had five passenger compartments and one guard's compartment. Third class carriages had either six passenger compartments or five, plus one for the guard from which he could apply brakes to all six wheels of his carriage. Two composites and four third class carriages passed into Great Western ownership in 1876. The composites had papier-mâché bodies, as did one of the third class carriages. Two of the other third class carriages had wooden bodies, and the fourth a body made of wood and iron.

A minute of 14th January, 1852, states that carriages were to be built using 'Mr Adams'' patent. William Bridges Adams (1797-1872) was a prolific inventor. As one might have expected, he designed bridge building systems but he also patented a design for a steam 'railmotor', the basis of *Fairfield*, built at his factory at Bow for the Bristol & Exeter Railway. Another of his patents, for paired engines, was adopted by Francis Trevithick for the Cornwall Minerals Railway. The West Cornwall saw merit in part of Adams' patent number 11715 of 24th May, 1847, for an underframe design that enabled six-wheeled, three-axled carriages to negotiate sharp curves. Under his patent, the centre pair of wheels were so mounted 'as to enable the wheels and axles to slide or radiate to follow curved lines of rail'.

It is not known exactly how many carriages the West Cornwall built, assembled or purchased, let alone how many incorporated Mr Adams' patent. In the report of the ceremonial opening of the main line in 1852 a 'monster' train of 32 carriages was alleged, in addition to the carriages of the Mayoral train. It is probable that many of the 'monster' train carriages were wagons into which benches had been fixed, for the occasion.

The livery of the locomotives, wagons and carriages has gone unrecorded, which suggests that it was probably orthodox. The only paint colour specified in West Cornwall advertisements for tenders for the supply of materials is brown - hardly a conclusive indication of the scheme for rolling stock. Bearing in mind the relative costs of pigments it is probable that brown and/or green were the chosen colours. Blue, which has been suggested, was an expensive and fugitive colour. The photograph of *Redruth* shows a fairly elaborate paint scheme with lined out panels to the sides similar to those found on early Great Western engines. Both it and the wagons in the photograph of Redruth station seem well cared for.

Incidents and Accidents

The WCR was neither better nor worse than contemporary small railways in its efforts to reduce the number of accidents or eliminate them altogether. In his *History of the Great Western Railway*, E.T. MacDermot describes the West Cornwall as having been equipped with 'semaphore signals [as] used on most narrow-gauge lines' and point indicators 'showing red or white'. At Penwithers Junction there was the additional protection of a signal locking frame to control access, which was approved for use by a Government Inspecting Officer. Level crossings over roads were manned from the earliest days - but not farm access crossings - and a sand drag was installed to prevent runaways on the steep incline down to the Hayle harbour sidings. In 1854, the WCR engaged the Electric Telegraph Co. to provide two wires at a cost of £125 per annum. Thereafter, the working of the main line was governed by forward clearance by telegraph, from station to station.

The West Cornwall maintained a service blessedly free from injury to passengers, but there were accidents. One occurred on the last Saturday of 1850 when a ticket collector, making his customary way along the outside of the carriages while the train was on the move, missed his footing between two carriages. He was later found lying injured across the rails between Hayle and Camborne and failed to survive the amputation of a leg.

Human life and injury seems not to have been greatly valued. In January 1851, another employee, 'Mr Stephens' was injured on a drawbridge at Copperhouse. He rejected the sum of £5 offered in compensation and the railway gave instructions for 'the best terms to be secured'. The outcome of his resistance is not recorded. Six months later the widow of Mr Roskilly, who was killed on the line, was awarded £10 'to be laid out to her best advantage'. This award could be compared with compensation of £7 10s. given to farmer Rowe in January 1851, for a cow killed when it strayed onto the line, due to the negligence of a crossing keeper. Farmer Rowe also lost two horses in the same manner, in December 1852, and received £20 for the pair.

Perhaps the most poignant incident featured one of Harvey and Company's wagon drivers, Read. Late one day in February 1854, Read was routinely placing his wagon in its shed, below the Hayle viaduct when the driver of the 6.25 pm train from Penzance, on the viaduct above him, also routinely sounded the engine's whistle for the brakes to be applied on the approach to Hayle station. The shriek of the whistle frightened Read's horse which stampeded, starting off at a furious rate. Read, acting intuitively to stop the horse, caught hold of its bridle but slipped and fell; a wagon wheel passed over his head and he died on the spot. The verdict of 'Accidental Death' hardly does justice to such a conspiracy of the fates.

In the unaccustomed dry season of 1853, West Cornwall engines caused several lineside fires. At Penponds, the thatched roof of Mr Bennett's house was set alight by a spark from a passing engine. A surveyor for the railway reported that replacing the thatch with a slate roof would cost £39 which was 'considerably more than the whole house was worth'. The railway settled with Bennett for £20 and doubtless the latter re-roofed with cheaper material. Lord Falmouth also put in a more serious claim that year for loss of a copse due to fire but the minutes give no indication how that was settled.

Gwinear Road was the setting for an alarming incident in October 1861, when a down working was deliberately derailed by vandals, who place an obstruction on the line. The incident was reported as follows in *The Falmouth Packet* on 12th October, 1861:

WEST CORNWALL RAILWAY - On Thursday night, the 3rd instant, as the 8.10 pm down train from Camborne was nearing the Gwinear Road Station, the engine was thrown off the line in consequence of some evil-disposed person having placed a stone on the rails, near the points. A reward of ten pounds has been offered for the discovery of the person who committed this most malicious act, by which life and property were endangered.

On 30th August, 1863, there occurred at Penwithers Junction the railway's most serious accident. The 7.15 pm train from Truro to Penzance was made up of eight carriages and a guard's van, headed by the Stephenson 2-4-0 tender engine *Truro*. William Eathorne, the *Truro's* driver, and John Johns, its fireman, were looking forward to returning home to Penzance, as was Thomas Olds 'acting as brakeman'. He was on the front of the engine to sand the rails because the track was greasy. Despite his efforts the train, having left Truro on time at 7.15 pm, had to set back to the station to put off three empty carriages.

On restarting, speed had been got up to 15 miles per hour on the incline out of Truro when, on rounding a curve, just before a bridge over the road from Higher Town to Bissow, a low truck was seen on the line. Sounding the alarm whistle twice, Eathorne threw the engine into reverse with the regulator wide open. The guard, Sampson, hearing the whistle, applied the brakes full on but their combined efforts failed to stop the train on the greasy track and *Truro* hit the truck. The wooden planking of the truck was smashed but a pair of its wheels on their axle jammed under *Truro*. This caused the engine to leave the rails, strike the parapet of the road bridge and, with the first two carriages of the train, plunge off the line and down 20 ft to the road below. The carriages were completely destroyed and *Truro* finally came to rest upside down.

Eathorne was trapped under the engine's firebox and died almost instantly, leaving a widow and six children. Olds was taken to hospital but died there of scalds and burns, two days later. *The Falmouth Packet* records that he died in Truro Royal Infirmary from 'shock to the nervous system'. The newspaper added that he had recently been appointed fireman, having originally worked as a porter at Penzance station. He was 'to have been married in few days time', and his mother, father and fiancee remained by his bedside until his death, 'praying with him all of the time'. John Johns jumped from the engine and escaped with minor injuries. No passengers were injured. The first five carriages had been kept empty at Truro because they were due to be set off at Camborne for an excursion the following day. For the same reason, two fortunate boys were removed at Truro from the leading carriage and placed further back in the train. Lastly, the coupling between the second and third carriages snapped under the strain of braking and the third and subsequent carriages remained on the track.

It transpired at the subsequent enquiry that a new goods siding was under construction, between Penwithers Junction and the Bissoe Road bridge, and a tipping wagon used in the siding's construction had been parked there, scotched by stones placed against the wheels. The siding was on a downward gradient leading to the main line and the stones had proved inadequate, in the Inspector's opinion, to hold the wagon in the exceptionally strong winds and it had been blown down the siding, coming to rest across the points on the main line, which were set in the main line's favour. The Inspector recommended the addition of chock-blocks on the siding, and a catch point and siding to divert runaways.

The Directors of the West Cornwall were not impressed by the Inspector's 'high wind' theory, believing sabotage to be the cause. Apparently other attempts at sabotage had been reported to them (presumably not made widely known 'in the public interest'). *Truro* was refurbished and served for a further 12 years and the total cost of the accident to the West Cornwall was over £2,000, a considerable sum.

The West Cornwall suffered minor derailments throughout its life and the condition of the permanent way was a constant source of anxiety. In August, 1864, in the last reported incident of that nature before the Associated Companies took over, the crowded 6.10 am train from Penzance was derailed while passing over a high embankment near Hayle. The engine and all the carriages left the line but the driver, quickly throwing the engine into reverse, brought the train safely to a halt. Not for the first time, perhaps, the pedestrian gait of the West Cornwall trains ensured no passenger was injured.

Directors and Staff

When the West Cornwall company was formed the first Board of Directors represented both local and City interests and of the nine persons named as 'Directors, or Provisional Committee' five had local connections. Over the years there were numerous changes to the composition of the Board but Edwin Ley and Louis Vigurs were the Board's stalwarts, Vigurs becoming Chairman in the Winter of 1853/4 and seeing the West Cornwall through to Associated Companies' ownership. His predecessors were Captain Moorsom, sometime engineer to the railway, and H.O. Wills (of Bristol and tobacco fame). The primary source of capital being London, the first Board meetings and management of the company were based there until the need for economising on management costs forced a move to Penzance, in 1855.

After the first, unsuccessful, application to Parliament the Board engaged Isambard Kingdom Brunel as Engineer to the line, responsible for its survey, construction and maintenance. The day-to-day running of the railway was in the hands of its Secretary and the Traffic and Locomotive Superintendents.

The London Secretary, Fitzgerald Church, did not move down to Penzance. His place was taken there by C.P. Charlton who was already traffic superintendent of the line, in succession to R.H. Pike, and combined the two roles. At the outset the locomotive superintendent, sometimes entitled 'Resident Engineer', was William Brunton and it is to him that much of the information we have about the railway's locomotives and rolling stock is due. Brunton, like his father, enjoyed a varied career. While Engineer of the West Cornwall he was also proprietor, with James and Joseph Tangye, of factories at Penhellic, near Pool, and Brymbo, near Wrexham for the manufacture of standard textile fuses, for mines. Latterly he was replaced by J.D. Sheriff who was himself succeeded, in the last year of independence, by Henry Appleby. Appleby stayed for the transfer of ownership to the Associated Companies and then departed to superintend the locomotive department of the Manchester, Sheffield and Lincolnshire Railway.

Nothing is known of the staff of the Hayle Railway, who were the backbone of the West Cornwall until the main line was completed. Then the staff numbers received a significant boost, as recorded in the Minutes. In an initial intake of 26 new appointments, Penzance station had five staff and Hayle, Camborne and Redruth four each. The temporary station at Higher Town, Truro is not named in the Minutes and may initially have functioned as an unstaffed halt.

The titles under which the staff were appointed indicate fine distinctions in the Board's perception of their duties and responsibilities. At Penzance the station master, Richard Simons, was the highest paid member of staff at a salary of £60 per annum. He had formerly been at Hayle. At the other stations along the line the chief functionary was styled 'station clerk' and received a salary of between £40 and £55 per annum (the clerk in Penzance was paid just £15 per annum). As befitted the source of the greater part of the railway's income, Hayle boasted a 'traffic manager', John Bone, who was paid £70 per annum. The salary of Mr Slater, locomotive foreman at Carn Brea, was raised to £126 per annum, reflecting increased responsibilities following the opening of the main line.

The larger stations had a 'policeman' on the payroll. Henry Armitage, at Penzance, was paid £1 per week and was also provided with a suit. Other policemen along the line, together with porters and gatekeepers received 'suitable clothes' in addition to their weekly salaries. The policemen had wider-ranging tasks than their titles suggest and it is probable that they were initially responsible for signals, and the general regulation of trains.

Over the years the staff numbers increased and, for example, 27 staff are listed in *The Penzance Directory* for 1864, the last year the West Cornwall functioned independently:

James Doyle Sheriff	*Engineer*	3 drivers
Charles Pearson Charlton	*Superintendent*	3 firemen
George Denbigh	*Accountant*	6 guards
Oakley Brighton	*Station master*	8 porters
		2 labourers
		1 occupation not given

The porters would have had general duties within the station, the labourers along the lineside. No account has been traced of the style of uniform adopted up to 1865.

Employment in the railway could be a job for life for the well-behaved, with a steady income and in later years, such benefits as (voluntary) membership of a Benevolent Fund. Literally a job for life - Thomas Berry, crossing gate keeper in 1851 at Illogan, on the Portreath branch was 78 at the time of the census and aided by his wife aged 81! For the staff at least, there were undoubted advantages in the transition from the West Cornwall to the Associated Companies and thence to the Great Western Railway.

Chapter Four

Loss of Independence - The Associated Companies and Great Western Railway Take Control

It could be argued that the Associated Companies were but the Great Western Railway writ large but it was in the first 16 years of the latter company's 'direct rule' that four of the most important railway developments in west Cornwall were completed. These, the laying of the St Ives and Helston lines, the re-building of Penzance station and the conversion of the broad gauge to the all-conquering 4 ft 8½ in., are referred to in later chapters. The concern in this chapter is with the general day-to-day operations of the former West Cornwall lines under Associated Companies and Great Western auspices, until the demise of the broad gauge, in May 1892.

The Conversion to Mixed Gauge

In May 1864, the South Devon Board Minutes recorded 'overtures which are considered to have been made for the lease by the Associated Companies of the West Cornwall Railway' and note that a meeting took place at Paddington between representatives of the South Devon, Bristol & Exeter and Great Western railways, to discuss the matter. In June, a lease proposed by the West Cornwall at three per cent per annum on its capital value was rejected by the Associated Companies as being too onerous.

The Chairman of the West Cornwall had already stated at a Shareholders' Meeting that the cost of conversion would be 'about £40,000' but this figure was too vague an estimate to be a basis for negotiations. Accordingly, H. Bush, Engineer at Lostwithiel for the Cornwall Railway, and J.D. Sheriff, resident Engineer of the West Cornwall, were instructed to prepare detailed reports and costings of the conversion. Bush submitted his report on 28th January, 1865, estimating the cost to be £74,184, after crediting £14,006 for old materials used. Sheriff's calculations came to £59,137, after crediting £17,370. The main difference between the two engineers was over the cost of strengthening the nine West Cornwall viaducts to take broad gauge trains - per Bush £17,149 and Sheriff £9,811. They agreed closely on the gross cost of relaying 5¾ miles of longitudinal road and 16¾ miles of Barlow rails with 11 ft cross-sleepered track - over £60,000.

Bush had experience of the engineering demands of broad gauge traffic on the Cornwall Railway and his report was accepted as a basis for negotiations. These culminated in the signing of Heads of Agreement on 18th April, 1865, which provided that the Associated Companies would work the West Cornwall from 1st July to 31st December, 1865, in return for 65 per cent of the receipts, and convert the line to broad gauge for an annual charge of £3,000. On 1st January, 1866, the West Cornwall could grant the Associated Companies a 1,000 year lease. Alternatively, it could make an immediate absolute transfer of the undertaking to the Associated Companies, or grant them a lease for three years, followed by an absolute transfer. Whichever option it chose, the West Cornwall would become a moribund company, receiving a perpetual rent-charge commencing at £21,000 and rising, in stages, to £25,000. From this, the West Cornwall would pay the annual charge of £3,000, interest on its outstanding debentures and dividends on its preference and ordinary shares. The rolling stock, plant and materials of the West Cornwall would be valued and paid for in cash or bonds. These terms received Parliamentary approval, under an Act of 5th July, 1865 (Vict. 18 & 29 cap. 219).

An absolute transfer was decided upon and, from 1st January, 1866, the West Cornwall ceased to be a railway operating company. Its locomotives, carriages, wagons, furniture and fittings were then valued by the arbitrator - Matthew Kirtley, of the Midland Railway - at £43,289 10s. 0d.

To watch over the interests of the three Associated Companies a 'West Cornwall Railway Joint Committee' was formed on 10th May, 1865, having two representatives from each company and meeting at Plymouth. For convenience the Committee will be treated in this account as if it were in full authority, though all major decisions required the approval of the individual associated companies.

The Committee's first task was to secure conversion of the West Cornwall main line to broad gauge. As narrow gauge running was also required for local mineral trains, the method to be adopted involved laying mixed gauge track from Penzance to the joint station at Truro. The Newham and other branches were to remain narrow gauge, except for the short spur to the Redruth yard, the former station of the old Hayle Railway.

On 10th August, 1865, the Committee instructed Bush to proceed with the work 'as early as possible'. He had a formidable task on his hands. The addition of a third rail was more complex than a full-scale conversion to broad gauge, the viaducts had to be strengthened with stone piers and sections of the trackbed had to be widened. It was not until September, 1866, that Bush was able to report that he had worked a broad gauge engine through to Redruth.

Impatient to see the conversion completed, the Committee decided to have a 'private' opening of the entire broad gauge main line on Friday, 19th October and offered the Mayor and Corporation of Penzance 125 return tickets to Truro for the appointed day. The Council accepted these with thanks, resolving also to take such steps as were necessary to celebrate the occasion.

At 10.25 am on 19th October, the Mayor and Council processed from the Town Hall to the station where a special train whisked them, and some 300 fellow citizens, off to Truro. Returning at 2.30 pm, they formed a procession with the Directors of the Associated Companies and 'any other gentlemen of the town who wished to' and made their way to the Town Hall to hear a formal address. This extolled the link between the coming of the broad gauge and the town's hopes for the local industries and 'a larger influx of visitors and tourists'. The Mayoral and Railway parties then partook of a *déjeuner* at the Union Hotel, in Chapel Street. This was a highly convivial occasion and, as at the opening of the West Cornwall, some 14 years earlier, the tables groaned with food and drink. Considerable stamina was needed, however, to pay attention to the many speeches and toasts for, as usual on such occasions, these were long and fulsome in their praise of the new venture and all directly or remotely connected with it.

Those in the town unfamiliar with railway matters might have been excused for thinking the official opening somewhat premature. It was not until 6th

Mazeppa, a South Devon Railway 4-4-0 saddle tank engine of 1859 vintage, built by Slaughter, Gruning, of Bristol, stands with a mail train at a disc and crossbar signal in west Cornwall. The mail van next to the engine is of a design in use on the mail trains from Penzance, the six-wheeled van has full length clerestory windows and, at the right-hand end facing the camera, pick-up apparatus for non-stop collection of mail.

Helston Museum

November that the first broad gauge goods train reached Penzance and the line had still not been passed for broad gauge passenger traffic. Hopes were raised on 12th and 13th December when Colonel Yolland was observed inspecting the line, only to be dashed when he pronounced himself dissatisfied. Broad gauge passenger train services finally commenced on 1st March, 1867. Until then the narrow gauge West Cornwall engines and carriages soldiered on, enjoying an 'Indian Summer'.

Once the main line was opened to broad gauge passenger trains, the Committee felt able to turn its attention to other matters. Among these were the improvement of facilities at Penzance. In September 1867, they advanced a scheme to reclaim from the sea 1½ acres of land at the back (eastern side) of Albert Pier, to extend the station seawards. The Penzance Council rejected this, instead suggesting that the station be built on newly-created plots of land on the landward end of the pier. These were behind the existing station and intersected by a road to the pier, prompting the Council also to propose restricting access to the new station to one train per half-hour. This was unacceptable to the Committee and they countered with a variation on the Council's scheme - to build over the existing pier road and replace it by a new road, further westward. This was accepted by the Council and in May 1868 it authorised purchase of the necessary parcels of land still privately owned. Rome was not built in a day, however, and the new Penzance station was not completed until 1880.

An inadequate station was not the Committee's only concern at Penzance. Towards the end of January 1869 there were fierce storms in Mount's Bay:

> . . . it was feared the railway viaduct would be carried away but the train came over safely at 10.45 pm, having been detained at Camborne. At 6.40 am on Sunday morning, as the Up train was ready to leave the station, the guards stopped her . . . [and] as it turned out, it was fortunate they [sic] proceeded no further. By seven o'clock the viaduct began to show signs of weakness from the violence of the waves, as the tide was at its height, and an immense body of water was beating against the timbers. In fifteen minutes it began to give way, and by half past-seven the greater [sic] half of it near Penzance was completely washed away. The train had to be detained . . .

The storm also brought down the railway's telegraph wires and the Penzance station master had to make his way through flood waters to Marazion, to arrange for relief trains. These reached the village station with some difficulty, the line in places being flooded to a depth of two to three feet. An omnibus service ferried passengers to and from Penzance.

The Committee's secretary wrote to Penzance Council, seeking re-alignment of the viaduct:

> The passage of trains during stormy weather has frequently been a source of great anxiety and occasions have, in former years and during the present season, occurred when it would not have been safe to allow the viaduct to be used at all.

The Council agreed to a re-alignment of the viaduct and a new, inshore, viaduct was brought into operation on 28th October, 1871. In the interim, trains to and from Penzance proceeded over temporary track, laid inland.

Fixed Points

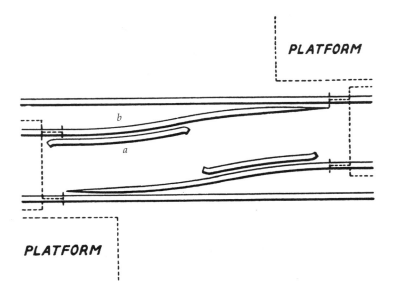

Conversion of the track by the addition of a third rail did not affect the running of broad gauge trains, but it was a different matter for narrow gauge trains. In the three rail system, trains of both gauges used one outside rail in common. At a station the common outside rail had to be the one nearest the platform and if, at the approach to the platform, this was not the case some means was needed to bring a narrow gauge train across. Moving points would have answered the case but the costs of installing and manning them would have been high so the solution adopted was to use fixed points, as shown above. On the approach to a platform the check rail (*a*), acting against the narrow gauge train wheels in concert with the change in direction of the uncommon narrow gauge line (*b*), forces the narrow gauge train from one outside common rail to the other. Fixed points were more elegant in conception than operation and it was essential that they were taken at very slow speed. Indeed, the system was only approved provided that narrow gauge trains taking fixed points at stations came to a halt before doing so. The sight of a narrow gauge train stepping across a fixed point is a highlight of any mixed gauge model layout!

While detailed planning and design of the new Penzance station carried on in the background, the Committee resurrected the oft-proposed scheme to connect St Ives to the main line. Their efforts culminated in an Act of 7th July, 1873, authorising construction of a broad gauge branch from St Ives Road (later St Erth) to St Ives. The Act described this line as being part of the West Cornwall Railway, but this was a legal quirk and did not signal any change in status of that moribund company. The work was put out to tender and on 17th April, 1874, the Committee awarded the contract to build the line to T. Lang, at a cost of £35,545. This line was to be the last significant purely broad gauge construction, though only four miles in length. The Committee's last involvement in the St Ives project was to recommend, after an inspection in July 1875, that there should be three stations only on the branch - at Lelant, Carbis Vale (later Carbis Bay) and St Ives.

In 1874 there was a late flourish by an independent spirit at Carn Brea. The Committee Minutes of 15th August, 1874, reveal that H.T. Ferguson, the broad gauge foreman there, had put up a shed without first obtaining permission. The cost of the shed was £600, about £30,000 in present day terms, and Ferguson was called before the Committee to explain his actions. The Minutes do not reveal what was said to him but they do record that his unauthorised initiative saved the Committee the cost of a more expensive building at Truro. Clearly, a man to watch.

Shortly before the Committee disappeared from the scene a fire caused extensive damage to the goods shed at Penzance. This not only resulted in a settled claim against the Imperial Insurance Company for £500 compensation, including £132 for damaged goods, but also stimulated the Associated Companies to look anew at the proposed development of Penzance station. A South Devon Minute of 30th March, 1876, records that 'after consideration, Mr Owen was instructed to prepare plans with the view to a general re-arrangement of the station at Penzance'. This suggests that it had not previously been thought necessary to make new arrangements there for handling goods and merchandise.

The Committee saw the Penzance-Truro line through a difficult period. It had also initiated important developments at Penzance and St Ives but outside events were colluding to prevent them seeing either through to completion. The Somerset & Dorset Railway, having driven on to Poole and Bournemouth, extended to Bath but found it had over-extended its finances and appealed to the Great Western Railway for help. In an episode reminiscent of their mishandling of negotiations over the Birmingham & Gloucester Railway, some years, earlier the Great Western was outsmarted by the joint efforts of the London & South Western and Midland railways. The loss of the Somerset & Dorset was a greater threat to the Bristol & Exeter than to the Great Western, but it was sufficient to sting the latter into bringing its western associates under direct control. Thus it was that, on 1st February, 1876, the Great Western became absolute owners of the West Cornwall and the Committee retired from the scene.

A broad gauge train on Redruth viaduct, *circa* 1875. The locomotive is thought to be *Stromboli*. If so, it was formerly *Juno* of the Great Western Railway, built in 1852 and sold to the South Devon Railway in 1872. The latter, having a *Juno* of its own, renamed the ex-GWR locomotive.
Great Western Society/Reed Collection

Redruth station, after broad gauge was added in 1866. The passenger facilities are as before but a hand crane has been installed to ease the loading and unloading of goods - which is still carried in narrow gauge rolling stock and of local origin.   *Cornish Studies Library*

Traffic

When the Associated Companies took control of the West Cornwall, in 1866, responsibility for operating both passenger and goods services was put into the care of the South Devon Railway. The most evident improvement for passengers was the removal of the irksome need to change trains if one was travelling beyond Truro. In other respects the services were much as before. The working timetable for June 1867 shows that three weekday passenger trains originated from Penzance. The 6.35 am departure had the sharpest timing, reaching Paddington at 6.15 pm. The second morning departure, leaving at 9.10 am, took 14 hours to reach the metropolis.

A passenger for London leaving Penzance on the afternoon train, at 3.05 pm, reached Paddington before most of London was stirring, at 4.35 am the following morning. Returning from London, there were just two through trains to choose from. The first left at 6.45 am and arrived at Penzance at 6.02 pm and the second, an overnight option, departed at 8.10 pm, arriving at Penzance with the mail at 9.25 am the following day.

The local broad gauge passenger service showed a useful acceleration over the West Cornwall days. The time taken to reach Truro from Penzance was slashed by 20 minutes, to 1 hr 30 min., still a less than exhilarating timing for a journey of 25 miles. The November 1867 working timetable shows a service from Penzance to Paddington virtually unchanged since June, but Truro was brought within 1 hr 18 min. of Penzance by the simple expedient of closing Carn Brea station! The same timetable includes a weekday narrow gauge passenger service leaving the joint station at Truro at 10.35 am and arriving at Penzance at 12.00 midday. The train then returned to Truro, leaving Penzance at 12.30 pm. It appears that this service was provided by a mixed rake, since the train originated from and returned to, Carn Brea and those return services are described in the timetable as 'Goods Trains'.

There were four narrow gauge goods trains in November 1867. Leaving Carn Brea at 7.40 am, the first train headed for Hayle, which it reached an hour and 10 minutes later. At 10.00 am a return train left Hayle for Redruth and so on until 5.30 pm when the final goods train returned from Hayle to Carn Brea, where the engine was shedded and made ready for the next day's work. This service was little different from that provided by the West Cornwall, and before it the Hayle Railway.

The November 1873 working timetable shows just one daily broad gauge goods service between Penzance and Plymouth, a very leisurely affair, leaving Penzance at 1.15 pm, taking three hours to reach Truro and almost seven hours between there and Plymouth. This was a pick-up goods service, stopping and shunting on demand - hardly evidence of a surge in traffic between the far West and the rest of England. A rule for enginemen dictated that 'The speed of Goods Trains must not at any time exceed 20 miles per hour' and the drivers quite clearly had little difficulty in complying with this particular requirement.

Goods traffic between Penzance and Newham was so depressed that the Committee inaugurated a novel economy measure, a mixed gauge goods train drawn by a narrow gauge engine. Narrow gauge wagons immediately followed

Redruth Station

This is the West Cornwall station in mixed gauge days. The photographs on pages 56 and 68 are taken from a point looking down towards Bond Street and Station Hill Road.

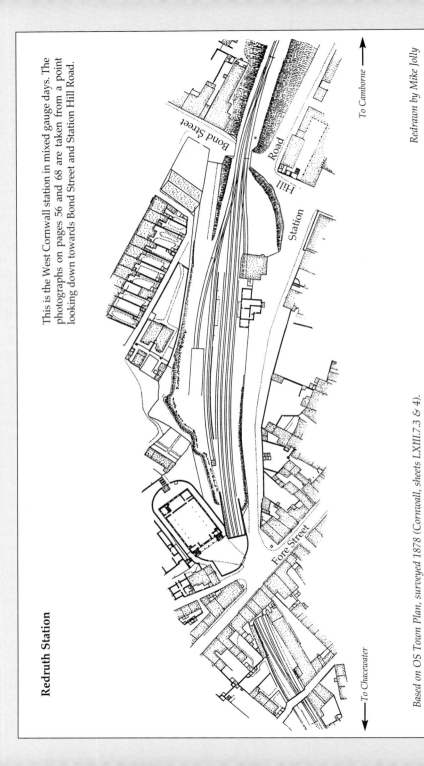

Bond Street

Hill Road

Station

Fore Street

To Camborne →

← To Chacewater

Redrawn by Mike Jolly.

Based on OS Town Plan, surveyed 1878 (Cornwall, sheets LXIII.7.3 & 4).

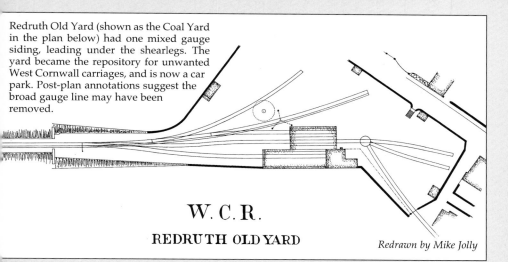

Redruth Old Yard (shown as the Coal Yard in the plan below) had one mixed gauge siding, leading under the shearlegs. The yard became the repository for unwanted West Cornwall carriages, and is now a car park. Post-plan annotations suggest the broad gauge line may have been removed.

W.C.R.

REDRUTH OLD YARD

Redrawn by Mike Jolly

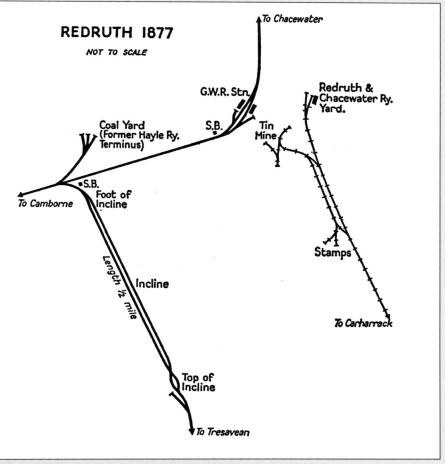

REDRUTH 1877

NOT TO SCALE

To Chacewater

G.W.R. Stn.

Redruth &
Chacewater Ry.
Yard.

S.B.

Coal Yard
(Former Hayle Ry.
Terminus)

Tin
Mine

S.B.

To Camborne

Foot of
Incline

Length ½ mile

Incline

Stamps

To Carharrack

Top of
Incline

To Tresavean

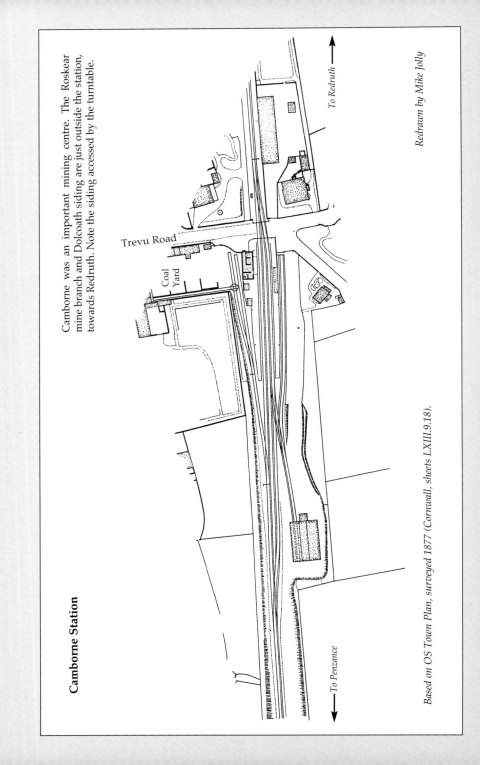

Camborne Station

Camborne was an important mining centre. The Roskear mine branch and Dolcoath siding are just outside the station, towards Redruth. Note the siding accessed by the turntable.

Trevu Road

Coal Yard

To Redruth

To Penzance

Redrawn by Mike Jolly

Based on OS Town Plan, surveyed 1877 (Cornwall, sheets LXIII.9.18).

the engine, and the last of these had extended buffers to match the first of the broad gauge wagons that made up the tail of the train. This phenomenon left Penzance at 3.15 pm and arrived at Truro at 6.20 pm, where any remaining narrow gauge wagons for Newham were separated from broad gauge wagons destined beyond Truro.

There were no narrow gauge passenger trains on Sundays and no goods trains, narrow or broad. Passengers on the day of rest had to be content with one morning and one afternoon through service to Paddington and just one through service in the opposite direction - and that overnight.

As an independent railway, the West Cornwall was required by the Government to file statistics relating to its passenger and goods traffic but, with the loss of independence, these details were submerged within those of the South Devon. The Minutes for that company show, however, that losses were incurred in many years. These were borne by the three Associated Companies, in equal shares.

Mixed gauge track reached Exeter by March 1876, virtually co-incidentally with the take-over of the West Cornwall by the Great Western. Long distance passenger services to and from Penzance were to be constrained for a further 16 years, until May 1892 by the exclusively broad gauge mileage from Exeter to Truro. In practical terms this meant that all passenger services to and from the far West were by broad gauge trains - the narrow gauge passenger train service between Penzance and Newham having been dropped from the timetable.

Timings were leisurely throughout the first 16 years of direct rule but there was a modest increase in the number of weekday services. In 1883, the first and second class weekday traveller from Penzance to London had three morning and one afternoon train to choose from, departing at 6.25, 10.00, 11.15 am and 3.50 pm. The pick of the four was the 'fast express' leaving Penzance at 11.15 am and arriving at Paddington at 8.10 pm. The 3.50 pm train was designated the 'night mail', somewhat ominously one feels in view of its afternoon departure time, but it lived up (or down) to its name by drawing into Paddington station at 4.35 am, the following morning. The 6.25 am train arrived at Paddington at 6.00 pm and this train, and the 'night mail' were open to passengers holding third class tickets.

The service from Penzance to London was little changed by 1890, the penultimate year of broad gauge operation. The 11.15 am train had by now become the 'Cornish express', and the 'night mail' departed at a more appropriate 5.00 pm. The latter train achieved a notable acceleration, not only departing 70 minutes later than in 1883 but also arriving at Paddington 35 minutes earlier, at 4.00 am.

The weekday passenger service from London to Penzance in 1883 and 1890 mirrored that in the up direction. In 1883 a 'fast express' left Paddington at 11.45 am, arriving at Penzance at 9.05 pm, a journey time of 9 hrs 20 min. Its successor in 1890, the 'Cornish express' departed at 10.15 am and drew into Penzance at 6.57 pm, cutting 38 mins off the 1883 running time. In both 1883 and 1890 there were additional services between Penzance and Plymouth.

The desire to travel on Sunday was barely recognised, there being just one train from Paddington to Penzance in 1883 and 1890, and two from Penzance to London (including a night mail in 1890). In 1890 an additional Sunday mixed train left Penzance at 2.05 pm, carrying passengers to Plymouth and perishable goods to London.

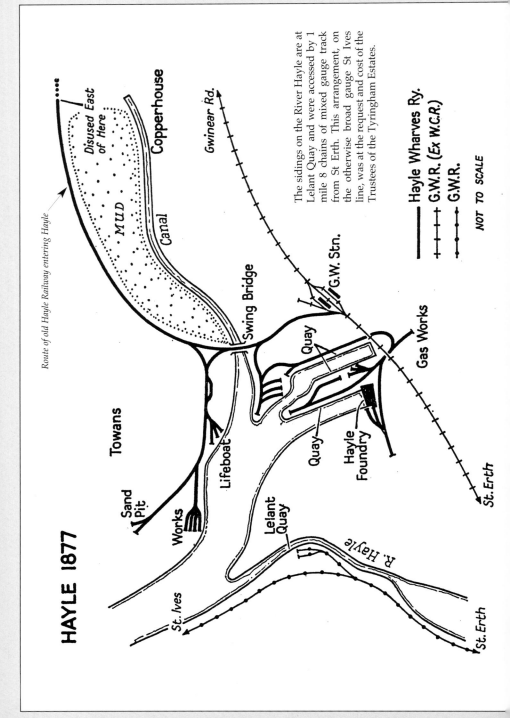

HAYLE 1877

Route of old Hayle Railway entering Hayle

Disused East of Here

MUD

Copperhouse

Canal

Swing Bridge

Gwinear Rd.

Towans

Sand Pit.

Works

Lifeboat

Quay

Quay

Quay

Hayle Foundry

G.W. Stn.

Gas Works

St. Erth

Lelant Quay

St. Ives

R. Hayle

St. Erth

The sidings on the River Hayle are at Lelant Quay and were accessed by 1 mile 8 chains of mixed gauge track from St Erth. This arrangement, on the otherwise broad gauge St Ives line, was at the request and cost of the Trustees of the Tyringham Estates.

Hayle Wharves Ry.

G.W.R. (Ex W.C.R.)

G.W.R.

NOT TO SCALE

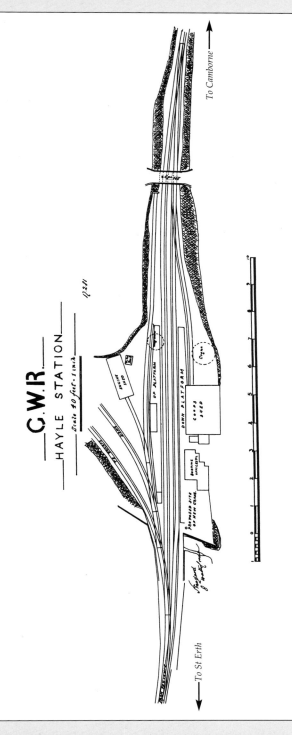

Hayle station, 1881, in mixed gauge days but with a one-engine narrow gauge shed for the wharves shunter.

Traced by Mike Jolly

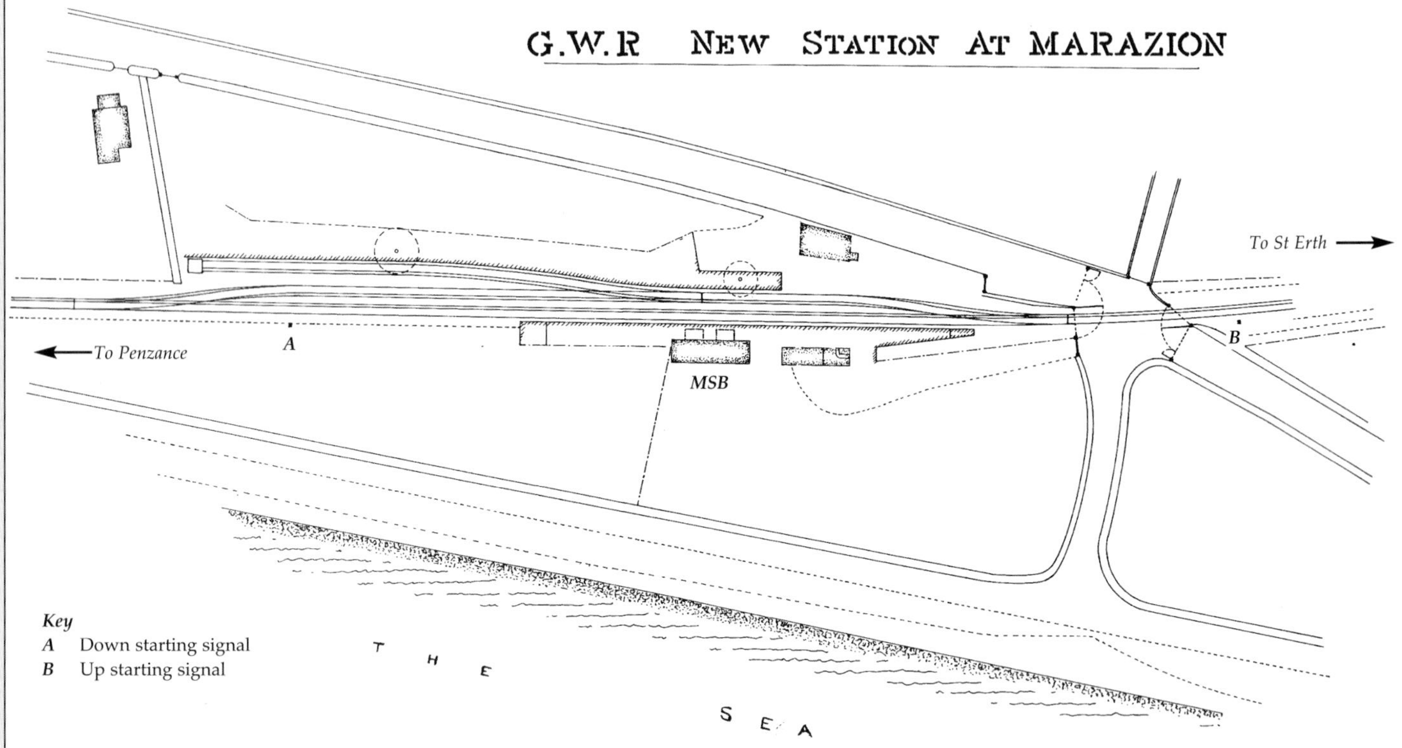

G.W.R NEW STATION AT MARAZION

To St Erth →

B

← To Penzance

MSB

T H E   S E A

Redrawn by Mike Jolly

The 'new' station of the drawing's title refers to the main station building only (MSB), which replaced the smaller building dating from West Cornwall days. There is no hint yet of a huge growth in market garden produce traffic that would require many additional sidings and transform Marazion into one of the busiest West Country stations in the 20th century.

Key
A   Down starting signal
B   Up starting signal

A

Broad gauge goods services in 1883 comprised two 'market' trains, departing from Penzance at 12.00 midday for Bristol and 12.30 pm to London and arriving at their destinations for the early morning markets. By 1890 the 12.30 pm departure was designated 'express fish, meat and perishables'.

During the whole of the period up to May 1892, local mineral trains ran between the mine branches, Hayle, Carn Brea and Portreath and these included a mixed broad/narrow goods train. The maximum permitted loadings of the goods trains in 1890, by way of example, were as follows:

Number of vehicles, including vans

			Mixed Gauge	Narrow Gauge Coal	Empties
Down Trains					
Redruth	to	Hayle	-	30	30
Truro	to	Newham	-	20	25
Newham	to	Carn Brea	-	20	25
Carn Brea	to	Portreath	-	25	30
Hayle	to	Penzance	20	-	30
Up Trains					
Hayle	to	Redruth	-	20	30
Camborne	to	Truro	30	-	30
Portreath	to	Carn Brea	-	20	25
Penzance	to	Hayle	27	-	30

All the above loadings were appropriate for a single tank engine but double-heading was allowed (hauling double the number of wagons). Also catered for in the rules was the haulage of a 'dead' engine - to count as four loaded wagons. It hardly seems likely there was much call for a 'maximum' loaded train, the poor health of the mining industry having led to a general run-down of services that had been the financial mainstay of the West Cornwall. The Portreath branch alone had a timed service in 1890, starting from and returning to, Carn Brea. Three crossing gates on the three mile branch formerly manned were by now opened and closed by the train guard, contrasting with the busy main line between Penzance and Truro, where there were 15 staffed signal boxes and level crossings.

Locomotives and Rolling Stock - Narrow Gauge

The Associated Companies inherited 11 locomotives from the West Cornwall, as shown in the table on page 83. Two, *Carn Brea* and *Hayle*, were immediately withdrawn from service and, within a week of the opening of broad gauge passenger services, the Committee set about the disposal of surplus Stephenson 2-4-0 tender engines. They first sought to exchange them for Great Western broad gauge wagons but this came to naught. Acting on advice from James Grierson, General Manager of the Great Western, they then advertised them on the open market, but nibblings from the Brecon & Merthyr Railway also came

This view of Penzance station is taken from an unusual vantage point, near the entrance to the goods shed (*see page 80*). The engine is *Antelope*, a 4-4-0 saddle tank supplied in 1859 to contractors responsible for providing motive power to the South Devon Railway by Slaughter, Gruning & Co., of Bristol. As Great Western Railway engine No. 2114, *Antelope* survived until December 1884. The leading carriage appears to be third class, of open type and illuminated by just one lamp. The man on the roof may be topping up its reservoir. The second carriage has six compartments, including one for luggage. The last carriage is third class and the short train is completed by a birdcage-roofed Bristol & Exeter Railway luggage van. The train is not drawn into the station and is, presumably, between services. In the foreground is the original West Cornwall Railway turntable, with broad gauge added. The track is a mixture of Barlow, bridge and Vignoles rail. The wooden construction against the retaining wall covers the entrance to the coke store (*see page 43*). Dating such an image precisely is difficult but the various elements of the train and station suggest a date *circa* 1868.

Morrab Library

An immaculate Bristol & Exeter 4-4-0 saddle tank engine backs on to carriages in the new (post-1880) Penzance station. The cabside number is not entirely clear, but the engine is one of a class of 26 built between 1855 and 1873. A useful type of engine which gravitated to the West Country as mixed gauge took over more and more of its home territory. The Bristol & Exeter engines never carried names, unlike their more westerly counterparts.

Penlee House Collection

G.W.R. PENZANCE STATION 1870-1871

Key

A Goods shed
B Engine shed
C Station
D Entrance to coke store, under road
E Weighing machine
F Smithy
G Steam ship office
H Refreshment room
I Signal box

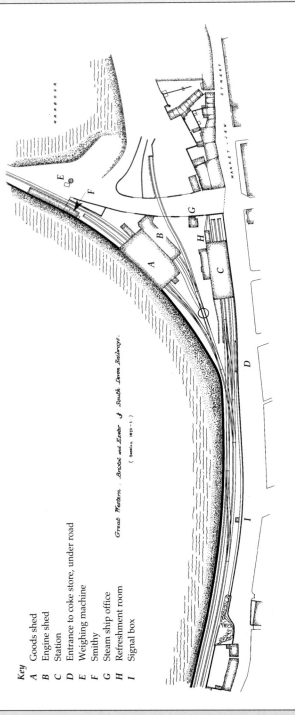

Great Western · Bristol and Exeter & South Devon Railways.

(Session, 1870-1.)

Redrawn by Mike Jolly

Plan prepared for Parliamentary Session 1870-1871

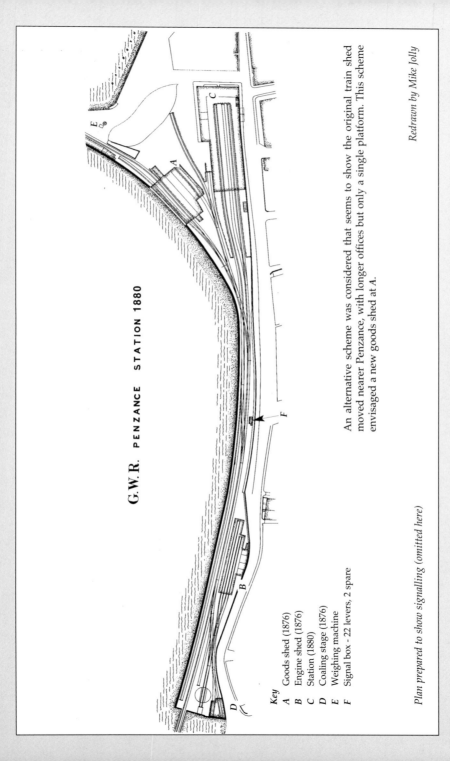

G.W.R. PENZANCE STATION 1880

Key

A   Goods shed (1876)
B   Engine shed (1876)
C   Station (1880)
D   Coaling stage (1876)
E   Weighing machine
F   Signal box - 22 levers, 2 spare

Plan prepared to show signalling (omitted here)

An alternative scheme was considered that seems to show the original train shed moved nearer Penzance, with longer offices but only a single platform. This scheme envisaged a new goods shed at A.

Redrawn by Mike Jolly

Penzance station, *circa* 1876-1879. For all that the tracks are mixed gauge, only broad gauge wagons are to be seen. The goods shed, against the sea wall, had already been enlarged twice by this time, as business increased. The building to the right of the goods shed is the first West Cornwall Railway engine shed, by this date superseded by a larger shed just outside the station. The small annexe at the front of the goods shed housed commercial staff. The disc and crossbar signal at the end of the single platform is a sign of South Devon Railway influence. The WCR favoured semaphore signals. The SDR saddle tank engine, visible below the solitary observer, is standing at the low platform that gave footplate access to the former coke store. Note that both up and down trains used the one platform. Services were infrequent! The scene at rail and road level is hardly one of frantic activity. Even so - was there a better way to spend a sunny afternoon than leaning on a wall overlooking a steam railway? *Penlee House Collection*

Penzance station, following the rebuilding of 1879/80. The new station extends further seawards and townwards than its predecessor *(above)*, allowing the provision of separate up and down platforms and a central carriage siding. The goods facilities are still cramped, however. Another scene of masterly inactivity but the number of interested spectators has increased threefold since the earlier view! *Penlee House Collection*

to nothing and it was not until November 1868 that the Committee finally disposed of some of its narrow gauge passenger engines and carriages. This came about when the Llynvi & Ogmore Railway, abandoning broad gauge in favour of narrow, agreed to exchange three of its broad gauge engines for *Mounts Bay, St Ives, Penzance* and *Helston*, plus some carriages. The Llynvi engines, *Ada, Una* and *Rosa* were taken into South Devon stock.

Of the usable narrow gauge locomotives taken over by the Committee just four were designated for goods and shunting duties, the main business of the railway. The West Cornwall had already recognised the need for more goods engines and the Vulcan Foundry was primed to build a new 0-6-0 tank engine for them, designed by Henry Appleby. The Committee confirmed the order, on 3rd November, 1865, and *Mars* was delivered a year later, at a cost of £2,370. The Committee also pursued negotiations opened by the West Cornwall with Hunt and Sacre, for the purchase of former London & North Western 0-6-0 tender engines. These were part of a class of 12 engines built by R.B. Longridge & Co. in 1846/7, for the Southern Division of that railway. Two such engines were ordered by the Committee in 1865. The first, *Nestor*, was delivered in September 1865 at a cost of £1,000. This proved satisfactory and a second engine, *Apollo*, was ordered that November, at a projected cost of £950.

Narrow Gauge Locomotives of the West Cornwall Committee

Name	WCR No.	GWR No.	Type	Maker	WCC Service*	Usage†	Wdn*
Ex-West Cornwall Railway							
Truro	3		2-4-0	R. Stephenson	1865-73	Pass.	1873
Hayle	4		0-4-2T	Stothert & Slaughter/WCR	1865-66	Pass.	1866
Penwith	5	2136	2-4-0	Stothert & Slaughter	1865-72	Pass.	1888
Carn Brea 2	6		0-4-2	Stothert & Slaughter	1865-66	Coal	1866
Mounts Bay	7	915	2-4-0	R. Stephenson	1865-68	Goods	1874
St Ives	8	918	2-4-0	R. Stephenson	1865-68	Pass.	1875
Falmouth	9	1384	2-4-0	R. Stephenson	1865-75	Goods	1881
Penzance 2	10	916	2-4-0	R. Stephenson	1865-68	Pass.	1875
Helston	11	917	2-4-0	R. Stephenson	1865-68	Pass.	1875
Redruth 2	12	2156	0-6-0	Slaughter, Gruning/WCR	1865-71	Coal	1887
St Just	13	1385	0-6-0	R. Stephenson	1865-75	Coal	1881
West Cornwall Committee							
Nestor		1387	0-6-0	R.B. Longbridge/LNWR	1865-75		1881
Apollo		1388	0-6-0	R.B. Longbridge/LNWR	1866-75		1881
Mars		1386	0-6-0T	Vulcan	1866-75		1881
Fox		1391	0-4-0T	Avonside	1872-75		1912
Cyclops		1389	0-6-0	R.B. Longbridge/LNWR	1874-75		1881
Ceres		1390	0-6-0	R.B. Longbridge/LNWR	1875-75		1881

Key
* There are no precise records of the dates on which locomotives were withdrawn from service or scrapped. The Associated Companies passed control of the West Cornwall lines to the Great Western Railway on 1st February, 1876.
† Per Engineer's return 30th September, 1864.

Mars, an engine commissioned from Vulcan Foundry by the West Cornwall Railway, but entering the service of its successors, the Associated Companies. This is an early photograph - the engine does not yet carry its Great Western number, 1386, which it held from 1876 until its withdrawal, in 1881. The scant weather protection is typical of the period.

Great Western Society/Reed Collection

Fox at Hayle. This is the only known photograph of the 0-4-0 Avonside saddle tank engine in its original form. *Fox* had several rebuilds over a life that extended to 1948. This photograph is undated but was taken some time between between 1872, when *Fox* was purchased by the West Cornwall Committee and 1876, when it became Great Western Railway locomotive number 1391. *Fox* was a light engine, weighing 18 tons when full, and well suited to its appointed task, shunting on Hayle wharves. The engine appears to be off the rails, which might explain the large gathering of workmen.

Cornish Studies Library

Following the exchange with the Llynvi & Ogmore and the purchases of *Mars* and the two former London & North Western engines, there was no further activity on the narrow gauge locomotive front until 1870, when the Committee sought once again to dispose of surplus engines. This time they also scouted the possibility of converting engines to broad gauge and *Penwith* and *Redruth*, being suitable candidates, both were converted. *Redruth* entered broad gauge service as a saddle tank in 1871 and *Penwith*, receiving the same treatment, followed a year later.

To replace *Penwith* on shunting duties at Hayle Wharves, the Committee ordered an 0-4-0 tank engine from Avonside on 23rd June, 1871. This engine, *Fox*, which cost £750, entered service at Hayle in 1872. It later found employment elsewhere in the West Country, on engineering and ballast trains, before moving to Weymouth. In 1912 *Fox* was sold to the Gloucester Railway Carriage & Wagon Co. Ltd, whom it served until scrapped in 1948. *Fox* had several rebuilds over its long life.

The Stephenson 2-4-0 tender engine *Truro*, which had been involved in the accident at Penwithers Junction in 1863, was retired in 1873. In the same year, approval was given by the Committee for the conversion of a locomotive for use as a stationary engine at Portreath, at a cost £1,400-£1,500 and it is possible, therefore, that *Truro* lived on in that guise. Of the original West Cornwall engines only *Falmouth* and *St Just* remained on home territory and survived to enter into Great Western hands, in 1876.

The London & North Western engines having made a good impression, two more were purchased from Hunt and Sacre, *Cyclops*, in 1874, and *Ceres*, in 1875.

In the independent West Cornwall days locomotives and rolling stock purchased 'up country' reached the railway by sea, to Hayle, often as kits to be assembled at Carn Brea. When the Committee took over, the narrow gauge operations of the West Cornwall were still isolated by broad gauge from the rest of the rail network, but they were not alone in this predicament. The Bristol & Exeter locomotive works were on the broad gauge line at Bristol and isolated from their narrow gauge engines used between Highbridge and Yeovil, between which places the Bristol & Exeter had laid a narrow gauge rail in an effort to prevent the Somerset & Dorset Railway reaching Bridgwater. In 1867 W. Brotherhood, of Chippenham, built for them at a cost of £698 'a broad gauge truck to carry narrow gauge engines to and from their place of service'. This had been designed by James Pearson, the Bristol & Exeter locomotive engineer. Taking advantage of the broad gauge link through to Truro the Committee hired this truck, with its men and tackle, in January 1868, to convey the four Stephenson engines to the Llynvi & Ogmore. The cost was two guineas per man-day.

To serve the mineral branches, the Committee continued the West Cornwall programme of upgrading the narrow gauge goods rolling stock. Some wagons were scrapped between 1865 and 1875 but the Committee also built, or rebuilt, 128 four ton capacity wagons and 16 six ton capacity covered goods vans at Carn Brea, which were allocated numbers from those withdrawn or scrapped. It was a different matter with the carriage stock, which became redundant early on, some carriages going to the Llynvi & Ogmore and others scrapped, leaving just three carriages to moulder away in the old Redruth yard until taken over by the Great Western.

Redruth, originally an 0-6-0 tender engine of the West Cornwall Railway, was rebuilt as a broad gauge saddle tank at Newton Abbot, in 1871, in which form she ended her days shunting at the Millbay goods yard.   *Great Western Society/Reed Collection*

Penwith, like *Redruth* originally a tender engine, was also converted into a broad gauge saddle tank at Newton Abbot and spent her last years at Millbay.

Great Western Society/Reed Collection

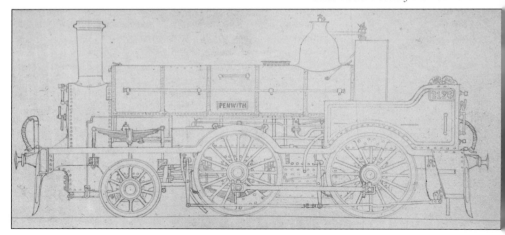

In 1876 the Great Western took over the motley collection of narrow gauge engines then serving the West Cornwall lines:

Falmouth	Stephenson 2-4-0 tender	built 1855
St Just	Stephenson 0-6-0 tender	built 1863
Mars	Vulcan 0-6-0 saddle tank	built 1866
Fox	Avonside 0-4-0 saddle tank	built 1872
Nestor, Apollo, Cyclops and *Ceres*		
	LNWR 0-6-0 tender	built 1846/7

Fox has already been mentioned; the other seven locomotives were all withdrawn in 1881.

As local narrow gauge operations were still an important part of railway activity in west Cornwall, replacement motive power was needed in 1881 - engines that could be conveyed there on broad gauge wagons and work on lightly-laid mineral lines. These restrictions point to the replacements coming from the '850' class of Wolverhampton-built 0-6-0 saddle tanks. Engines of this class were to be found throughout the Great Western's Southern Division and earned a good reputation for hard work. The first locomotive in the class was built in 1874 and the last in 1895, but the batch probably of most significance to west Cornwall was of eight locomotives built in 1881, numbers 1901 to 1908. If needed, further confirmation that the '850' class locomotives were suited to conditions in Cornwall came the following year, when four such engines, numbers 1909, 1915, 1918 and 1919, were allocated to the Cornwall Minerals Railway.

Passenger and long distance goods services being entirely served by the broad gauge, the Great Western's only other narrow gauge concern was with the goods wagons used on the mineral branches, and for purely local traffic. At the takeover in 1876 these comprised the following:

Type	*Built*	
	Pre 1865	*Post 1865*
Box wagons		10
Mineral wagons	130	128
Coal wagons	32	
Low-sided wagons	2	
Covered goods		20
Timber trucks	34	4
Brake vans	7	2

The goods rolling stock had been designed with the particular needs of the local mineral lines in mind and a comprehensive maintenance programme at Carn Brea ensured the fleet was generally in good order. These were sufficient reasons for the Great Western to retain the, admittedly unorthodox, local rolling stock. Indeed, though narrow gauging in 1892 brought 'foreign' wagons into Cornwall some of West Cornwall origin survived into the 20th century, latterly carrying warnings that they were not to be used east of Truro.

As for the independent days of the West Cornwall Railway there is no record of the livery of either the locomotives or the rolling stock in the Committee days and this applies equally to the stations and other buildings, whose structures are reasonably well-known, but colour schemes not. It is possible that the South Devon colour scheme was applied when repainting of locomotives was necessary. Its locomotives were painted dark green, with a black panel line, having a thin white line on either side. Buffers and buffer beams were vermilion. The frames were painted brown, picked out with red and black.

The Llynvi & Ogmore Railway

As previously noted, four of the West Cornwall 2-4-0 Stephenson long boiler engines - *Mounts Bay, Penzance, Helston* and *St Ives* - along with some carriages. were transferred to the Llynvi & Ogmore Railway in 1868.

The four locomotives had cost new over £6,000 but in 1873, when the Llynvi was taken over by the Great Western, their value had fallen to £3,200. Having been rebuilt in 1865 by the West Cornwall Committee, *Mounts Bay* remained a tender locomotive throughout its life but the other three locomotives were converted by the Llynvi into saddle tanks. *Mounts Bay* was scrapped in 1874 and *Penzance, Helston* and *St Ives* in 1875. The boiler from *Helston* entered stationary service, at Llanelly.

Eight carriages were also transferred to the Llynvi in 1868. Two were composites of 16 ft 10 in. and 16 ft 3 in. length respectively, each having one first class and two second class compartments. The remaining six were third class carriages, 18 ft 9 in. long and having four compartments. The third class carriages were condemned between 1874 and 1876.

Locomotives and Rolling Stock - Broad Gauge

Until 1876 the services provided by the Associated Companies over the tracks of the Cornwall and West Cornwall railways were the operating responsibility of the South Devon Railway. For 17 years, until 1st July, 1866, the South Devon locomotives were provided by contractors, latterly Messrs Evans, Walker and Gooch. When the last contract ended, shortly before the West Cornwall lines were made broad gauge, 40 of the contractors' locomotives were acquired by the South Devon. By the time the Committee bowed out, in 1876, the South Devon had acquired a further 45 broad gauge locomotives.

Broad gauge locomotives were shedded at Penzance and Truro, with repair facilities at Carn Brea. A shearlegs over a broad gauge siding at the old Redruth yard may also have been used for light repairs, or wheel-changing. The identities of the South Devon locomotives used over the West Cornwall lines are known only from the occasional photograph, or record of a noteworthy event, until a valuation was made of locomotives and rolling stock at 1st February, 1876, when direct control was assumed by the Great Western.

The valuation is summarised in the table below. Of the 11 locomotives listed as allocated to the West Cornwall on 1st February, six were purchased new by the South Devon in 1866, three were bought second-hand in 1868 and the remaining two, *Penwith* and *Redruth*, were former West Cornwall narrow gauge engines. The second part of the table is a list of engines actually rostered at Penzance and Truro on 1st February, 1876. A comparison between the two lists reveals only one engine, *Rosa*, common to both and the balance between passenger and goods engines is significantly different in the two lists. It is also noticeable that the engines rostered at Truro and Penzance were generally older than those 'allocated' and it seems possible that the allocation in the first part is a book-keeping justification of the take-over price to the Great Western!

Name	GWR No.	Type	Maker	Built	Miles ,000s*	Wdn	Usage
Allocated to West Cornwall Railway (5 passenger, 6 goods)							
Gorgon	2122	4-4-0ST	Avon	9/66	351	5/92	Pass.
Pluto	2123	4-4-0ST	Avon	10/66	333	5/92	Pass.
Titan	2126	4-4-0ST	Avon	10/66	357	12/86	Pass.
Zebra	2127	4-4-0ST	Avon	10/66	362	5/92	Pass.
Penwith	2136	2-4-0ST	Stothert & Slaughter	/53	91	12/88	Pass.
Rosa	2145	0-6-0ST	Slaughter, Gruning	/63	163	10/85	Goods
Ada	2146	0-6-0ST	Slaughter, Gruning	/62	170	6/86	Goods
Una	2147	0-6-0ST	Slaughter, Gruning	/62	140	12/86	Goods
Remus	2154	0-6-0ST	Avon	11/66	241	12/86	Goods
Romulus	2155	0-6-0ST	Avon	11/66	198	5/92	Goods
Redruth	2156	0-6-0ST	Stothert & Slaughter/WCR	/65	88	6/87	Goods
Rostered on West Cornwall Lines (6 passenger, 3 goods)							
At Penzance							
Lynx	2109	4-4-0ST	Haigh	4/59	512	12/76	Pass.
Gazelle	2110	4-4-0ST	Slaughter, Gruning	5/59	529	6/85	Pass.
Cato	2118	4-4-0ST	Slaughter, Gruning	9/63	387	10/77	Pass.
Castor	2121	4-4-0ST	Slaughter, Gruning	6/65	316	9/82	Pass.
Juno	2153	0-6-0ST	Slaughter, Gruning	12/64	243	6/84	Goods
Achilles	2165	0-6-0ST	Avon	12/73	60	4/05	Goods
At Truro							
Damon	2101	4-4-0ST	Haigh	2/52	562	12/76	Pass.
Giraffe	2112	4-4-0ST	Slaughter, Gruning	6/59	486	10/77	Pass.
Rosa	2145	0-6-0ST	Slaughter, Gruning	/63	163	10/85	Goods

* The mileages given may be from new, or last rebuild.

Only one rostered broad gauge locomotive could be described as being in the first flush of youth. *Achilles*, a convertible, was built when the writing was clearly on the wall for broad gauge, and it saw service as a narrow gauge engine after conversion in 1893. The list of locomotives rostered gives a clear indication of the sluggish demand at the time for broad gauge goods trains needed to convey west Cornwall products and fish beyond Truro.

Apart from the nine engines at Truro and Penzance on 1st February, 1876, there are a few instances where broad gauge locomotives can be identified as being on West Cornwall rails during the tenancy of the Associated Companies. Writing for Oakwood Press, in 1968, G.H. Anthony credited *Lance*, a cabless 4-4-0 tank engine built by Longridge and Co. in 1851 for the South Devon, with the honour of

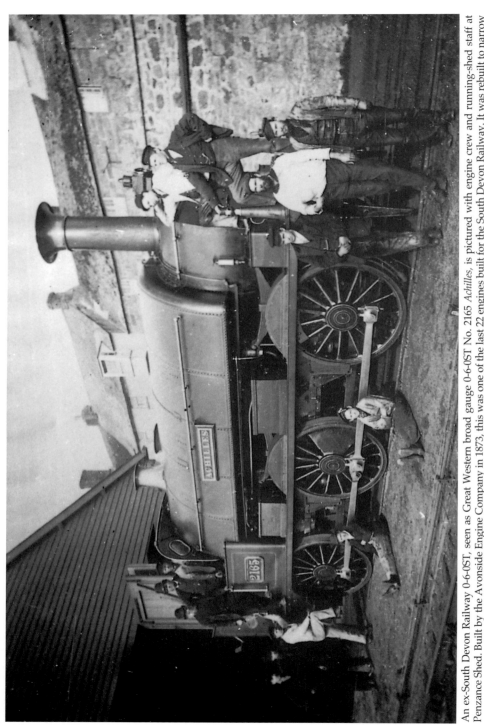

An ex-South Devon Railway 0-6-0ST, seen as Great Western broad gauge 0-6-0ST No. 2165 *Achilles*, is pictured with engine crew and running-shed staff at Penzance Shed. Built by the Avonside Engine Company in 1873, this was one of the last 22 engines built for the South Devon Railway. It was rebuilt to narrow gauge in 1893 when it was renumbered 1324, and in April 1905 No 1324 was sold to the Glyncorrwg Colliery Company in Wales.   *P.Q. Treloar Collection*

A poor quality image of *Dido*, a South Devon 0-6-0 saddle tank engine approaching Marazion station. *Dido* was built in 1860 and withdrawn in 1877. The 'All Clear' signal is given to the driver by the staffman on the platform, his arm held horizontally, as the rules required. Judging by the bunching of the first wagon against the engine, the train has been braking on its approach to the station and it may be that the two men to the left are waiting for an afternoon's shunting.

drawing the first broad gauge passenger train into Redruth, on 1st March, 1867. However P.J.T. Reed, writing for the Railway Correspondence & Travel Society, gave the accolade to *Sedley*, a brand new 4-4-0 saddle tank from Avonside. What is certain is that there is a very old photograph of *Lance* at Redruth. Another photograph shows *Dido*, an 0-6-0 cabless saddle tank dating from the South Devon contractors' days, drawing a goods train into Marazion station, in 1867.

Two other certainties come from the Committee minutes. On 10th November, 1868, these record that *Rocket*, a Longbridge 4-4-0 saddle tank of 1851 vintage, broke a driving wheel tyre between St Ives Road and Marazion. The same source reveals that *Osiris*, a 22-year-old Stothert & Slaughter 4-4-0 saddle tank, was purchased for £1,500 on 13th August, 1875, for conversion into a stationary engine for Portreath incline. One would like to think she made her last journey into Cornwall under her own steam.

There is scant evidence concerning the passenger rolling stock used over West Cornwall metals in the period 1866-75. In 1866, the South Devon purchased a number of new and second-hand carriages and it is likely that these were acquired with the West Cornwall needs in mind:

Lance heading possibly the first broad gauge train at Redruth, in 1866. 'Possibly' because *Hedley* has also been credited with that honour. There appears to be only one carriage attached to the engine, suggesting this may be an inspection train, rather than the first public service. Whatever, this is a fine period piece and the anxiety of everyone to get into the picture leaves little doubt that some worthy event has been recorded for posterity.

Royal Institution of Cornwall

11 six-wheeled brake third class carriages, built by Metropolitan Carriage & Wagon Co., Birmingham (MCW). These had six compartments. Length 27 ft 9 in.

4 six-wheeled brake second class carriages, built by MCW. These had five compartments plus one luggage compartment. Length 30 ft 9 in.

16 six-wheeled 'Meat vans' and 1 six-wheeled passenger brake van, formerly GWR 'Short iron third class carriages'. Length 21 ft 10 in.

The Great Western valuation of West Cornwall broad gauge stock at 1st February, 1876, lists 14 carriages. There is no indication where the count took place.

Two six-wheeled composites having two first class compartments, two second class, and one central compartment for luggage. Length 27 ft 8 in. These were purchased from the Great Western in 1873, for £240 each, and were built by them in 1854. The bodies were of wood and papier mâché construction.

Four six-wheeled third class carriages. Two were former Llynvi & Ogmore carriages and two originated with the Great Western. The Llynvi carriages reputedly dated from 1866 and had six compartments. The Great Western carriages dated from 1852 and 1857, respectively, and had five passenger compartments and one compartment for luggage. Length 27 ft 8 in.

Eight four-wheeled carriage trucks. These were built by the Great Western in 1849 and purchased by the Committee in 1873.

It is possible that the rakes of carriages making up most trains to and from Penzance originated on South Devon lines, or beyond, and were only overnight at the western terminus. As with the locomotives, an appropriate charge would have been made by the South Devon to the West Cornwall for their use. Together with other costs (and income) they would have been divided three ways by the Committee, between the Associated Companies.

The rolling stock position is clearer when it comes to broad gauge goods wagons, of which 248 were allocated to the West Cornwall:

No.	Type	Maker
20	Open box, wooden	Shackleford
155	Open box, wooden with iron frame	Shackleford
30	Open tilt, iron	Waddington
10	Furniture van trucks	Great Western
1	Shunting truck	West Cornwall
1	4-wheel timber truck	
12	6-wheel timber truck	Brotherhood
16	Goods brakevans	
3	Shunting vans	West Cornwall

The policy of the Great Western and its allies appeared to be that no item of rolling stock should be scrapped if there was a chance of it being used in a new incarnation. Early carriages might descend down the scale until they found use as shunting vans (as the three above). Carriage trucks, to enable the gentry to take their carriages with them for use at their destinations, might end up in humbler service as furniture van trucks.

In later years, the Great Western developed the broad gauge goods services from West Cornwall to the point where trains of purpose-built wagons and vans were used to convey fish and market-garden produce from Penzance to

London. These trains received special mention in the working timetables. In the Committee's day perishable goods were carried by passenger trains and, in exceptional circumstances, by special trains.

The gradual conversion of broad to narrow or mixed gauge track (which, as already noted, had reached Exeter by March 1876) was followed by a reduction in the older broad gauge locomotive stock. Thus, 50 engines of the Bristol & Exeter and South Devon railways were scrapped between 1880 and 1885, and a further 36 between 1886 and 1890. One consequence of these changes was that Bristol & Exeter engines started to serve as far west as Penzance and a passenger used to the dark green, named South Devon engines 'up front' had to become accustomed to plain black Bristol & Exeter engines, sporting only numbers - such was the austere policy of that railway's locomotive engineer!

The increasing weight of the remaining broad gauge expresses, and a shortage of goods and general traffic engines, led to the building of convertible engines which, after broad gauge was eliminated, might live on in narrow (4 ft 8½ in.) gauge form. Convertible engines came down to west Cornwall, most notably Armstrong's standard 0-6-0 double-framed saddle tanks. Some of these, numbered in the ranges 1238 to 1257 and 1566 to 1580, had already put in several years on the narrow gauge, before being converted to broad gauge as a temporary measure, between 1884 and 1888. Including their original use on the narrow gauge, these engines must be accounted one of the most successful, if unglamorous, products of the broad gauge era, being at home on both passenger and goods services.

The growth in traffic, following the adoption of broad gauge, forced the railway to build a new engine shed just outside Penzance station and, with it, a coaling stage and water tower. The water tower is atop the building to the right of this picture. The 1880 plan on page 81 shows how cramped the new engine shed and other facilities were, but the Penzance boundary ran just behind the site and enforced economy in planning. 'Dean Goods' 0-6-0 No. 2314 is seen in the foreground. This locomotive dates from 1883, as built it had a domeless-boiler, but this had been replaced during the 1890s.   *GW Trust Collection*

In Associated Companies days the South Devon was responsible for providing both locomotives and rolling stock for the broad gauge passenger trains (though some rolling stock, on long-distance trains, might originate beyond Plymouth) but when the Great Western took over, and as the broad gauge mileage shrank, more modern carriages reached the far West. These included convertible stock, having narrow bodies on broad gauge frames.

Overall, the period from 1876 to 1892 can be viewed now as one of transition. The decline of broad gauge, sentiment aside, was to be welcomed and no more so than in the far West. It is easy to forget, when looking at photographs of the majestic London expresses, that broad gauge imposed severe limitations on both the Great Western and its passengers who, unless they kept to the London main line, were faced with the inconvenience of a gauge change at some point or another along the way. And where passengers suffered, goods and merchandise did likewise, to the disadvantage of businesses in the old West Cornwall area.

Incidents and Accidents

On 17th September, 1867, there was a 'collision' at Hayle. Guard Penna, concerned that his passenger train was going too fast, applied the brakes strongly with the result that the couplings parted between two of the carriages. The rearward carriages fell back, only to crash into the front half of the train when the driver, seeing what had happened, brought it quickly to a standstill. No-one was injured. Driver Hill was fined a nominal 10 shillings for driving too fast and the Secretary was instructed to issue an 'Order' that guards were not, as a rule, to apply their brakes unless signalled to do so by the driver in the usual manner.

At Penwithers Junction, scene of the most serious accident in West Cornwall days, the inherent stability of broad gauge engines and trains was sorely tested in April 1869 when the 3.00 pm up mail train was turned into the narrow gauge Newham branch, fortunately without injury to the passengers or serious damage to the train. The only other incident reported concerned a boy named Harvey, who was committed to trial for injuring guard Butler by throwing a stone at St Just. Nothing changes.

Chacewater station served an area once noted for its tin mines - the immediate vicinity being literally honeycombed with former mine workings. The proximity of these subterranean workings occasionally led to subsidence or 'runs', and on 22nd January, 1874 The West Briton reported a curious incident in which an unfortunate railwayman had almost lost his life:

> On Thursday night a run took place on the West Cornwall Railway, near the Chacewater station. An old shaft ran in to a depth of about ten fathoms, close under the permanent way, and carried a man also. It appears that one of the servants of the Company, named Roskilley, on his way to the station about half-past six on Friday morning, saw a dark object, but could not make it out. On going nearer, he found it to be an open shaft, and unfortunately fell into it to a depth of about six fathoms. Here he remained calling out lustily.

Two photographs of an accommodation crossing on the West Cornwall mixed gauge. There is no indication as to why these photographs were taken, where or when! As to why, a possible explanation is to record the scene of an accident. The WCR and its successors met several claims for compensation for animals, killed when straying on the line. The disc and crossbar signal and warning notice are prominent, the latter on the furthest side of the track from the open, ungated road access and possibly of little help to man or beast. There is a fine house in the background that might enable the location to be pinpointed - does it still stand?

(Both) Royal Institution of Cornwall

A lad passing heard cries and could see no one, but at length made out the man, who called upon him to go to the station as fast as possible, and stop the train just then due. This was done, and assistance sent by the station master to the poor fellow Roskilley, who was got out much bruised and greatly frightened. The shaft appears to be an old one connected with Wheal Busy Great Audit, and was unknown to the authorities. Having been properly secured, the trains were sent on without much delay.

The railways of Cornwall have operated safely for a period of one and a half centuries, no passenger having been killed as a result of an accident within that period. There have, on the other hand, been numerous incidents involving derailments, breakaways and equipment failures, and on Saturday 8th January, 1876 *The Falmouth Packet* reported the following mishap that had recently taken place at Camborne station:

COLLISION ON THE WEST CORNWALL RAILWAY - A serious accident occurred on the West Cornwall Railway on Thursday. The guard's van of a goods train broke away while being shunted at Camborne, and dashed down the incline westwards. It was brought up when close to Penpounds Viaduct [sic] by coming into collision with a goods train advancing in the opposite direction, and the line was instantly strewn with merchandise, and remained obstructed for some hours. The engine-driver and stoker escaped, but the guard received injuries.

Staff

The introduction of broad gauge services to west Cornwall was supported by a nucleus of South Devon staff. Initially three broad gauge engine drivers were based at Penzance - Messrs Clatworthy, Westlake and Thomas. At Carn Brea, William Finney was installed as foreman under H.T. Ferguson (of unauthorised building fame). G.S. Denbigh (in 1864 the line's Accountant was promoted superintendent of the line (£300 per annum) and J.D. Sheriff as Engineer (£350 per annum). Henry Appleby, the last West Cornwall locomotive engineer, stayed on under the South Devon regime for little over a year, before moving in 1867 to the Manchester, Sheffield and Lincolnshire Railway.

For the tenure of the Associated Companies the majority of the general staff in West Cornwall were local men. The time had not yet come when staff would move around the country with promotion. Staffing at Penzance from the inception of the West Cornwall to 1891 is considered further in Chapter Eight.

There is a very well-known photograph generally misdescribed as staff of Penzance station *circa* 1876-1892. The wide variety of uniforms in this photograph suggest that 'make do and mend' was well and truly in vogue since no two uniforms are alike.

Cornwall and West Cornwall Railways.

B

To _____

_____ }
Viaduct Ganger. }

Station, _____ day of _____ 187__

Repairs of _____ Viaduct No. _____ .

I have received your Requisition No. ____ , and will block

the Line from _____ to _____

after the ____ m ____ Train has reached that Station.

Station Master.

Rules for gangers and others employed on the permanent way May 1872

Forty-nine rules, some of which are summarised below, applied to employees of the South Devon, Cornwall and West Cornwall Railways:

General
2. No rails to be removed or work done which will interfere with free use of line without an order in writing, except in the case of an emergency.
9. Immediate assistance to be rendered by all men on the line following an accident.

Signals
11. All men signalling trains to stand facing them, if possible, preferably on elevated footing.
12. The signal 'All Right' consists in holding one arm in a horizontal position pointing across the line of rails on which the train is running, or by exhibiting a white flag [at night a white light held steadily, facing the train - Rule 15].
13. The caution signal to 'Go Slowly' consists in holding one arm straight up or by exhibiting a green flag [at night a green lamp - Rule 16].
14. The danger signal 'To Stop' consists in holding both arms straight up or by exhibiting a red flag [at night a red light - Rule 17 - or, in the absence of a red light, the violent waving of a light horizontally indicates danger - Rule 18].

Gangers
28. During very stormy weather gangers must keep their district watched by day and by night.
34. Trains preceding an unscheduled special train will show a double red disc behind (at night time two red lights). If two trains pass showing double reds it means two special trains follow.
36. The special train itself shows one red and one green disc behind (at night time one red and one green light).
49. Notice - Six days notice to be given on either side, except in case of misconduct, when notice is immediate.

Chapter Five

Subsequent History of the West Cornwall Line

As we have seen, the Great Western Railway and its allies assumed full responsibility for the West Cornwall line in 1866, and the West of England main line was thereby brought under unified management and control. For 325¼ miles, this long artery of communication extended from Paddington to Bristol via the old GWR main line, and then continued south-westwards to Exeter over the Bristol & Exeter line; from Exeter, the route continued via the former South Devon and Cornwall Railway lines to Truro, from where the West Cornwall route formed the final link in the long chain of broad gauge lines between Paddington and Penzance.

The Paddington to Penzance line was, by any definition, a major component of the Victorian railway system, its great distance being exceeded only by the two Anglo-Scottish trunk lines - neither of which was controlled by one company, as was the case with the Great Western main line to the far West.

Completion of the System

Before abandonment of the broad gauge there had been two additions to the railway system in west Cornwall. First of all, on 1st June 1877, a broad gauge branch was opened between St Erth station (formerly St Ives Road) on the WCR main line and St Ives, a distance of 4 miles 72 chains. The line was single track throughout, with intermediate stations at Lelant and Carbis Bay.

The new branch line was worked independently of the main line, with a limited number of through trips to and from Penzance for operational purposes. These through workings were normally in the form of empty stock workings or light engine movements. In 1883, the St Ives branch was served by 11 up and 11 down workings between St Ives and St Erth, the journey time being 15 minutes. By July 1894 the train service had been reduced to nine trains each way on weekdays, with two extra workings on Mondays only.

The St Ives branch was a success from its very inception, and in addition to carrying large numbers of summer visitors to St Ives, the line also conveyed large amounts of agricultural produce such as broccoli. Fish traffic was, in the early years, of even greater importance. St Ives was one of the largest fishing ports in Britain, and catches big enough to fill 2,000 or 3,000 hogsheads (52½ gallon casks) were by no means unknown. As each hogshead contained about 2,200 fish, it will be seen that these enormous catches would have totalled anything up to 6,000,000 fish! The largest catch was 12,000,000 fish, recorded in 1851.

These huge catches were probably counter-productive, in that they depressed prices, and defeated the object of fishing for profit. Unrestricted fishing resulted in severely depleted fish stocks and, on 8th January, 1891 *The West Briton* reported that 'not a single pilchard' had been caught by a seine net during the previous year. The decline of pilchard fishing was accompanied by a severe depression in the Cornish tin mining industry. The long-term future of the West Cornwall Railway and its branches then became closely linked with the development of tourism.

The local railway system was completed on 9th May, 1887, when an 8 mile 67 chain standard gauge branch was opened between Gwinear Road and Helston. The line was constructed by an independent company known as the Helston Railway Company, but its train services were worked by the GWR under the provisions of an operating agreement. The Helston Railway was financed by local landowners. Its leading supporters included William Bickford-Smith MP, W. Molesworth St Aubyn and the Revd Sir Vyell Vyvyan. These gentlemen clearly hoped that their new branch line would enable farmers to send their produce to the London markets.

The railway was single track throughout, with intermediate stations at Praze and Nancegollan. The largest engineering feature on the new line was the Cober viaduct, near Helston. This impressive structure had six 50 ft arches and a total length of 370 ft. The Helston branch had a service of seven trains each way in 1894, the normal journey time being around 25 minutes. An additional stopping place was opened at Truthall in 1905.

The Great Blizzard of 1891

Snow is rarely seen in West Cornwall, which is noted for its mild and equable climate. Occasionally, however, severe blizzards may be experienced, and on these occasions communications are often disrupted. One such snow storm commenced on Monday 9th March, 1891 and, by the end of the day much of the countryside was buried in deep snow drifts. The down 'Flying Dutchman' had left Paddington in clear weather, but on arrival at Plymouth the snow drifts were already five feet deep. The conditions worsened as the broad gauge express continued its westwards journey behind South Devon 4-4-0 saddle tank No. 2128 *Leopard* and, on approaching Camborne station, the locomotive was derailed. Further progress was impossible and those aboard the stranded train were helped through the drifting snow to nearby Camborne, where they were given emergency accommodation in the local hotels.

Earlier the up 'Dutchman' had set out from Penzance with about 80 passengers, including several babies. The train passed safely along the West Cornwall line, but conditions were so bad that the engine was brought to a halt by fallen telegraph wires at St Germans, on the Cornwall Railway section. The passengers were obliged to spend the night in the station building at St Germans, though on the following day the severely delayed train was able to reach Plymouth, where it was terminated as a result of the severe weather conditions.

There were further problems on branch lines such as the Helston route, which was blocked by 15 ft snow drifts. The evening service from Helston to Gwinear Road, for example, became completely stuck in the cuttings between Praze and Nancegollan, and the stranded passengers were forced to spend the night in the train. On the following morning, the train crew and one passenger were able to

The South Devon Railway assumed responsibility for West Cornwall operations in 1866, on behalf of the Associated Companies and 4-4-0 saddle-tank engines such as the 1872 built convertible *Leopard*, seen here at Penzance, became a familiar sight on WCR lines. *Leopard* was never converted to narrow gauge, her last melancholy duty being a shunter at Swindon's broad gauge graveyard. As a result, she was one of the last two active broad gauge engines, not being cut up until June 1893.   *Great Western Society/Reed Collection*

reach the safety of a neighbouring farm. Towns such as Helston and Falmouth were, by this time, cut off from the main line - while the West Cornwall and Cornwall routes were themselves blocked by immense snow drifts.

On 12th March, 1891, *The West Briton* reported that that the River Fowey had frozen over, while the terrific snow storm at St Austell had caused the suspension of nearly all business transactions, and a stoppage of the clay works. At Bodmin, the drifts were said to be up to 20 ft deep, and at Falmouth two colliers had been driven ashore 'at the back of Messrs Grose & Sons' premises, and were literally jammed between the boundary wall of Mrs Downing's garden . . . the stern of one of the vessels breaking down the garden wall, while her bow demolished a good portion of the Cabmen's Rest at the end of the tank adjoining the King's Arms Hotel premises'.

The disruption lasted for almost a whole week and in that time the railway, postal and telegraph systems were paralysed. Sadly, the loss of all communications had imperilled life at sea, in that it was virtually impossible to summon help for stricken vessels that had become trapped at various places around the treacherous Cornish coast. The worst loss of life occurred at Penare Point on Tuesday 11th March, when the four-masted steel sailing vessel *Bay of Panama* was driven ashore at the height of the tempest. Local rescue parties managed to save 17 seamen with the aid of a 'rocket apparatus' and breeches buoy, but the master, his wife and 18 seamen were drowned.

News of the wreck was brought to Helston by a man on horseback, but as the telegraph wires were down and the railway out of action he had to walk through the snow storm to Falmouth. 'On the way he encountered enormous difficulties', reported *The West Briton*:

> . . . for a mile and a half or two miles he had to crawl along on his hands and knees through the snow. His face became coated with ice, and several times he had to break the ice from his eyes, whilst icicles hung from his ears. More dead than alive he came across a cottage in the occupation of a mason named Combellack. Here, he rested until daylight on Wednesday morning, when he pursued his journey and arrived in Falmouth about nine o'clock.

In the meantime, enormous efforts were being made to clear the impacted snow from the West Cornwall main line. This led to a unfortunate incident at Chacewater, where a locomotive had become entrapped in the huge snow drifts. A relief engine had been sent out to help clear the line, and it was decided that this could best be achieved if the rescue engine charged into the 15 ft drifts at full speed. This dramatic method of snow clearing was usually quite effective, but on this occasion the pilot engine ploughed into the drift with such force that it collided violently with the trapped locomotive. William Richards, a brakesman, was thrown off the engine and sustained serious back injuries.

Towards the end of the week the wind died down, and communications were slowly restored. The Helston branch was re-opened on Saturday 14th March, and the 200 men who had toiled for two days to clear the line were welcomed by loud cheers when they finally entered Helston. On the Falmouth branch, a locomotive was employed to plough through the drifts, and a reporter from *The Royal Cornwall Gazette* described how:

> Our drivers put on extra steam and our party cheered again as we cut through the white banks scattering snow on either side like foam from the bow of an ocean liner. The sight was beautiful, the white undulating surface of tile snow stretching away on every side, except when relieved by the bare branches of the trees, or the solitary, half-starved cattle and sheep prowling about looking for a morsel of something green.

By Sunday 15th March, the unexpected crisis was virtually over, and on the following Monday the local railway system was more or less back to normal. The 'Great Blizzard' would nevertheless be remembered for years afterwards as one of the worst storms to hit Cornwall.

New Viaducts and Doubling

The Great Western lost no time in initiating a programme of renewals and improvements on the West Cornwall line, one of the most obvious changes put into effect during the later years of the 19th century being the progressive elimination of timber viaducts such as those at Blackwater, Redruth and Hayle. These were, in general, replaced by conventional stone-built viaducts, the seven-span masonry viaduct at Blackwater being typical of the new structures provided on the former West Cornwall line under Great Western auspices.

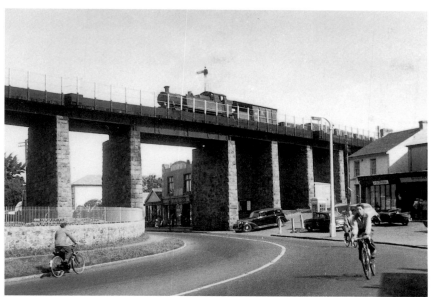

Hayle viaduct *c.* 1954, with a '45XX' class 2-6-2T crossing with the Hayle Wharves branch goods train.   *P.Q. Treloar*

Apart from Penzance viaduct - which had been replaced in 1871 following storm damage - the first timber viaduct to be rebuilt was that at Angarrack, a masonry structure being brought into use (on a new alignment) in 1885. The Guildford and Hayle viaducts were replaced in 1886, followed by Penwithers in 1887, and Chacewater, Blackwater and Redruth viaducts in 1888. Penponds, the last major viaduct to be replaced on the West Cornwall line, was rebuilt in 1899-1900, a single line over the new viaduct being brought into use in September 1899, with full double track working from the following January.

Another important change carried out by the Great Western concerned the doubling of the line between Truro and Penzance. This was, however, a somewhat protracted process, and it may come as a surprise to discover that the final section of double track was not installed on the West Cornwall route until April 1930.

Chronologically, the first sections to be doubled were those between Truro and Penwithers, and Marazion and Ponsandane, which were both tackled in 1895. The line between Redruth and Camborne was doubled in a number of short operations between 1894 and 1898, while the Hayle to St Erth section was converted to double track in September 1899.

The remaining single track sections were doubled at intervals during the next 30 years, the various sections being brought into use as shown in the following table:

Doubling of the Line 1900-1930

Section of Line	Date of Doubling
Camborne to Gwinear Road	January 1900
Chacewater to Scorrier	December 1902
Angarrack to Hayle	December 1909
Drump Lane Goods Yard to Redruth	December 1911
Baldhu to Chacewater	July 1913
Penwithers Junction to Baldhu	July 1914
Gwinear Road to Angarrack	June 1915
Ponsandane to Penzance station	July 1921
Hayle to Marazion	June 1929
Scorrier station to Drump Lane	January 1930

Further alterations and improvements were put into effect at Truro, Penzance, and at many of the intermediate stations, most of the original West Cornwall station buildings being entirely rebuilt in the years following the Great Western takeover. At Truro, for example, the former Cornwall Railway station was swept away, and in its place the GWR provided a typical, late Victorian red brick station, with ample accommodation for goods and parcels traffic.

At the western end of the line, Penzance station was similarly reconstructed in dressed granite, the new facilities being completed in 1880 at a cost of around £6,000. The intermediate stations, meanwhile, were rebuilt and remodelled as necessary - Marazion and St Erth being lavishly reconstructed in granite, while Camborne was provided with a standard red brick booking office and waiting room block in the same architectural style as neighbouring Truro.

Elsewhere, the Great Western added a variety of new facilities for both passenger and goods traffic, one of the most important additions made to the local system at this time being an entirely new goods station at Drump Lane, Redruth, which was brought into use on 17th June, 1912 as a replacement for the original goods yard at Redruth station, itself replacing the yard formerly the station of the old Hayle Railway. (These and other details will be examined in greater depth in Chapters Six and Seven.)

The signalling arrangements provided in West Cornwall and Associated Companies days had been fairly basic, semaphore signals favoured by the West Cornwall and disc and crossbar signals by its successors, and although rudimentary home and stop signals were in use at stations and junctions, interlocking was unknown, (apart from a simple form of interlocking at Penwithers Junction). In the 1880s and 1890s, however, the Great Western introduced a fully modernised signalling system, with standard Great Western signals and signal boxes in place of the earlier 'station signals', 'time interval' system and control by telegraph clearance from station to station from 1854.

As a general rule, the signal boxes erected by the GWR from the 1890s onwards were of two basic types, being either gable-roofed cabins with small-paned windows, or hip-roofed structures with distinctive five-paned window frames - the latter type being constructed from the turn-of-the-century onwards, whereas the gable-roof cabins were typically built during the 1890s.

Narrowing the Line

When first introduced the broad gauge of 7 ft 0¼ in. had been a far-sited innovation which, if properly developed, would have resulted in an ultra-safe, high-speed railway system that would have been the envy of the world. Unfortunately, the majority of lines built throughout the United Kingdom (and indeed in most other countries) were constructed to the 'coal wagon gauge' of 4 ft 8½ in., and this eventually became the standard gauge in England, Scotland and Wales (a wider gauge of 5 ft 3 in. being adopted in Ireland).

The Great Western Railway and its subsidiaries remained loyal to the broad gauge for many years, but it soon became clear that they would to comply with the national standard of 4 ft 8½ in. In fact, many West Country travellers (and even some railway shareholders) had long argued that it would be better for all concerned if the GWR system were 'narrowed' to permit through running to all parts of the national railway network, and in 1892 the Great Western Chairman announced that the broad gauge would at last be abandoned.

It was decided that the entire system west of Exeter would be converted to standard gauge in one gigantic operation, which would be carried out on the weekend of 20th-22nd May, 1892. To facilitate this operation, the company stopped all incoming Cornish goods traffic several days before the designated conversion weekend, though loaded wagons and empty stock were worked eastwards until Thursday 19th May. On the mixed gauge West Cornwall line, purely narrow gauge goods traffic was handled until the eve of conversion on Friday 20th May but, thereafter, the entire system was shut down until the following Monday.

As the appointed time drew near empty stock trains worked northwards to Swindon while, in the reverse direction, an endless procession of engineering trains conveyed men and equipment into Devon and Cornwall. The last up broad gauge passenger train left Penzance at 6.30 pm on Friday 20th May, and this working reached its destination at Plymouth by 10.25 pm. In the down direction, the final passenger service was the 8.40 pm from Plymouth to Liskeard - though as far as the West Cornwall section was concerned, the very last passenger train appears to have been the 8.25 pm branch service to St Ives.

Once these scheduled services had reached their destinations, a series of empty stock workings conveyed all redundant broad gauge rolling stock out of Cornwall - the final train from Penzance being run 35 minutes late at approximately 9.45 pm, when empty passenger vehicles were sent eastwards behind two locomotives.

All public services ceased late in the evening of Friday 20th May, and in the next few hours some 5,000 men worked non-stop to convert over 170 miles of broad gauge trackwork. Many sidings had already been narrowed while, to further expedite the work, 4 ft 8½ in. gauge locomotives had already been transferred to Newton Abbot, Plymouth and Carn Brea Yard, in order to work the first standard gauge services during the following week. On Saturday 21st May an emergency service was worked over the West Cornwall line between Truro and Penzance, with road connections to and from Falmouth.

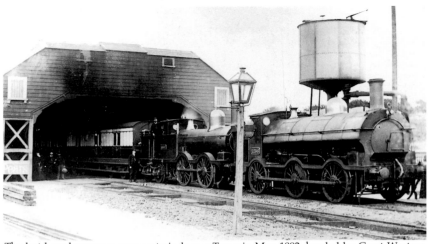

The last broad gauge passenger train leaves Truro in May 1892, headed by Great Western Railway-built locomotives Nos. 1256 and 3557. No 1256 was an Armstrong standard class 0-6-0 convertible which started life in 1877, as a narrow gauge engine. It was converted to broad gauge in 1887 and re-converted to narrow gauge in 1892. No. 3557, seen here as an 0-4-4 back tank, started life as an 0-4-2 saddle tank but was converted in 1891. After barely a year it was again converted, this time to narrow gauge.   *Great Western Society/Reed Collection*

The huge conversion operation was successfully completed by the evening of Sunday 22nd May, and on Monday 23rd May the West Cornwall line (together with the rest of the Great Western system west of Exeter) was re-opened to public traffic as a purely standard gauge route. The first narrow gauge passenger train left Truro at 7.50 am with three carriages and a guard's van supplied from the Cornwall Minerals line.

The ending of the broad gauge did not pass unrecorded, and the conversion operation attracted much attention in the local press. On Monday 23rd May 1892, for example, *The West Briton* printed the following report:

> Traffic on the Great Western Railway between Falmouth and Exeter was suspended in the early hours of Saturday; it was resumed this morning, and in the interval over 200 miles of line in Cornwall and Devon were converted from broad to narrow gauge. About 5,000 were engaged in the work, which was under the superintendence of Mr T.H. Gibbons, the Divisional Engineer.
>
> It was thought by many that the Great Western Company were attempting the impossible in arranging to carry out such a gigantic undertaking in so short a time; but the staff organised for the occasion proved themselves equal to the emergency, and before they dropped their tools last night all the main lines were in readiness for the resumption of traffic this morning.
>
> The night mail from Paddington to Penzance started at the usual time last night, and experienced no delay on the journey.

The paper also provided some interesting details regarding the vast labour force that had been transported into Devon and Cornwall to carry out the conversion work. Many men had camped-out in station waiting rooms, goods sheds or even in tents beside the line - over 80 workers being accommodated in and around Truro station, as recorded in the following extract from *The West Briton:*

Of the men who were imported, eighty four were lodged at the Truro station, where they were accommodated in two large tents and in the goods shed. Some of the men reached Truro station early on Thursday, but the greater portion came on Friday morning, and, like their comrades who arrived on the previous day, they found an abundant supply of hot oatmeal awaiting their arrival.

In general, each of the men engaged, on the conversion operation had brought with him his own food, but to prevent hardship (and keep up morale) the GWR also provided a supply of thin porridge made from oatmeal, sugar and water - over 10 tons of oatmeal being obtained, for this purpose! As a further gesture, each man was offered a straw-filled palliasse and two coarse blankets, while Mr Wills (a Great Western Director and member of the W.D. & H.O. Wills tobacco company) donated 5,000 two ounce packets of tobacco.

On a footnote, it should perhaps be mentioned that, at the time of the 1892 gauge conversion, much of the Great Western system had already been adapted for mixed gauge operation. On the Paddington to Penzance main line, for instance, mixed gauge was available between Paddington and Exeter and (as we have seen) on the West Cornwall section between Truro and Penzance. However, the line from Exeter to Truro remained a purely broad gauge route which, with its various branches, comprised over 170 miles of 7 ft 0¼ in. gauge track.

Much of the work carried out during the weekend of 20th-22nd May took place on this entirely broad gauge section, but the great conversion had obvious implications for mixed gauge lines such as the West Cornwall route which were part of the wider broad gauge system; in all 213 miles of 7 ft 0¼ in. gauge trackwork were involved in conversion. The St Ives branch had been (almost) entirely broad gauge. A photograph of the line at Carbis Bay, taken some time after conversion, shows 'mixed' gauge track, suggesting that the narrowing there was more than just a 'moving in' of broad gauge rail. It may even have been that this isolated line was given a third rail some time before May 1892. Where, as on the West Cornwall main line, narrow gauge was already in place the task facing the Great Western was more straightforward - the superfluous broad gauge rail being removable at leisure.

The 'Cornish Riviera Express'

Although the demise of the broad gauge was widely-mourned throughout the West of England, the gauge conversion brought in its wake a considerable improvement in standards of passenger comfort. Even before the conversion the Great Western company had been constructing comfortable bogie coaches which were at least the equal of any vehicle running on rival lines. Full corridors, as such, were not yet provided, though the best coaches were equipped with lavatory compartments reached by side gangways. For several years prior to the conversion, the company had been building coaches with 'narrow' bodies on broad gauge underframes, which could quickly converted to standard gauge when the time for full conversion arrived.

The up 'Cornishman' is pictured leaving Penzance *c.* 1899 with Great Western 'Duke' No. 3273 *Amorel* in charge. This locomotive was rebuilt as a 'Bulldog' in February 1902.

P.Q. Treloar Collection

Penzance station looking west *circa* 1912. The 'Cornish Riviera Express' stands in platform one.

Lens of Sutton Collection

The first Great Western corridor trains appeared on the Birkenhead and South Wales main lines, but in June 1893 improved coaches were introduced on the 10.15 am service from Paddington to Penzance and the balancing 10.45 am service from Penzance to London. These coaches, which were gangwayed with separate compartments and smoking saloons, ran as a four-coach set, a fifth coach being conveyed to and from Truro for Falmouth traffic.

At the time of the gauge conversion the 10.15 am from Paddington - known semi-officially as 'The Cornishman' - was one of two prestige workings between Paddington and Penzance, the other being the celebrated 'Flying Dutchman'. Except for a short period in 1867-69, when it was withdrawn as an economy measure, the latter train had departed from Paddington at 11.45 am without a break since the 1860s. In May 1892, immediately after the gauge conversion, the 'Flying Dutchman' was accelerated by 15 minutes to become the fastest train in the world at that time; it reached Plymouth at 6.00 pm and Penzance by 9.00 pm.

Further progress came in the summer of 1904 when the GWR introduced a new 'Limited' express from Paddington, which reached Plymouth in 4 hours 27 minutes having run non-stop from London; Penzance was reached at 5.10 pm, exactly seven hours after leaving London. As the new train was intended primarily for Cornish holiday traffic, it called *en route* at Truro, Gwinear Road and St Erth, from where travellers could change into the branch line trains to Falmouth, Helston and St Ives respectively.

The train was at first provided only during the summer months, but from 1906 onwards it became an all-year-round working. At the same time, it started to run via the Great Western's new cut-off line through Westbury, the timings from Paddington to Plymouth being slashed to just 4 hours 10 minutes, while Penzance was reached in 6 hours 40 minutes.

As an imaginative marketing ploy, the Great Western had run a 'name the train' competition in *The Railway Magazine*, and several entries had suggested a 'Riviera' theme. In the event, there were two joint winners, the suggested names being 'The Cornish Riviera Limited' and 'The Riviera Express', though in practice the train soon became known to the travelling public as 'The Cornish Riviera Express'. (Railwaymen, in contrast, usually called it simply 'The Limited'.)

Two 4-4-0s head an express across the old viaduct over the beach at Penzance. Note the 'Dreadnought' coaches in the train.   *P.Q. Treloar Collection*

The down 'Cornish Riviera Express' approaches Marazion headed by 'Hall' class 4-6-0 No. 5926 *Grotrian Hall* in May 1940.   *B.A. Butt*

BR 'Britannia' class 4-6-2 No. 70019 *Lightning* arriving at Penzance with the 'Cornish Riviera Express' in October 1951.   *B.A. Butt*

From 1906 onwards, 'The Cornish Riviera' left Paddington at 10.30 am, and this became its traditional time of departure throughout the years. The train was then composed of luxurious 68 ft 'Dreadnought' coaches, which were corridor-fitted and built to the maximum width permitted by the generous Great Western loading gauge. The train was equipped with electric light, and seat reservations were used for the first time - a feature of the service that has continued to this day.

The 'Cornish Riviera Express' was, from its inception, a prestigious, luxury working that catered unashamedly for a wealthy, upper middle class clientele. The new train soon replaced the 'Flying Dutchman' as the flagship express service between London and Penzance, though the 'Cornishman' was revived in 1935 as a relief service for the 'Cornish Riviera Express' leaving Paddington at 10.35 am and serving various intermediate stations east of Plymouth by slip coaches.

The 'Cornish Riviera Express' had, meanwhile, developed into a multiple-destination service that ran non-stop to Plymouth, slipping coaches at Westbury, Taunton and Exeter, and then dropping off through portions for Falmouth at Truro and St Ives at St Erth. By the mid-1920s the train had grown into a heavy 14-coach formation, with through coaches for Weymouth, Minehead, Ilfracombe, Kingsbridge, Newquay, Falmouth, St Ives and Penzance - the total weight on leaving Paddington being some 500 tons (although this was progressively reduced as the various through portions were slipped or detached *en route* to Penzance).

The 'Cornish Riviera Express' was always seen as a showpiece train, not only on the Paddington to Penzance run but also in terms of Great Western publicity, and the company made sure that its very best locomotives and rolling stock were available for this celebrated long-distance working. In 1935, for example, two trains of special 'Centenary Riviera' stock were built as part of the company's hundredth birthday celebrations. These new vehicles were designed with maximum comfort in mind, with large, plate glass windows through which travellers could admire the countryside passing. The 'Centenary Riviera' stock was no less than 9 ft 7 in. wide, full advantage having again been taken of the Great Western loading gauge (which was of course a legacy of the broad gauge).

Although the 'Cornish Riviera Express' always ran from Paddington to Penzance, the precise pattern of operation has varied over the years, some resorts being served by through portions while others were omitted. However, as far as the West Cornwall line was concerned Truro, Gwinear Road and St Erth were usually served - though Gwinear Road and even Truro were omitted at certain times. Further alterations were effected on summer Saturdays, to cater for the exceptional numbers of holiday-makers to resorts such as Newquay and St Ives.

Road Motor Services in West Cornwall

The Great Western Railway was a noted pioneer in the field of rural motor bus services, the company's first scheduled road motor service having been introduced between Helston and the Lizard in August 1903. By 1904 the company was operating 36 buses (more than in the whole of London) and these vehicles effectively carried the railway into remote, under-populated areas which would have been unsuitable for conventional railway operation.

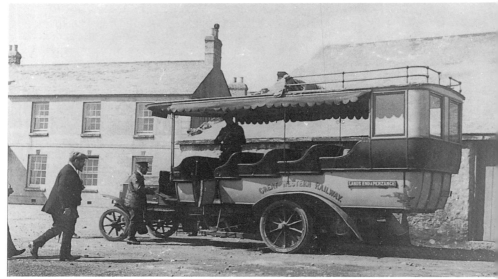

GWR observation car or covered charabanc; notice 'Lands End & Penzance' route board at the
rear.   *R.M. Casserley Collection*

An early GWR single-deck bus fitted experimentally (?) with seats on the roof and a vertical
ladder (fitted at the rear) in order to get there. The vehicle is seen outside the Woolcock's
Commercial Hotel in St Just.   *John Cummings Collection*

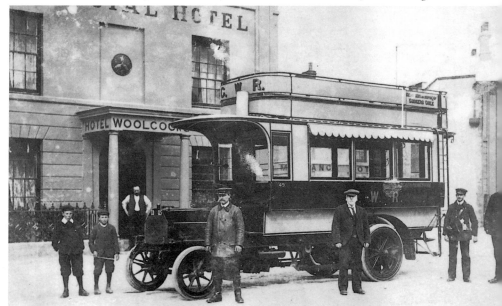

There was a rapid expansion of Great Western motor bus services after World War I and, within a few years, regular services were in operation in West Cornwall and elsewhere. Penzance and Helston both became major centres of the company's 'road motor' operations, typical services being from Penzance station to Land's End, Porthcurno, St Just and Zennor. There was also a useful cross-country service between Penzance and Falmouth via Marazion, Ashton, Breage, Porthleven, Helston, Longdowns, Mabe and Penryn.

The first vehicles used on these services were Milnes-Daimler 16 or 20 horse power buses, but other makes soon appeared and, by the late 1920s, the vehicles operating on the Penzance-based road motor services were as shown below:

Some GWR Motor Buses used on the Penzance routes *c*.1928

GWR No.	Reg. No.	Type	Notes
216	T6680	AEC/YB	Rebuilt as lorry
230	E3413	AEC/YB	Rebuilt as lorry
234	AX1414	AEC/YB	Rebuilt as lorry
260	XK9103	AEC/YB	Rebuilt as lorry
261	XK9930	AEC/YB	Rebuilt as lorry
265	XL1794	AEC/YB	Rebuilt as lorry
266	XL1793	AEC/YB	Rebuilt as lorry
276	LX8263	AEC/YB	Rebuilt as lorry
280	LX9743	AEC/YB	Rebuilt as lorry
282	XO7577	AEC/YB	Rebuilt as lorry
286	XM9791	AEC/YB	Rebuilt as lorry
452	BH7725	AEC/YB	Lorry, fitted with charabanc body for summer work only
460	BH7724	AEC/YB	Lorry, fitted with charabanc body for summer work only
521	XL8004	Burford 30 cwt	St Ives Hotel bus
811	XW1877	Burford 30 cwt	Rebuilt as a lorry
819	XW4564	Burford 30 cwt	Rebuilt as a lorry
854	XY2107	Burford 30 cwt	Rebuilt as a lorry
859	XY7431	Burford 30 cwt	Rebuilt as a lorry
867	XY7439	Burford 30 cwt	Rebuilt as a lorry
884	YK3813	Burford 30 cwt	Rebuilt as a lorry
885	YK3814	Burford 30 cwt	Rebuilt as a lorry
917	XY7442	Thornycroft 30 cwt	To Western National
939	YK3833	Thornycroft 30 cwt	To Bristol Tramways
1037	AF4747	Ford 1 ton van	To Western National
1038	RL5818	Albion	To Western National
1039	RL7159	Albion	To Western National
1040	AF1558	Studebaker	To Western National
1041	FK3196	Overland	To Western National
1112	RL6278	Albion	To Western National
1204	YR1154	Maudslay ML3	To Western National
1217	YR6416	Maudslay ML3	To Western National
1220	YH3792	Maudslay ML3	To Western National
1233	UC4239	Maudslay ML3	To Western National
1235	UC4863	Maudslay ML3	To Western National
1236	UC7505	Maudslay ML3	To Western National
1239	UC7506	Maudslay ML3	To Western National
1245	YH6818	Guy FBB	To Western National

A busy scene showing GWR bus No. 64 AF 647 being loaded in preparation for departure from Penzance station to Land's End. Driver Westlake stands in front of the vehicle.

John Cummings Collection

Driver Forrest and conductor Dai Jones pose next to their vehicle, an AEC bus, No. 220 BX 918 outside the station at Penzance. The board on the front indicates a subsequent departure for Land's End. Note the bicycle on the roof of the bus.   *John Cummings Collection*

These Great Western motor buses were usually adorned in a variant of the GWR coaching stock livery, though photographic evidence suggests that some vehicles had carried an overall brown livery during the earlier period of road motor operation.

The railway bus services were at their peak during the 1920s, by which time a multiplicity of routes had been introduced. Some of these services actually competed with the railway, though this element of competition could be contained so long as the bus services concerned remained in railway hands. When that ceased to be the case, the railway found it had aided its competitors by establishing so many useful, door-to-door services.

By the later 1920s the GWR was one of the largest bus operators in the country and it seemed, at the time, that the company would continue to expand and develop its huge road motor fleet as an important adjunct to the rail network. Unfortunately, the undoubted success of the Great Western bus fleet led to complaints from the road transport industry to the effect that the GWR (and other railway companies) did not have Parliamentary consent to operate road services, and for this reason the railway bus routes were said to be illegal.

There was an element of truth in the allegation of illegality, and to formalise the situation whereby the Great Western could operate its road services, the company decided to seek Parliamentary approval for its extensive road transport operations.

Nancherrow Hill, St Just was 'troublesome' in the early days of GWR buses. The road surface does not seem much better c.1925.   *John Cummings Collection*

From the 1920s the GWR used some Maudslay vehicles for its bus services to and from Penzance, and at Land's End, during a coastal tour, we see driver Thomas and conductor Hill with Maudslay ML3B coach (Regn No. YV 8565) standing outside Land's End Hotel. The 'board' on the front of the bus indicates that the coastal tour will include Zennor, Gurnard's Head, Morvah, Pendeen, St Just, Land's End and Sennen Cove.   *John Cummings Collection*

In 1928 the Great Western Railway (Road Transport) Act was passed, and this allowed the railway company to own, work and use motor vehicles in its own right. The 1928 Act also enabled the company to enter into agreements with other parties for the operation of road-based motor transport services and, by virtue of these powers, the Great Western Railway acquired a substantial interest in the National Omnibus & Transport Company. As part of this arrangement, all Great Western motor buses in an area bounded by Penzance and Moretonhampstead were transferred to that undertaking on the understanding that the bus company would not compete with the railway.

This agreement, which had been reached after much detailed negotiation, was supposed to lead to much greater co-ordination between road and rail services; it nevertheless signalled the end of the GWR road motor services, and by 1933 all Great Western motor bus services had been handed over to bus companies - the routes in West Cornwall being operated by the newly-created Western National Omnibus Company, which had been formed jointly by the GWR and the National Omnibus & Transport Company.

In retrospect, the formation of the Western National bus company probably did lead to a degree of co-operation between road and rail transport in rural areas, but at the same time the bus company continued to operate at least some routes in competition with the railway - such as that between Penzance and St Ives.

Most of the Great Western motor buses in Cornwall were handed over to the Western National company, while the bus crews were transferred to the new undertaking while retaining their existing conditions of employment and pension rights. Some older vehicles, however, remained in railway use as motor lorries, their original bus bodies being replaced or rebuilt as necessary.

Rural Delivery Services

Country stations such as Gwinear Road and Marazion had traditionally been seen as railheads for the surrounding area, carriers or railway cartage agents being employed to run horse-drawn road feeder services to outlying farms and villages. In the 20th century the Great Western started to take direct control of these local cartage services. Horse transport was used for many years, but in 1910 the Great Western introduced its first motor parcels van, and in the 1920s country lorry services were established at specially-selected railheads throughout the system.

In February 1928 *The Railway Magazine* reported that arrangements had been made for 'about one hundred country lorry services', which would enable farmers, village store keepers and others to get their parcels and perishables to and from the railway, special low collection and delivery rates having been fixed for distances of up to 10 miles.

One of the first of these new railheads was centred on Penzance, and similar 'Country Lorry Centres' were also established at Helston, Redruth and Truro. These stations soon acquired fleets of road delivery vehicles, the lorries in use being of various types, including vans for general parcels and cartage work, and flat-bed trucks for container traffic. Many of the vehicles employed were articulated, with three-wheel tractor portions capable of hauling a variety of two-wheeled trailers.

In addition to the more remote destinations served by the country lorry services, the Great Western also provided free collection and delivery services in and around larger population centres such as Penzance, Redruth and Truro. Other, more sparsely-populated villages or hamlets were served by country carriers or by Western National buses - the employment of the latter being a useful and practicable result of the agreement whereby the Great Western Railway Company had relinquished its own bus services under the terms of the 1928 Road Transport Act.

In order to assist railway staff in deciding on the best collection and delivery arrangements for specific consignments, the Great Western provided an 896-page guide entitled *Towns, Villages & Outlying Works Etc. Served by the Great Western Railway*, and this large green volume listed all places served by the company, together with the mode of conveyance from the nearest GWR station. Goods and parcels for Penzance, for example, were sent to Penzance station - from where the company's road vehicles were used for the final free delivery. Consignments destined for nearby Newlyn, on the other hand, were delivered by lorry or cartage service, while the more remote destinations of Lamorna (5 miles from Penzance station) or Land's End (10 miles) were served both by lorry service and by Western National buses - goods being collected or delivered by railway lorry, while parcels were sent by bus.

Some further information from the book of *Towns, Villages & Outlying Works* is given in the following table, which provides a useful insight into the way in which the Great Western Railway served West Cornwall by road and rail.

Some Typical Goods and Parcels Collection and Delivery Arrangements, 1938

Location	Distance from station	Delivery arrangements
Camborne	-	Free cartage service
Chacewater	1 mile from Chacewater	Cartage service
Gwinear	1¼ miles from Gwinear Road	Lorry service
Kea	2¼ miles from Truro	Private carrier
Lamorna	5 miles from Penzance	Lorry service and Western National bus
Marazion	1½ miles from Marazion	Railway cartage service
Penzance	-	Free cartage service
Portgwarra	10 miles from Penzance	Lorry service and Western National bus
Portreath	4 miles from Redruth	Lorry service and Western National bus
Prussia Cove	4 miles from Marazion	Private carrier
Pulsack	2½ miles from Hayle	Lorry service
Redruth	-	Free cartage service
Roskear	¾ mile from Camborne	Free cartage service
Tredavoe	2½ miles from Penzance	Lorry service
Tredinnick	4 miles from Penzance	Lorry service and Western National bus
Treen	8½ miles from Penzance	Lorry service and Western National bus
Tregavara	2½ miles from Penzance	Lorry service
Treleigh	1½ miles from Redruth	Lorry service and private carrier
Trevenson	1 mile from Carn Brea	Cartage service
Trispen	4 miles from Truro	Private carrier
Truro	-	Free cartage service

The Development of Tourist Traffic

When first constructed in the early years of Queen Victoria's reign, the Hayle and West Cornwall railways had carried a heavy goods and mineral traffic but, with the decline of the Cornish mining industry, in the later years of the 19th century freight traffic became less important. At the same time, large numbers of Cornish people left their native land in search of new work in Australia, North America or South Africa, and this inevitably resulted in a diminution in the level of local passenger traffic. In the event, Cornwall and its economy was saved from further decline by expansion of the china clay industry and, particularly in the far West, by the growth of the Cornish holiday industry - and in the latter case the West Cornwall Railway played an important role.

By the 1870s and 1880s small fishing villages such as Cadgwith and Mullion had been 'discovered' by increasing numbers of summer visitors, while neighbouring Coverack was said by *The West Briton* to be 'filled' with lodgers for 'most of the summer'. Most of these summer visitors travelled into Cornwall by the Great Western Railway and its subsidiaries, and in the next few years the Great Western itself began to promote tourism as a means of stimulating passenger traffic.

Branch lines such as the St Ives route were built, at least in part, with summer tourist traffic in mind, and in the case of St Ives the Great Western even purchased a large hotel - the Tregenna Castle - as a means of encouraging summer (or off-season) visitors into the area. One of the first vistors to the Tregenna Castle Hotel was Sir Daniel Gooch (1816-1889), the Great Western Railway Chairman, who took rooms in the new hotel in September 1878. Sir

Daniel was much impressed by the very high standard of accommodation, and on 22nd September, 1878 he wrote the following note in his private diary:

TREGENNA CASTLE ST IVES - We left Penzance this morning and came here . . . The situation of this house is very fine; it is a castle within its own grounds of about 70 acres, a great part of which are gardens and woods with pretty, shaded walks. The Great Western Company have taken it and opened it as a hotel to encourage the traffic in the west.

The house feels more like a private home than a hotel; the views from it are very fine, looking over the town and bay of St Ives and along the coast as far as Trevose Head. With the bright sunshine today the view was lovely.

The emphasis placed by the Great Western on luxury hotels such as the Tregenna Castle and prestige express train services such as the 'Cornish Riviera' underlines the fact that, until the 1920s and 1930s, the Cornish holiday industry was geared primarily to the needs of the better off. It was the custom, in those days, for people to book accommodation for all or part of the summer, and whole families would then migrate to the seaside with their children, nannies, servants and mountains of luggage. As far as the working class was concerned, 'holidays' would have been no more than occasional day trips to the coast - the distances covered being relatively small.

Some destinations, notably St Ives, became popular venues for day trippers; church outings and Sunday school 'treats', for example, became something of a Victorian institution, and in summer time the large sandy beaches in and around St Ives were often thronged by hundreds of families from the neighbouring Cornish towns.

In later years, the development of holidays with pay gave rise to the annual seaside holiday and, by the 1930s, seaside resorts such as St Ives, Penzance and Marazion had become very busy during the summer season of July and August. Saturdays were the 'change-over' days in which people began or ended their holidays, and many extra trains were provided to cater for the large numbers of additional summer travellers. Most of the Cornish resorts were served by through coaches from Paddington, and on occasions the 'Cornish Riviera Express' was run in as many as five portions to cater for the extraordinary numbers of summer Saturday travellers!

World War II brought an end to the summer holiday trade, but, thereafter, holiday traffic resumed in the late 1940s and early 1950s. At a time when few British families had access to a motor car, the railways carried many thousands of summer visitors, and the West Cornwall line and its branches were probably at their peak as holiday routes during the early British Railways period. Sadly, by the end of the 1950s, car ownership was increasing rapidly and the age of mass holiday transportation by railway was drawing to a close.

Motive Power in the Great Western Period

The engines used on the West Cornwall line after its conversion to standard gauge in 1892 included the 3521-3560 series 0-4-4 tanks (some of which were formerly broad gauge engines), plus a few 'Stella' class 2-4-0 tender engines and

A portrait of '1076' class 0-6-0 saddle tank No. 1247 at Penzance. *P.Q. Treloar Collection*

An unidentified 0-6-0 pannier tank stands in Penzance station during a shunting manoeuvre. The original timber goods shed can be seen to the left; this was superseded by the new goods yard at Ponsandane, after which the old goods yard area was used mainly for flowers, parcels and perishable traffic. *Lens of Sutton Collection*

other converted 2-4-0 tender locomotives. Standard gauge goods locomotives at work in Cornwall in the period following the gauge conversion included 'Dean Goods' 0-6-0s, Armstrong double-framed 0-6-0s, double-framed 0-6-0 saddle tanks, single-framed 0-6-0 saddle tanks of the '1854' class, and a few domeless tank engines of the '1813' class.

Most of the engines used on the broad gauge were scrapped after the gauge conversion, though the '3521' class 0-4-4Ts and other 'convertibles' were adapted for standard gauge use. The '3521' class 0-4-4Ts, which had never been particularly successful, were reconstructed as 4-4-0 tender engines following serious derailments at Bodmin Road on 16th April, 1895, and near Falmouth on 31st October, 1898. In this heavily rebuilt form, they survived for many years in the Truro area, the Falmouth branch being one of their main areas of operation.

At the end of the Victorian period, the West Cornwall route was worked mainly by 4-4-0 and 0-6-0 classes, the 4-4-0s being employed on passenger work. The 'Duke' class 4-4-0s deserve a special mention in this context. These attractive double-framed 4-4-0s were introduced in 1895 especially for South Devon and Cornwall express work. At that time, locomotives were normally changed at Exeter or Plymouth, and the 'Dukes' were intended for use west of Newton Abbot. The class totalled 60 engines, Nos. 3264 *Trevithick*, 3272 *Fowey*, 3283 *Comet*, 3284 *Isle of Jersey* being some typical examples. The engines were used for piloting long after they had been displaced from front rank passenger duties.

Another well-known 4-4-0 type used on the West Cornwall route was the 'Bulldog' class of engine, in effect improved 'Dukes'. 'Bulldogs' were double-framed engines with 5 ft 8 in. coupled wheels and 18 inch by 26 inch inside cylinders. Nos. 3371 *Sir Massey Lopes* and 3453 *Seagull* were among the 'Bulldog' class 4-4-0s allocated to Truro Shed during the early 1920s, while sister locomotives Nos. 3376 *River Plym*, 3379 *River Fal*, 3395 *Tasmania* and 3406 *Calcutta* were stationed at Penzance at that time. Some other 'Bulldogs' recorded on the West Cornwall line included Nos. 3377 *Penzance* and 3398 *Montreal*.

The 4-4-0 classes were subsequently replaced, on front rank passenger services, by the Churchward '43XX' class 2-6-0s, which were introduced in 1911 and soon became well-known in the far West. They were true mixed traffic engines and worked both passenger and freight services; an improved version with side window cabs was later introduced. Numerous examples of these Churchward Moguls appeared on the West Cornwall main line, including Nos. 4386, 4397, 5307, 6318, 6319, 6354 and 6373.

Main line freight traffic was worked by a number of locomotive types, ranging from Armstrong and Dean standard goods 0-6-0s to the powerful Churchward '28XX' 2-8-0s that remained at work in Cornwall until comparatively recent times. The 0-6-0s were replaced by sturdy, outside-framed 'Aberdare' 2-6-0s during the Edwardian era, and these distinctive locomotives handled main line freight traffic on the West Cornwall line until their replacement by '28XX' class 2-8-0s. The 'Aberdares' were shedded at Laira, Truro, Penzance and St Blazey, Nos. 2601, 2620, 2621, 2639, 2642, 2658, 2675 and 2674 being among those employed in Cornwall at different times during the 1920s and 1930s.

'1701' class 0-6-0 pannier tank No. 1799 on shunting duties at Penzance station. This locomotive was originally built as a saddle tank in 1895 and was rebuilt in 1919 into the form we see here.

'Duke' class 4-4-0 No. 3325 *St Columb* outside the east end of the 1876-built engine shed at Penzance. This locomotive was subsequently rebuilt into a 'Bulldog' class' locomotive in 1908 taking the number 3316.   *GW Trust Collection*

A busy moment at Truro *circa* 1912 as 'Bulldog' 4-4-0 No. 3432 *River Yealm* stands in the down main platform, while a rebuilt '3521' class 4-4-0 waits in platform 3 (*left*) with a stopping train. The Falmouth branch train stands in its bay platform on the extreme right.

Lens of Sutton Collection

An unidentified 'Duke' class 4-4-0 stands in the up platform at Penzance. This locomotive is seen in rebuilt form with domeless boiler and top feed. In the down platform a rake of London & North Western Railway coaches can be seen. *P.Q. Treloar Collection*

An unidentified 'Bulldog' class 4-4-0 approaches Penzance *circa* 1906.

A fine portrait of 'Bulldog' class 4-4-0 No. 3410 *Columbia* in Penzance station.

Rail Archive Stephenson

The local branch lines were worked by a varied assortment of GWR tank locomotives during the early years of the 20th century. The Helston branch, for example, was typically worked by 'Metro' class 2-4-0Ts, Armstrong '517' class 0-4-2Ts or by various 0-6-0 saddle tank classes. Engines known to have appeared on the line included '517' class 0-4-2Ts Nos. 569, 831, 1158 and 1163, all of which were stationed in the West Cornwall area in the years following World War I.

The most distinctive locomotives seen on the St Ives and Helston branch lines during the early years of the 20th century were two picturesque and curiously-elongated 0-4-4Ts that had been built at Swindon specifically for use on short feeder branches. Carrying the numbers 34 and 35, these two small tank engines were alternated between the St Ives and Helston lines, but it appears that they were not particularly successful, and the design was not perpetuated.

In 1904 the Great Western constructed a prototype 2-6-2 side tank locomotive with outside cylinders and 4 ft 1½ in. coupled wheels. Ten similar engines emerged from Wolverhampton works in 1905. These 11 locomotives - which subsequently became the '44XX' class - were intended for use on steeply-graded branch lines, their large boilers, short-coupled wheelbases and small wheels making them ideally-suited for use on Cornish routes such as the St Ives, Helston and Falmouth branch lines.

The first small Prairie to appear in West Cornwall was No. 3103 (later 4403), which arrived in February 1906 from Wolverhampton works, and started work on the St Ives branch. In the next few years, the '44XX' class 2-6-2Ts were widely used on the local branch lines, Nos. 4401, 4403, 4405, 4406, 4409, 4408 and 4409 being among those used in the area at various times between 1906 and 1925. The '44XX' class engines were later joined by the visually-similar, but slightly larger '45XX' class Prairies, which had arrived in west Cornwall in considerable strength by the 1930s, and eventually replaced the '44XX' class on local branch line duties.

The '45XX' small Prairies soon became well-established in west Cornwall, and it would probably be true that in the eyes of most enthusiasts, they were the Cornish branch line engines *par excellence*. Numerous engines of this class were used in the area, including Nos. 4505, 4523, 4532, 4554, 4561, 4569, 4574, 4581, 4588, 4589, 5500, 5515, 5526, 5533, 5537, 5562 and 5573. There were normally about a dozen '45XX' class locomotives stationed at Truro at any one time for employment on the local branch lines, the engines concerned being '4500' series engines with 1,000 gallon tanks, and the slightly heavier '4575' sub-class with sloping-topped 1,300 gallon side tanks.

There was a further concentration of nine or ten '45XX' class engines at Penzance, some of these being sub-shedded at Helston and St Ives to work the local branch lines. In 1947, for instance, Nos. 4509, 4537, 4540, 4545, 4548 and 4574 were shedded at Penzance, with Nos. 4500 and 4566 at St Ives, and 4525 at Helston. These locomotives were rotated between the three sheds, the branch engines being regular changed for boiler washouts and other routine maintenance work. The small Prairies were classified as 'Yellow' engines under the GWR weight restriction system, and this ensured that they could work on all of the Cornish branch lines.

Penzance station during the Edwardian period, showing Great Western steam railmotor No. 45. These self-propelled vehicles were used on the nearby Perranporth branch for several years. They were in many ways the ancestors of today's single-unit diesel railcars.

Lens of Sutton Collection

GWR small Prairie '44XX' class 2-6-2T No. 4406 in Penzance Shed yard.

P.Q. Treloar Collection

An up postal train is seen here just north of Marazion headed by a Churchward 4-6-0 'Star' class locomotive in August 1924. *P.Q. Treloar Collection*

'4300' class 2-6-0 No. 5308 leaves Penzance with a train for Liverpool in August 1924. Note the ex-London & North Western Railway stock. *P.Q. Treloar Collection*

No. 4957 *Postlip Hall* approaches Marazion station with a down stopping train in May 1940.
B.A. Butt

A general view of the engine shed at Long Rock, Penzance in the 1930s.
Lens of Sutton Collection

Large Prairies were not normally associated with Cornwall, although in practice Churchward '3150' class 2-6-2Ts had appeared on main line passenger and goods workings from around 1912 onwards. There was, however, an influx of large 2-6-2Ts into the area in 1935, these engines being pressed into use on the Cornish main line while Penzance turntable was under repair. The engines involved were mainly London Division '61XX' class 2-6-2Ts such as Nos. 6160, 6162, 6163, 6164 and 6166. *The Railway Magazine* reported that the engines were all in excellent condition, having been sent to Cornwall 'fresh from building or overhaul at Swindon'. The 2-6-2Ts worked all services, including the 'Cornish Riviera'.

There was another influx of '61XX' class large Prairie tanks during World War II, several examples being seen in Cornwall around the period 1943-45. The engines involved included Nos. 6112, 6141, 6145, 6146, 6153 and 6164. Again, these archetypal London Division locomotives were ostensibly sent to the far West during turntable work at Penzance, though in practice some of them remained in the area for several months. One of their regular duties is said to have been on oil fuel supply trains to and from a large Fuel Reserve Depot that had been established at Swanvale, on the Truro to Falmouth line.

The Great Western favoured 4-6-0 locomotives for long-distance express work, but large engines of this kind did not appear regularly on the West Cornwall line until the 1920s, the usual practice being for main line services to change engines at Plymouth. In 1925, however, *Saint Martin*, the prototype 'Hall', was tried out on the 'Cornish Riviera Express' between Plymouth and Truro. The results having been deemed a success, 'Hall' class 4-6-0s were used in Cornwall in increasing numbers following their introduction in 1929. Some typical examples included Nos. 4900 *Saint Martin*, 4901 *Adderley Hall*, 4902 *Aldenham Hall*, 4903 *Astley Hall* and 4904 *Binnegar Hall*, all of which were allocated to Penzance by 1929.

In the 1930s, the 'Hall' class 4-6-0s were perhaps the most characteristic main line passenger locomotives on the West Cornwall line and in these years they appeared regularly on parcels, mail and 'perishable' services, as well as main line passenger duties. In general, the 'Halls' worked between Plymouth and Penzance, around 25 members of the class being shedded at Laira, Truro and Penzance at that time. The maximum load for a 'Hall' class 4-6-0 on the Cornish main line was 364 tons, which represented up to 10 or 11 bogie vehicles, though it is said that the maximum permitted loads were sometimes exceeded.

Seasonal consignments of flowers or broccoli invariably resulted in short term operational problems and in these circumstances some extra-long trains were sometimes assembled. In this context, one former Penzance driver recalled an occasion when an up 'perishables' service set out for Paddington behind a trusty 'Hall' class locomotive and, although the load was already a dozen vehicles, further vans were added at just about every station *en route* to Plymouth. The train soon became so long that 'you couldn't see the end of it' on many of the sharper curves, yet further vans were coupled up at every intermediate stopping place. In due course the mammoth train became so long that it would not fit into any of the intermediate loops or sidings between Liskeard and Plymouth. Unfortunately, the up 'Riviera' was now rapidly gaining on the slower perishable train, and when asked if he could reach Plymouth before the express, the driver laconically replied, 'I think we can keep in front of it'!

'Hall' class 4-6-0 No. 4946 *Moseley Hall* stands simmering at Penzance Shed in May 1952. Notice that the locomotive still carries 'GW' and the Great Western crest on its tender, but on its smokebox door it boasts BR shedplate '83G' indicating that this was a Penzance-allocated engine.

Hawksworth 'County' class 4-6-0 No. 1023 *County of Oxford* leaves St Erth with a down stopping train on 15th September, 1951.   *B.A. Butt*

The 'Grange' class 4-6-0s were introduced in 1936 as replacements for the '43XX' class mixed traffic engines. The new engines were soon at work on Cornish passenger and fast freight services, Nos. 6801 *Aylburton Grange*, 6827 *Llanfrechfa Grange* and 6829 *Burmington Grange* being allocated to Penzance by 1938. No. 6829 was later transferred to Truro, while Nos. 6825 *Llanvair Grange* and 6838 *Goodmoor Grange* had been sent to Penzance by 1941. The 'Granges' were very similar to the 'Hall' class 4-6-0s, albeit with slightly smaller wheels of 5 ft 8 in. diameter.

The famous 'Castle' class 4-6-0s appeared on main line express workings on the WCR route in the period immediately before World War II. The regular performers included Nos. 4087 *Cardigan Castle*, 4097 *Kenilworth Castle*, 5024 *Carew Castle*, 5028 *Llantilio Castle* and 5057 *Earl of Waldegrave*. These very capable locomotives were larger and more powerful than the 'Halls' and 'Granges', with 6 ft 8½ in. diameter coupled wheels and four 16 inch by 26 inch cylinders. The locomotives and tenders weighed 126 tons 11 cwt, but as 'Red' engines under the GWR system, the 'Castles' could work through to Cornwall, and over all other parts of the Great Western main line network.

Another Great Western 4-6-0 type seen in the area were Hawksworth's handsome, but somewhat under-valued, 'County' class locomotives. Introduced in 1945, these engines were intended for fast mixed traffic work and, as such, they could perhaps be described as 'super Halls'. They were certainly used on Hall-type duties and in this capacity they became familiar sights on the West Cornwall line. In 1947, Nos. 1019 *County of Merioneth* and 1022 *County of Northampton* were allocated to Penzance, while Nos. 1004 *County of Somerset*, 1006 *County of Cornwall* and 1009 *County of Carmarthen* were at Laira. Sister engine No. 1023 *County of Oxford* was stationed at Truro.

Motive Power in the British Railways Era

The Nationalisation of Britain's railways on 1st January, 1948 did not bring about any major or immediate changes on the West Cornwall line, and for the next few years the route remained a bastion of Great Western motive power. The new 'Britannia' class 4-6-2s were tried briefly on the 'Cornish Riviera Express' and other top link services around 1951-52, but they were not appreciated by the former GWR enginemen and, after a few months, the new Pacifics were transferred elsewhere. There was, thereafter, considerable variety in terms of motive power, with regular appearances by 'Castles', 'Counties', 'Halls' and 'Granges' on the West Cornwall main line.

There was, by that time, a sizeable allocation of 'Grange' class 4-6-0s at Penzance, and by September 1955 these included Nos. 6800 *Arlington Grange*, 6801 *Aylburton Grange*, 6808 *Beenham Grange*, 6809 *Burghclere Grange*, 6824 *Ashley Grange*, 6825 *Llanvair Grange*, 6826 *Nannerth Grange* and 6837 *Forthampton Grange*. The Hawksworth 'Counties' were regularly employed on the 'Cornish Riviera Express' and other important workings, some random sightings from the mid-1950s being Nos. 1006 *County of Cornwall*, 1008 *County of Cardigan*, 1010 *County of Caernarvon* and 1023 *County of Oxford*.

'Grange' class 4-6-0 No. 6801 *Aylburton Grange* on shed at Penzance on 24th June, 1951.
R.S. Carpenter Collection

The tank engines at rest inside Penzance Shed on 26th September, 1956 include a Hawksworth '94XX' class 0-6-0PT, Churchward '57XX' class 0-6-0PT No. 9748 and a Churchward '45XX' 2-6-2T.
H.C. Casserley

'Castle' class 4-6-0 No. 4095 *Harlech Castle* passes Gwinear Road with an up passenger working.
N. Stead Collection

'Castle' class No. 7031 *Cromwell's Castle* pulls away from Penzance along the shore of Mount's Bay with the 11.00 am 'Royal Duchy' on its way to Paddington, 9th September, 1959.
P.Q. Treloar

'45XX' 2-6-2T No. 4547 is seen being turned on the turntable at Long Rock on 26th September, 1956. *R.M. Casserley*

Hawksworth '94XX' class 0-6-0PT No. 9434 is seen on station pilot duties at Penzance *circa* 1958. *P.Q. Treloar*

In the 1950s, there seemed to be no clear pattern in the employment of 4-6-0 classes in Cornwall, and lineside observers at Penzance or elsewhere could usually be sure of seeing a procession of 'Halls', 'Counties', 'Castles' and 'Granges' on main line passenger duties. 'Castle' class 4-6-0 No. 4037 *The South Wales Borderers* was at that time allocated to Penzance for use on the 'Cornish Riviera' and other express workings, while other locomotives seen in the area included Nos. 1002 *County of Berks*, 6872 *Crawley Grange*, 6809 *Burghclere Grange*, 6857 *Tudor Grange*, 6852 *Headbourne Grange*, 4929 *Goytrey Hall*, 5972 *Olton Hall*, 5964 *Wolseley Hall*, 5021 *Whittington Castle* and 6869 *Resolven Grange*.

Lack of space precludes a detailed analysis of the rolling stock employed on the Penzance main line, suffice to say the 'Riviera' and other prestige workings were always formed of the very latest Great Western bogie vehicles. Dean clerestories, 'Dreadnoughts', 'Toplights', and the special 'Centenary' stock constructed for the 'Riviera' service all appeared at Penzance, and when displaced from regular main line duties, older vehicles were often given a new lease of life as branch line or excursion stock. After Nationalisation, these GWR vehicles were gradually replaced by BR Mk I coaches which, for several years, were painted in the traditional Great Western chocolate and cream livery.

The St Ives branch was often worked by two coach 'B-set' formations incorporating pairs of steel-panelled brake composite vehicles. One of the sets employed on the line was composed of coaches 6462 and 6463, both of which were 9 ft 3 in.-wide, bow-ended vehicles. They were 61 ft 2 in.-long, with five third class compartments, one first class compartment, and a combined guard's & luggage compartment. Other B-sets employed in West Cornwall during early 1950s included coaches 6464 and 6461, 6445 and 6446 and 6168 and 6175, all of which were 61 ft 2 in. bow-ended vehicles dating from the early 1930s.

The GWR Electrification Scheme

Most locomotive enthusiasts now look back on the 1930s as a 'Golden Age' of steam operation on the Paddington to Penzance main line. At the time, the reign of the steam locomotive seemed destined to last for ever, and it comes as something of a surprise to find that the Great Western had considered electrifying the main line between Taunton and Penzance. In February 1938, the company announced that, in view of the high cost of steam coal, Messrs Merz & McLellan, the famous consulting engineers, had been engaged to prepare a report 'on the economic advantages of electrifying the company's main line between Taunton and Penzance, and the branches connected thereto'.

The suggested electrification scheme would have involved the GWR main line between Taunton and Penzance, together with the secondary or branch lines to Kingswear, Newquay and Fowey, and the various china clay lines. Other branches, including the St Ives, Helston and Falmouth routes, were not considered suitable for electrification, and these would probably have remained steam-worked. It was assumed that the 3,000 volt ac overhead system would be employed, and that 164 electric locomotives would be required, the largest of

Two of the North British type '2' diesel-hydraulics (later class '22') await departure from Penzance with the London mail train which also includes two milk tanks *circa* 1959. Beyond the train, steaming away, is '45XX' class 2-6-2T No. 4552 on station pilot duties.   *P.Q.Treloar*

A 'Warship' class diesel-hydraulic (*right*), No. D828 *Magnificent*, prepares to run-round its train in platform 3, while a Swindon cross-country diesel multiple-unit waits in platform 1.
                                                                          J.W. Stevens-Stratton

these being 2-6-6-2s with a weight of about 140 tons, while the others would be smaller types for use on freight and mixed traffic duties.

In June 1939, *The Railway Magazine* reported that Merz & McLellan had completed their detailed investigations, and concluded that 'in nearly every case, the average annual traffic density throughout the year is insufficient to justify the capital cost of electrification'. The consultants estimated that the capital cost of implementing the electrification scheme would be £4,361,100, while the annual working expenses for the electrified lines would be £473,077 per annum. However, this was little better than the £573,577 required for steam operation, and in view of this very small anticipated saving the Great Western decided to continue operating its West of England line with steam locomotives.

It is by no means clear why the Great Western should have selected the West of England main line as a likely candidate for electrification, when it was manifestly clear that the route was subject to heavy seasonal traffic flows, interspersed with less hectic periods of operation. Experience with other railway electrification schemes had already shown that lines which carried heavy, all-year-round traffic flows were ideal candidates for electrification, and one must therefore ask why the GWR did not consider the use of electric traction on the busy London to Reading and South Wales route?

It has been suggested that the West Country electrification scheme was merely a ploy to exact lower prices from the coal companies, and if this was indeed the case it follows that there was never any real likelihood of the Taunton to Penzance line being converted to electric operation. In any case, the outbreak of World War II on 3rd September, 1939 put an end to all such modernisation schemes and when the West Cornwall route was finally modernised, in the 1960s, it was with the aid of diesel traction, rather than electricity.

The Diesel Era in West Cornwall

The 1950s and 1960s were the era of cheap oil fuel and, in these circumstances, it is easy to see the attraction of diesel power. In the late 1950s it was announced that the Newton Abbot to Penzance main line and its branches would become one of the first parts of the railway system to be completely dieselised.

The first diesel-hauled passenger train to work through to Penzance ran on 21st April 1958, when 'Warship' class A1A-A1A No. D600 *Active* headed a test working through Cornwall. On the following day this same engine left Penzance with the up 'Cornish Riviera Express'. Thereafter, diesels appeared in Cornwall in increasing numbers, the D800-870 series 'Warship' class Bo-Bos being used on many express workings during the 1960s. Nos. D800-832 and D866-870 were later designated class '42' under the British Railways 'TOPS' scheme, while Nos. D833-865 became class '43'. These 78 ton locomotives were classified as 'Red' engines under the former-GWR route colour system.

Another diesel class used in West Cornwall during the 1960s was the North British Locomotive Company type '2', which later became better-known as TOPS class '22'. The NBL type '2s' were slab-ended Bo-Bos, numbered in the D63XX series from D6300 to D6357, and like other early Western Region diesels

A train is seen arriving in Penzance from Paddington in this scene dominated by 'Warship' class locomotives in May 1968.   *G.F. Heiron*

'Western' class diesel-hydraulic No. 1071 *Western Renown* emerges from Penwithers tunnel at the head of a down express during the mid-1970s, the train is composed of Mk I coaching stock in blue and grey livery.   *N. Stead*

they were diesel-hydraulics rather than diesel-electrics. The new engines were designated 'Yellow' locomotives under the colour-coded route system, and as such they were considered suitable for employment on branch lines and secondary services, as replacements for the familiar '45XX' class small Prairies.

In 1962, the Western Region introduced a class of powerful Co-Co diesel-hydraulics, weighing 108 tons, and suitable for use on important main line passenger services such as the 'Cornish Riviera Express'. These engines were numbered in the D1000-D1073 series, and all 74 locomotives carried the class name 'Western', plus an individual name which, in many cases, harked back to the days of the broad gauge (such as *Western Courier* and *Western Thunderer*). The 'Westerns' - later class '52' - replaced the 'Warships' on top link services, and by the 1960s and early 1970s they were handling most of the long distance passenger services between Paddington and Penzance.

Sadly, the reign of the Western Region diesel-hydraulics was destined to be remarkably short, and in the mid-1970s the 'Westerns' were withdrawn for scrapping or preservation, their duties on the West Cornwall line being taken over by 2,700 hp English Electric class '50' Co-Cos that had themselves been displaced from express passenger duties on the West Coast Main Line by electrification.

The demise of the 'Warships' and (more especially) the 'Westerns' was the cause of some regret among railway enthusiasts but, within a few years, the class '50s' had achieved a degree of popularity. This was due, at least in part, to the evocative 'Warship' names that were applied to these locomotives after their transfer to the Western Region. Although intended as a tribute to the maritime traditions of the West Country, names such as *Ajax*, *Thunderer* and *Achilles* were also old Great Western names, and this enlightened naming policy seemed to underline the awesome continuity of railway history in the far West of England.

The Brush-Sulzer type '4' Co-Co diesel-electrics (later class '47s') were first introduced in 1962, and this versatile class was soon in use over much of the British Railways system. In Cornwall, the class '47s' were used on many long-distance workings between Penzance and the North of England. On 28th March, 1972, for example, class '47' No. 1620 was noted leaving Penzance at the head of the 7.25 am to Leeds, while on 22nd August, 1981, sister engine No. 47105 was observed in charge of a Penzance to Manchester working. Class '47s' have also worked the 'Cornish Riviera Express' - on 27th March, 1972, for instance, No. 1597 powered the down 'Riviera' between Paddington and Penzance.

The introduction of High Speed Train sets from the late 1970s led to a marked reduction in the number of locomotive-hauled trains, and by the 1980s these versatile units had assumed control of virtually all long distance services between London and the far West - though class '47s' and class '50' Co-Cos continued to appear on passenger workings, sleeper services, and long distance cross-country workings to the North of England.

Conventional diesel multiple units were comparatively rare in the west Cornwall area, though Pressed Steel class '117' three-car units were used on the St Ives branch for many years. Other multiple unit types used on this line during the 1980s and early 1990s included Birmingham Railway Carriage & Wagon Co. class '118' units and Derby class '115' sets.

A double-headed express waits in the up platform at Truro; the leading locomotive in class '52' No. D1054 *Western Governor*, while the train engine is English Electric class '50' No. 50034 (later named *Furious*).   *N. Stead*

Class '47' Co-Co No. 47484 *Isambard Kingdom Brunel* arrives at Penzance with a stopping train from Plymouth on 21st September, 1983. The formation consisted of four Mark I coaches comprising a brake second, second, composite and a full brake vehicle.   *S.C. Jenkins*

A Western Region HST set stands in platform 1 at Penzance on 20th May, 1981.   *S.C. Jenkins*

A general view of Penzance station, with class '50' No. 50031 *Hood* in the foreground on 17th November, 1984. In the background is another class '50', and a 350 hp class '08' diesel shunter.
P.G. Barnes

Dmu set No. L842 passes Penzance signal box as it departs from Penzance with the 5.05 pm train for St Ives, 26th March, 1994.   *P.G. Barnes*

A view of the west end of Truro station in March 1996. A Cross-Country HST set stands in the up main platform, while a class '117' unit occupies the Falmouth branch bay.   *S.C. Jenkins*

In recent years the introduction of modern diesel multiple units such as the class '158' two-car sets has resulted in the development of longer distance stopping services between Penzance, Bristol and Cardiff. In October 1990, for instance, a two-car class '150' Sprinter unit was rostered to work a service which left Penzance at 5.25 pm and then called at all stations to Liskeard before continuing northwards as a semi-fast working to Cardiff (arr. 11.08 pm).

It would also be appropriate to mention the humble 0-6-0 diesel locomotives that have been used for shunting duties at Penzance. In steam days, these duties were carried out by 0-6-0 pannier tanks, but since the 1960s British Railways class '08'diesel shunters have been employed. These 0-6-0 diesels were the last locomotives to be stationed at Penzance, the allocation in 1981-82 being Nos. 08641 and 08644.

By the early 1990s all long distance passenger services on the West Cornwall line were being worked by HST units, with class '43' power cars at each end. Inter-City Great Western services to and from Paddington were formed of eight-car sets, while Inter-City Cross-Country workings between Penzance, Bristol and the North were typically formed of seven-car sets.

Regional Railways South Wales & West services between Penzance, Bristol and beyond were worked by two-car class '158'units, while branch and local services were usually worked by class '150' units, class '153' single units or by older class '117', suburban units. Some of the latter sets appeared, for a short time in red, white and blue Network South East livery, but the most popular class '117' unit was undoubtedly No. 117305 - a three-car chocolate and cream-liveried set formed of cars 51368, 59520 and 51410, which worked on Cornish branch lines during the mid-1990s.

Large main line locomotives are now rarely seen in Cornwall, the last regular workings being sleeper services and Rail Express Systems (RES) mail services to and from Penzance, which were hauled by class '47s' in RES red and grey livery. These services were later taken over by the English, Welsh & Scottish train operating company.

A class '158' set No. 158822 stands in the up platform at Hayle on 21st September, 1996.
S.C. Jenkins

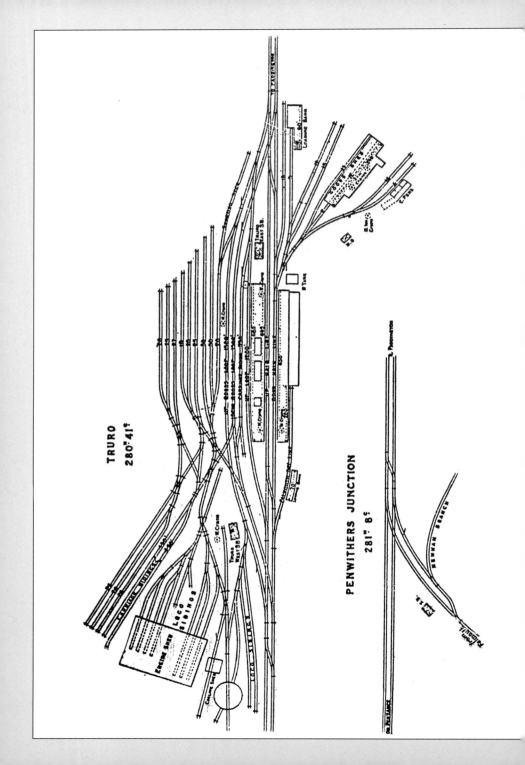

Chapter Six

The Stations and Route -
Truro to Carn Brea

Having outlined the history of the West Cornwall Railway, it would now be convenient to examine the stations and route of this historic line in greater detail. The following chapters will therefore take readers on an imaginary guided tour of the route from Truro to Penzance. As the West Cornwall route is still an integral part of the modern railway network, it is possible to use the present tense for the actual route description, although the past tense must obviously be employed when dealing with stations or other features that have been closed or removed in recent years.

Truro Station

In railway terms Truro has always been regarded as an important traffic centre on the main line from Paddington to Penzance. Its passenger receipts have traditionally been the best in Cornwall, while the station served as a nodal point for branch line services to Falmouth and Perranporth. It also boasted a short goods branch to the quays at Newham, which added operational interest to the local railway system prior to rationalisation in recent years. Historically, Truro was served by two constituent companies of the GWR, the standard gauge West Cornwall line running westwards to Penzance, while the broad gauge Cornwall Railway was conceived as an eastwards link to Plymouth.

Newham was, as we have seen, the easternmost extremity of the West Cornwall Railway but, in 1859, most West Cornwall passenger services were diverted into the newly-opened Cornwall Railway station. The latter station thereby became Truro's main passenger facility - though the old West Cornwall station at Newham remained in being for many years thereafter as a goods yard. Our description must therefore commence at the former Cornwall Railway station, which remains in operation as a busy rail centre.

Situated a little under 300 miles from Paddington (via Bristol), Truro is a relatively large station. It is laid out on an approximate east-to-west alignment in an elevated position on the north-west side of Truro. The station is sited at the bottom of a dip, with 1 in 70 gradients to the east and 1 in 66 gradients to the west of the platforms. The approach from the east is spectacular, in that trains pass over the majestic Truro viaduct; with a length of 1,290 ft, it is the longest viaduct on the former Cornwall Railway, and it provides excellent views of Truro Cathedral and the distant Truro River as trains slow for their final approach to this busy Cornish station.

When first opened as the western terminus of the broad gauge Cornwall Railway, Truro featured a range of stone buildings on the down side. The station was approached by single lines in each direction, the western end of the station being laid with mixed gauge trackwork to accommodate the standard gauge West Cornwall trains. There were, at that time, three through platforms

The main down side buildings at Truro, seen from the south around 1912. These extensive red brick buildings were authorised on 18th November, 1896 at a cost of £5,500, and completed by 1900. The final cost was approximately £7,300. The original Cornwall Railway station, erected by Olvers of Falmouth, had incorporated an overall roof similar to that at Falmouth.

Lens of Sutton Collection

The main down side station buildings at Truro in the 1930s. These buildings were of standard Great Western design.   *Lens of Sutton Collection*

and a shorter bay, with a 'third line' between the main up and down platform lines, and two mixed gauge loop lines to the north. There was a small goods yard on the down side, and a wooden engine shed on the up side of the station.

The original layout was modified and enlarged throughout the 19th century, although the basic configuration remained the same, in that the down platform was always a side platform while the up platform was an island with tracks on either side. One fairly significant change concerned the position of the engine shed, which was originally sited to the north-east of the passenger station, but was later moved to a new site on the west side of the station between Penwithers tunnel and an area known as 'Dobb's Field'.

In the 20th century the layout at Truro incorporated three through platforms and an additional bay on the down side for Falmouth branch trains. The platforms were numbered in sequence from one to four, platform one being the Falmouth branch bay, while platform two was used by down main line services between London and Penzance. Platform three, to the north, was used by Newquay and Perranporth branch workings, while platform four, on the far side of the station, was served by up main line trains to Plymouth, Exeter and beyond, these platforms formed the two sides of an island.

In 1912 platforms two and three were extended from 484 ft and 450 ft to 634 ft and 600 ft respectively, at a cost of £398. Further lengthenings increased platform two to 650 ft, while platforms three and four were extended to 685 ft. Platform four was served by a 1,200 ft loop, which diverged from the up main line at the west end of the station and rejoined it at the east end of the platform.

The up loop line was flanked by four long parallel lines, one of which was used as a carriage siding, while two others functioned as up and down goods loops; the goods loops were linked to the main lines by double track junctions at each end, and they were therefore able to serve as by-pass lines for goods traffic. A further line, on the north side of the goods loops, was known as No. 1 Siding and although arranged as a loop with connections at each end this line was also equipped with a shunting neck at its east end, which was referred-to as 'No. 1 Dead End'.

The goods loops incorporated a series of crossovers and siding connections, by means of which trains were able to enter an array of parallel sidings on the north side of the station; these extended eastwards, and they were used mainly for storage and marshalling purposes. Six further sidings extended westwards to provide additional stabling facilities for passenger vehicles. The latter sidings were authorised on 12th December, 1912 at an estimated cost of £3,338, and they were brought into use around the end of 1913; the two longest sidings had a length of 430 ft and 450 ft respectively.

The station was lavishly equipped with an extensive range of station buildings, the main block being sited on the down side. In architectural terms, Truro was a typical late Victorian Great Western station, with standard red brick buildings and a projecting platform canopy. The main building was a single-storey structure with a hipped, slated roof, two of its bays being graced by elegant, French-style towers. There was, in addition, a raised clerestory or cupola over part of the building, while the entire roofline was punctuated by elaborate ironwork and tall brick chimney stacks with 'oversailing' upper courses.

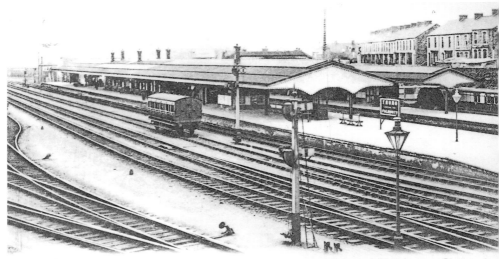

Truro   *Gt. Western Station.*

A general view of Truro station from the north, probably around 1912. The platform canopies
were subsequently extended.   *Lens of Sutton Collection*

Truro station, looking east from the footbridge *circa* 1900.   *Lens of Sutton Collection*

There were additional buildings on the up side and these too dated from the great rebuilding that had been carried out by the Great Western company at the end of the Victorian period. Facilities on the up side, included waiting rooms, staff accommodation and toilets, the main buildings being covered by extensive platform canopies. The construction of these buildings was authorised on 18th November, 1896 at an estimated cost of £5,500 although, in the event, extra expenditure of £1,872 8s. 1d. was incurred before the new station facilities were completed in 1900. The platform coverings were further extended in 1936 with the aid of cheap government loans.

The up and down sides of the station were linked by two standard Great Western plate girder footbridges, one of these being strategically situated at the eastern extremity of the station, while the other was sited near the centre point of the platforms. Both of these characteristic GWR structures were roofed and glazed, so that travellers crossing the line to reach their trains were fully protected from the vagaries of the Cornish weather.

There were no luggage lifts or other labour-saving devices, but most passengers were happy to carry their hand baggage over the footbridges - which were equipped with wide gangways and broad wooden treads. Heavier items could be moved across the running lines on barrow crossings, two of these being provided.

On a footnote, it is interesting to note that, on 1st June, 1912, Truro became the very first station in Cornwall to issue penny platform tickets for the benefit of friends or relatives wishing to greet travellers or say goodbye within the confines of the station. Until that time, most local stations had been 'open' stations at which non-travellers presumably walked onto the platforms without any form of payment.

In steam days Truro was signalled from two standard Great Western-style signal cabins known as Truro East Box and Truro West Box. Both were typical brick-and-timber hipped-roof boxes with distinctive five-paned windows, which were supposed to give the signalmen an unimpeded view; boxes of this same general type were built throughout the Great Western system from the turn-of-the-century onwards. The West box was situated to the north of the goods loops at the west end of the station, while Truro East box was sited to the east of the island platform. The station was originally signalled with Brunelian disc and crossbar signals, but these were later replaced by standard Great Western lower quadrant semaphores.

The goods yard was entered via a trailing connection from the down main line, and it contained a number of dead-end sidings, one of which ran into a large goods shed with a 240 ft internal loading platform. A further siding, on the north side of the yard, terminated beside a loading bank, while another siding served a cattle loading dock. Three further sidings were available for 'mileage', or wagon load traffic, which was normally loaded or unloaded by coal merchants or other local traders. A hand crane was provided within the goods shed, and there was also a 12 ton yard crane for handling timber, steel or other heavy consignments.

In addition to the two station footbridges, a lengthy pedestrian footbridge spanned several tracks at the western end of the platforms and provided an

Truro station during the 1930s, showing an unidentified '45XX' class 2-6-2T in platform 3, with what appears to be the Falmouth portion of the 'Cornish Riviera Express'.

Lens of Sutton Collection

Truro station, looking west towards Penzance around 1950. The point visible to the left gave access to the goods yard.   *Lens of Sutton Collection*

excellent vantage point for youthful 'spotters', who were afforded a bird's eye view of the adjacent locomotive shed and sidings. The shed was of stone construction, with a ridge and furrow roof and had three roads, and offices and a repair shop immediately to the north; an adjoining part of the structure contained three further roads which served as a carriage and wagon shop.

Facilities at the engine shed included the usual Great Western-type coaling plant, with a raised coaling stage beneath a large water tank and a high-level wagon road which was served by a steeply-graded ramped siding. The nearby turntable was originally of 55 ft diameter but, in 1924, a new 65 ft turntable was installed at a cost of £4,999. Access to the engine shed and associated sidings was via a trailing connection from the up goods loop, or by means of a reverse shunt from the adjacent sidings. In 1947, at the end of the GWR period, Truro had an allocation of 22 locomotives, including five 4-6-0s, four 0-6-0PTs and a dozen 2-6-2 Prairie tanks. In British Railways days the shed was coded 83F.

In 1921, Truro Shed had an allocation of 19 locomotives of various kinds. Among them were '517' class 0-4-2Ts Nos. 1159 and 1165, '43XX' class 2-6-0 No. 5307, Armstrong 0-6-0 No. 1188, and a number of 'Duke' and 'Bulldog' class 4-4-0s. Like other Great Western traffic centres, Truro was the home of several 0-6-0 pannier tanks which were used for local freight and shunting work, and also for branch line passenger duties. In 1947, Truro's allocation included '1701' class 0-6-0PT No. 1753 and '655' class 0-6-0PT No. 1782, together with more modern '57XX' class engine No. 5779 and '74XX' class pannier No. 7422. Pannier tanks noted at Truro in British Railways days included Collett '57XX' class locomotives Nos. 3702, 3709, 4622, 5744 and 5779, together with Hawksworth '94XX' class panniers Nos. 8421 and 8473.

These versatile engines appeared sporadically on local passenger trains; in July 1960, for instance, Collett 0-6-0PT No. 3709 was noted at work on the Falmouth branch train, while on 10th July, 1961 the same engine was photographed at the head of a Perranporth branch working. At other times, the '57XX' class 0-6-0PTs typically worked local goods traffic, the rarely-photographed Newham goods branch being one of their usual haunts, though Truro's large stud of '45XX' class 2-6-2Ts were equally likely to appear on Newham goods trips. In addition to Truro's usual allocation of 0-6-0PTs and 2-6-2Ts, there was also a handful of larger Great Western 4-6-0 locomotives. In 1947, these included 'Hall' class 4-6-0s Nos. 4906 *Bradfield Hall*, 4929 *Goytrey Hall*, 4936 *Kinlet Hall* and 6931 *Aldborough Hall*.

The station was liberally-supplied with locomotive watering facilities, standard Great Western-type water columns being sited at convenient places around the station and yards. There was a water column at the east end of the island platform, together with two more at the Penzance ends of platforms two and three; the column at the end of platform three was later moved along the line to a new position near the West signal box. Other water columns were sited in the locomotive yard, and between No. 1 Siding and the goods loops on the north side of the station; these were fed from a raised metal tank at the east end of the down platform.

Truro was one of the busiest stations in Cornwall, its passenger receipts being the best in the county (though St Austell was busier in terms of freight traffic).

THE WEST CORNWALL RAILWAY

An early view of the 1900-built engine shed at Truro. The locomotive·is probably a '3521' class 4-4-0.   *GW Trust Collection*

The former Truro East signal box, which now controls the entire station. This *circa* 1900 box was typical of GWR practice during the early 20th century.   *S.C. Jenkins*

Truro issued around 130,000 tickets a year during the period 1903-1938; in 1913, for example, the station issued 149,577 tickets, while in 1930 150,529 tickets and 417 season tickets were issued. In the later 1930s, there was an apparent decline in bookings, though in reality this was due to the increased use of season tickets. By 1938, ordinary bookings were down to 108,930, whereas season ticket sales had risen to 2,151 per annum. The Falmouth branch typically issued about 100,000 tickets per annum during the period under review.

Truro's goods traffic amounted to around 23,000 tons a year during the 1930s, though there was a dramatic rise during World War II, which was sustained during the British Railways era. In 1941 and 1942 the station handled 35,572 and 32,272 tons of freight respectively, rising to an average of 80,000 tons per annum during the period 1947-1952. In part, this enormous increase can be explained by the fact that Truro was then being developed as railhead for the surrounding area, but at the same time it is manifestly clear that Truro was handling far more goods traffic in the 1950s than it had handled at any previous time in its history.

As a railway employment centre, Truro rivalled Penzance as the most important station in Cornwall. In 1935 Truro employed 90 people under station master W.H. Blamey, while in 1938 the staffing establishment had increased to 98. In 1950 there were 18 clerical and supervisory staff, plus 4 relief staff and 136 'wages' staff, making a grand total of 158 employees in the passenger and goods stations alone. In addition, there were numerous other employees in the locomotive and permanent way departments.

Those employed at this busy Cornish station during the inter-war period included passenger guard H. Smith, goods guard F.W. Packer, porter N.E. Hicks, signalman George Colwill, signalman W.J. Johns, clerks L.P. Lewis and L.J. May, shunter J. Reynolds, wagon repairer G.T. Bellinger, inspector J.Westaway, signal lineman A. Tozer, ganger T. Dunstone, motor driver R.J. Collier and engine cleaner H. Tidball. The station master during the early 1960s was Mr T.A. Collins, who had earlier worked at St Austell.

The pages of *The Great Western Railway Magazine* provide an interesting glimpse of everyday life at the station during the Great Western era, and one senses a distinct 'family' atmosphere in the reports of weddings, retirements and similar events, the following extract being a typical example from the February 1924 issue:

At Truro station, recently, Mr J. Westaway, formerly inspector there, who retired a few months ago after forty years service, was presented with a case of pipes, and a tobacco pouch, and Treasury notes. The gift was subscribed for by as many as 130 members of the staff of all departments.

A similar extract, from the 1924 *GWR Magazine*, recalls a lifetime of diligent service on the part of a retiring signalman, who had served at Truro for well over three decades:

At the age of sixty-five, Mr George Colwill, signalman at Truro, retired in November. He had been in the service of the company for 47 years, worked as a signalman for over 43 years, and spent 35 years at Truro. During the whole of his service he was never once absent from duty through sickness.

He ascribes his wonderful good health to his having made it an invariable rule to take proper rest, and to his life-long total abstinence. The occasion of his retirement was marked by the staff of the station presenting him, on December 7th, with a walking stick, together with an umbrella for Mrs Colwill.

In common with numerous other stations throughout the country Truro has declined in recent years, but the run-down has not been excessive, and the station remains in being as a busy traffic centre. There have nevertheless been many changes, most noticeably the closure of the locomotive sheds in 1965, and the elimination of most of the sidings on the north side of the station. In connection with this rationalisation of facilities the West signal box has been closed, control of the remaining signals and connections being concentrated in the former East signal box.

In its present-day form Truro has three platforms, platforms two and three being used by main line traffic, while platform one, on the down side of the station, continues to serve as the Falmouth branch bay. The extensive station buildings survive intact, albeit with modified internal arrangements in that the ticket office and travel centre now occupy the eastern end of the main downside building. The footbridges linking the up and down sides of the station have been retained. At the west end of the station, Falmouth branch trains use the down main line in order to reach their own route at Penwithers Junction, bi-directional working arrangements being in force from the platforms, through Penwithers tunnel.

The goods yard on the down side has been abandoned, but goods traffic can still be handled as and when necessary in two long sidings which extend along the north side of the passenger station on land formerly occupied by carriage and storage sidings. This new freight handling facility was opened in 1972 as a 'wagon load' terminal, and as originally constructed the modernised goods yard included a siding link to an adjacent warehouse. Vehicular access to the freight terminal is by means of a level crossing, with full length lifting barriers controlled from the adjacent signal box.

There has, in practice, been no regular freight traffic from Truro or Falmouth for many years, though occasional bulk consignments are still dealt with by the EWS train operating company. The remaining sidings at Truro have latterly handled military stores and calcinated seaweed, while Falmouth has dealt with containerised coal traffic and trainloads of scrap material from Falmouth dockyard. In August 1994, for instance, a large quantity of military stores was delivered by rail, while in the following year trainloads of hopper wagons were noted in the yard in connection with the above-mentioned seaweed traffic.

Truro continues to enjoy an excellent train service which is in many ways better than that provided during the heyday of steam operation! Four train operating companies now provide the services, First Great Western providing express workings between Paddington and Penzance, while Virgin Trains operate long distance cross-country services such as 'The Cornishman' between Dundee and Penzance. At the same time, the Wessex train operating company contributes useful long-distance stopping services on the Great Western main line and a frequent service on the Falmouth branch, while mail services and occasional freight trains are worked by the English Welsh & Scottish train operating company.

Penwithers Junction

As intimated earlier, additional goods-handling facilities were available in the former West Cornwall terminus at Newham. To reach Newham goods station, trains proceeded westwards through the 70 yd Penwithers (or Higher Town) tunnel, beyond which the Falmouth branch diverged from the West Cornwall main line. It is noticeable that Falmouth services enjoy a straight run on to the branch, whereas main line trains are faced with a sharp right-hand curve; this is an interesting legacy of the original Cornwall Railway, which had been planned as a main line link from Plymouth to Falmouth.

In broad gauge days, the Newham branch had left the West Cornwall line by a junction on the north side of the physically-separate Cornwall Railway route to Falmouth, and then crossed the single track Falmouth line on the level. This arrangement was transformed in 1893 when a new junction was installed between the Newham branch and the Falmouth line. The direct route from Penzance to Newham was thereby severed, with the result that access to and from Newham goods station could only be obtained by means of a reverse shunt from the Falmouth branch. The junction was worked from a standard Great Western gable-roofed signal box on the down side of the main line in the 'V' of the junction between the West Cornwall route and the Falmouth branch.

Much later, there were further alterations at Penwithers Junction. In 1971 the connections between the Penzance main line and the Falmouth branch were modified to provide bi-directional working over the down line from Truro station through Penwithers tunnel to the actual point of bifurcation - in effect a reversion to the pre-1893 situation! This present-day junction is controlled from the surviving signal box at Truro, with a colour light signal to control movements between the Falmouth line and into the station (branch trains now have to run 'wrong line' on the down main line in order to reach their bay platform).

The Newham Branch

The Newham branch ran generally eastwards from its junction at Penwithers to the riverside terminus at Newham. The line was 2 miles 33 chains in length, and single track throughout. Newham, which had been the easternmost limit of West Cornwall Railway operations from 16th April, 1855 until most trains were diverted into the Cornwall Railway station on 11th May, 1859, was used exclusively as a goods station after September 1863. The station boasted a wooden 'Brunel' style overall roof, together with a hip-roofed timber station building and a single platform.

The track layout at Newham incorporated a run-round loop beside the former passenger platform, with a goods shed and one or two quayside sidings. The history of Newham station is long, but undistinguished. West Cornwall Railway Directors' reports provide a few glimpses of the station in operation. For instance in September 1864 it was reported that 'a new five ton crane had been erected on the quay at Newham', together with what was described as an 'ore hutch'. Much later, in Great Western days, extra warehouse accommodation was provided at the goods station for the benefit of local traders, who were allowed to rent

Impatient to reach Truro and not willing to wait for the Cornwall Railway, mired in financial problems, the West Cornwall Railway decided to build its own station there at Newham, by the side of the Truro river. This was served by a short extension of its main line. The station was opened in 1855 amid hopes that it would generate profits from its closer access to the town and sea-borne traffic. It was not to be. The returns were disappointing and the West Cornwall lost no opportunity in negotiating joint usage of the new Truro station of the Cornwall Railway, from 1859. Newham, never converted to mixed gauge, stuttered on with a vestigal passenger service until 16th November, 1863. From then until post-nationalisation Newham was a goods-only branch. In this undated view of Newham we see a double-framed 4-4-0 locomotive of what is believed to be a member of the '3521' class in its final rebuilt state. This would date the picture as being post-1892.

Royal Institution of Cornwall

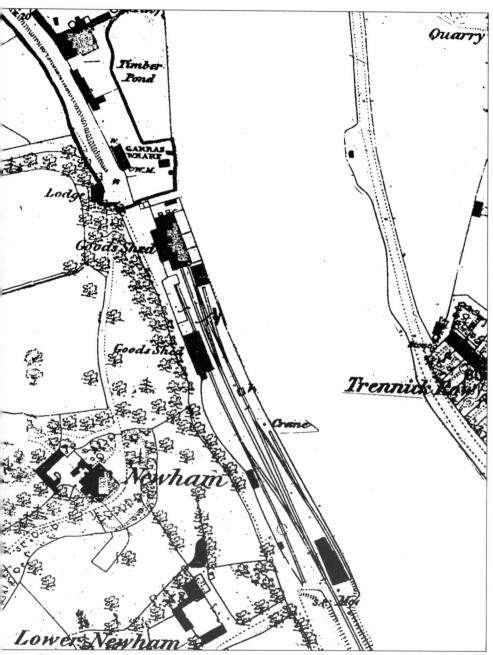

Newham terminus.   *Reproduced from the 25", 1879 Ordnance Survey Map*

This view of Newham, taken in 1938, shows the train shed little changed, the single platform *in situ*, serving duty as a loading bay.   *Great Western Society/Reed Collection*

Chacewater station, looking east towards Paddington during the Edwardian period, around 1912. This station became a junction in 1903, when the first section of the Perranporth branch was opened from Blackwater Junction to Perranporth. The main down platform can be seen to the right, while the island platform, with its outer face for branch traffic, can be seen to the left of the picture.   *Lens of Sutton Collection*

storage space on a so-called 'fixed space' agreement. The station remained busy throughout the early British Railways period but, sadly, this historic West Cornwall terminus was closed to all traffic in November 1972.

Chacewater

From Penwithers Junction, the West Cornwall route continues, as a double track main line, on a ruling gradient of 1 in 80 which extends for about three miles towards Chacewater.

Heading westwards, trains soon reach the 124 yards-long Penwithers viaduct, which was rebuilt as a masonry structure in 1887. Beyond, the railway continues its ascent, and then drops towards Chacewater on a series of falling grades. Nearing the station, trains cross two more viaducts, the first of which, known as Chacewater viaduct, is 99 yards long and 52 ft high, while the second - the seven-arch Blackwater viaduct - is 132 yards long and 68 ft high.

In West Cornwall Railway days Chacewater (5 miles 18 chains from the Cornwall Railway station at Truro) had been no more than a wayside station but, in July 1903, the Great Western opened a new branch line to St Agnes and Perranporth, and Chacewater was thereby transformed into a country junction.

The Perranporth line actually left the West Cornwall route at Blackwater Junction (to the west of Chacewater station), a triangular junction being provided so that trains could reach Perranporth from either the Truro or Redruth directions. Two years later, in 1905, the Perranporth line was extended to Shepherds - from which point up-graded mineral lines enabled passenger trains to reach Newquay.

The Chacewater to Newquay route was worked by steam railmotors for several years, but these were subsequently replaced by conventional locomotive-hauled trains. In 1924, the junction at Blackwater was removed, the branch being extended eastwards into Chacewater station as a single line. This arrangement persisted until the closure of the Perranporth route in 1963.

Chacewater station had three platform faces, the main station building being on the down side. Its goods facilities comprised two sidings, serving the usual coal wharves, cattle pens and loading docks; the yard crane was capable of lifting two tons.

The layout at Chacewater was fairly simple. The main down platform was a side platform, but the up side was an island, the additional platform face for branch services to Newquay and Perranporth being served by a loop from the up main line. Goods facilities consisted of a small yard and associated headshunt on the down side, while the up and down main lines were linked by crossovers at each end of the station; there was, in addition, a short dead-end spur at the eastern end of the loop line.

The passenger facilities consisted of a range of simple wooden buildings on the down side, which contained the usual booking office, waiting room and toilet accommodation for both sexes. A typical Great Western type covered footbridge gave access to the up platform, which was itself equipped with a solidly-built waiting room and toilet block. The latter building was of attractive

Chacewater station, looking west towards Penzance on 4th June, 1920. The main station building, just visible beyond the plate girder footbridge, was badly damaged by fire in 1947, and a new building was then erected in its place.   *Lens of Sutton Collection*

A later view of Chacewater station, showing '45XX' 2-6-2T No. 4565 in the branch platform at the head of a local working.   *N. Stead Collection*

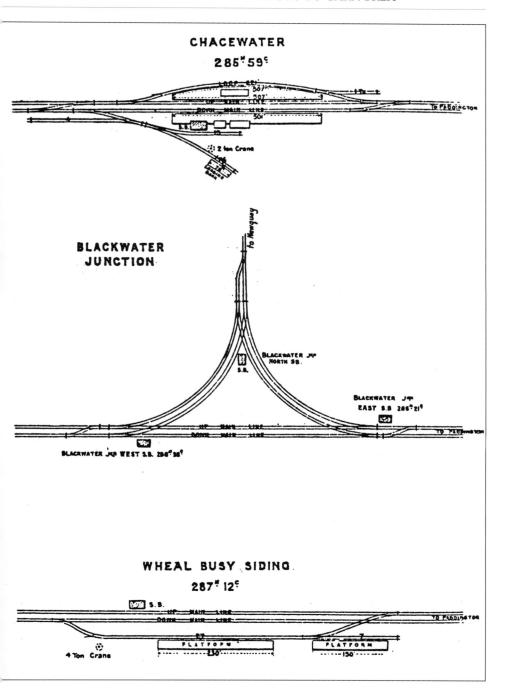

CHACEWATER

285ᵐ 59ᶜ

BLACKWATER JUNCTION

WHEAL BUSY SIDING.

287ᵈ 12ᶜ

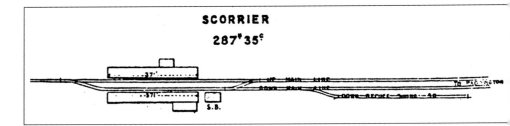

A panoramic view of Scorrier looking east towards Paddington, probably in the 1920s or 1930s. The up side waiting room (*left*) was a later addition. *Lens of Sutton Collection*

The down platform at Scorrier, in the early 1900s; the original West Cornwall Railway station building can be seen to the left of the later stone-built structure with the hipped-roof. Scorrier station was 6 miles 74 chains from Truro; it had two 371 ft platforms for up and down traffic and a small goods yard. The station was placed under the control of the Chacewater station master in 1933. *Lens of Sutton Collection*

'snecked' stone construction, and it boasted commodious canopies on both sides for the benefit of waiting travellers.

In February 1947, the downside buildings were damaged by fire, but new buildings were provided in the 1950s. The station was originally signalled from a gable-roofed signal cabin on the down platform, but this box was subsequently replaced by a hip-roofed cabin with five-pane windows, which was brought into use in 1914. The platforms were lit by simple oil lamps for many years, but these were later replaced by paraffin vapour lamps suspended from tall concrete posts.

In the early 1920s, Chacewater had a staff of 10, including two leading porters, two porters, one class four station master and five signalmen. In 1924, the staffing establishment was reduced to seven, following the removal of Blackwater Junction, and a consequent reduction in the number of signalmen.

Chacewater was never a particularly busy station, and its average passenger bookings during the period from 1930 to 1938 were only 15,600 a year. Freight traffic was of minimal importance, and in most years the goods yard dealt with little more than 1,000 tons of coal, minerals and general merchandise per annum. The station was closed in October 1964.

Scorrier

After Chacewater, the West Cornwall route runs north-westwards for a short distance, before curving south-westwards at the site of the abandoned Blackwater Junction. Thereafter, the line runs roughly south-westwards for many miles, this same general heading being maintained for much of the journey to Penzance. The approaches to Scorrier are on a stretch of 1 in 60 rising gradient but, once past Scorrier, the route descends towards Penzance - though as mentioned earlier these favourable grades are punctuated by several sharp ascents as the line follows the undulations of the local terrain.

Scorrier, the next stopping place, was 6 miles 74 chains from Truro. One of the smallest intermediate stations *en route* to Penzance, Scorrier had originally been known as 'Scorrier Gate'. In later years at least, the station had no cattle pens, end loading docks or yard crane, though the 1938 Railway Clearing House *Handbook of Stations* reveals that a private siding connection to the nearby Wheal Busy mine was, at that time, still available for use; this siding was sited ¼ mile to the east of the station, at 6 miles 51 chains.

Mention of Wheal Busy serves as a reminder that, during the first half of the 19th century, Scorrier station had served a busy mining district, famous not just for tin, but also for copper mines. Indeed, the transport needs of local mines had brought rail communication to Scorrier as early as 1812 - by which time the horse-worked Poldice tramway from Portreath had been extended as far east as Scorrier House. This tramway - which was probably of 4 ft gauge - was later extended to serve the productive copper mines at Poldice.

Sadly, the demise of Poldice mine during the 1860s led to a dearth of traffic on the tramway, and this little-known line was closed around 1866. On 1st January 1874, *The West Briton* reported that thieves had been stealing 'the short railway bars forming the old line . . . between Scorrier and St Day'. As the line was not in use, 'no great amount of inconvenience' had been occasioned, but Messrs Williams, the owners of the line, had asked the local police to investigate these worrying thefts, and *The West Briton* report ended with the pious hope that the property would remain unmolested, 'or the thieves speedily captured'.

Scorrier consisted of two platforms for up and down traffic, each of which was 371 ft in length. The main station building was on the down platform and there was a small waiting room on the up side. The station was signalled from another standard hipped-roof signal box, this characteristic Great Western structure being sited immediately to the east of the down platform.

Until 1930, Scorrier was of operational significance in that it marked the end of the double track section from Truro, the short section westwards to Redruth being single line. However, in that year the Great Western doubled the line between Scorrier and Redruth, a distance of just over 1½ miles, this work being undertaken as part of an unemployment relief programme sanctioned by the Government. With the completion of this work, the Great Western main line was equipped with double or multiple track throughout its length from Paddington to Penzance, a distance of 305 miles via Somerton (except for the short section of single track across the Royal Albert Bridge at Saltash).

For administrative purposes, Scorrier came under the control of the Chacewater station master after February 1933. In that year the station issued 14,565 tickets , this figure being typical for the middle 1930s - though bookings had dropped to 11,199 by 1938. The goods traffic handled at Scorrier in the later 1930s was less than 1,000 tons per annum. In 1936, a typical year, the station dealt with just 989 tons of freight, most of this being in the form of inwards or outwards general merchandise traffic. Coal traffic amounted to only 31 tons, which would have filled just three wagons.

In 1903, Scorrier had employed eight men, but the labour force had been reduced to five by the mid-1920s. In March 1925 these comprised two signalmen at the station proper, and two porter-signalmen at Wheal Busy Siding. This modest staffing establishment was, at that time, controlled by a class five station master.

Two of those employed at the station around 1960 included G.M. Bunney and F.T. Harris, both of whom were signalmen. By that time, the amount of traffic being handled had fallen still further, and it came as no surprise when Scorrier was listed for closure in the 1963 Beeching Plan. The closure was carried out as planned in October 1964, when Scorrier and three other West Cornwall Railway stations were deleted from the British Railways network.

Redruth

Running through a semi-industrial landscape, punctuated by the characteristic stone-built engine houses of the Cornish tin mining industry, down trains soon reach Redruth, some 9 miles 5 chains from Truro. The main station building here is situated on the up side; of brick construction, it is a modernised version of the Great Western 'standard' design. The down side building, in contrast, is a timber-framed structure clad in horizontal weather boarding. The station is approached through the 47 yds-long Redruth tunnel, and the up and down platforms are linked by a lattice girder footbridge.

Redruth formerly had a full range of goods facilities, with ample provision for the carriage of coal, cattle and general merchandise traffic. There were loading docks, cattle pens, a goods shed and a 6 ton yard crane, while a private siding served the West of England Bacon Company's nearby premises (later purchased by Messrs C. & T. Harris of Calne).

The evolution of Redruth station was a somewhat complex process spanning several decades. When first opened by the West Cornwall Railway, on 11th March, 1852, the station had been a passing place on the WCR single line, with simple wooden buildings on the up platform and a timber goods shed, both of these structures being of standard 'Brunelian' design. This first West Cornwall station survived for many years, but major changes were put into effect in 1912, when the Great Western opened a new goods yard at Drump Lane, some 33 chains to the east of the passenger station.

The planning and construction of new goods depots did not normally attract much publicity. There was, however, considerable interest in the progress of the new works at Drump Lane, and on 21st June, 1912 the following report appeared in the pages of *The Falmouth Packet*:

REDRUTH'S NEW GOODS STATION - The new goods station, which has occupied nearly two years in erecting and laying out for the Great Western Railway at Drump, Redruth, was on Monday opened for traffic. It contains a very commodious brick building for the goods shed, and up-to-date facilities are provided in the sidings for the training and detraining of cattle and heavy goods, the whole covering a large area.

Redruth has, up to the present, been badly provided for both as regards the passenger accommodation and goods and cattle facilities, and it is hoped that the removal of the goods depot to Drump will result in the company using the space thus left at their disposal in the provision of a station worthy of the trade and size of Redruth, on which matter the company has several times been approached by the town.

The facilities in Drump Lane goods yard consisted of a long reception loop and a second, parallel loop line serving a large red brick goods shed. Another siding served a loading bank and end-loading dock, while two further sidings were available for coal or other forms of 'mileage' traffic. The goods shed was a standard Great Western structure, with a 160 ft internal loading platform and three cart entrances; its external dimensions were approximately 160 ft by 49 ft at ground level, and it was covered by a gabled, slated roof. A partially-glazed canopy extended for 135 ft along the south side of the building, affording ample wet weather protection for the three cart entrances.

A gable-roofed extension projected beyond the west gable of the main block, and this contained office and toilet facilities on the ground floor, with a storage loft above. A corresponding extension at the opposite end of the building provided staff messing accommodation, and there was a small checker's office within the main part of the structure. The goods shed also contained two 1 ton 10 cwt hand cranes, while a much larger 5 ton yard crane was conveniently sited beside the mileage

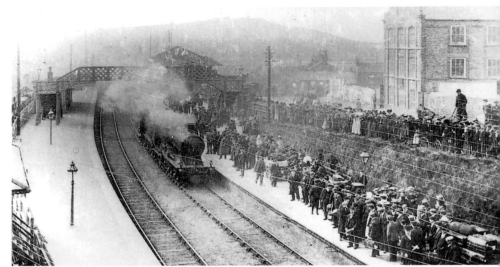

A general view of Redruth station, showing large numbers of travellers on the up platform; these may be emigrants bound for South Africa, Australia, or some other part of the distant Empire.   *Lens of Sutton Collection*

Another general view of Redruth station, photographed in the early 1900s, and looking west towards Penzance. In 1912, the GWR opened a new goods depot at Drump Lane, and the original goods yard was then run-down, though not entirely superseded. The large goods shed was demolished, but a loading platform and associated sidings were retained.

Lens of Sutton Collection

Redruth station at the end of the Victorian era. The gentlemen in the slouch hats are members of the Local Rifle Volunteers - the 19th century predecessors of the present-day Territorial Army.
Lens of Sutton Collection

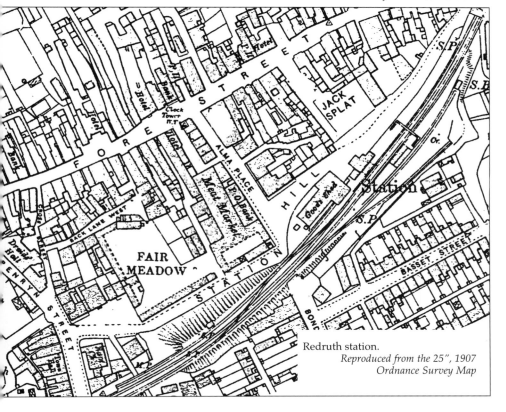

Redruth station.
Reproduced from the 25", 1907
Ordnance Survey Map

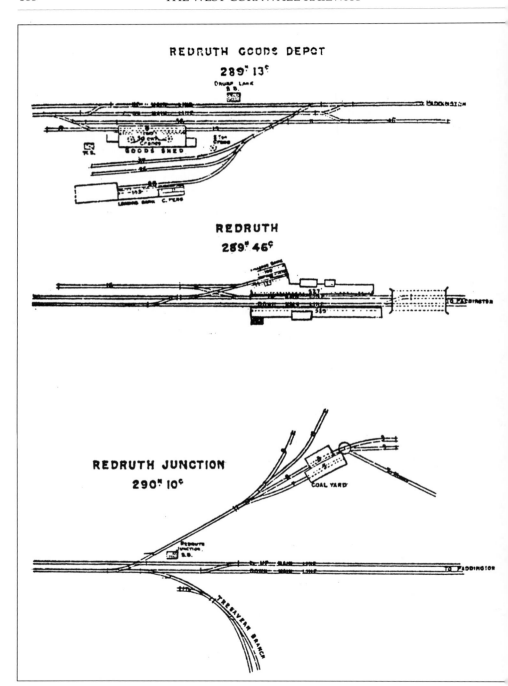

sidings. The new goods yard was signalled from Drump Lane signal box - a standard Great Western type cabin situated on the up side of the running lines.

Most goods handling facilities were removed from the passenger station following the opening of the new goods depot, though a dead-end siding was retained on the up side, together with a short spur which terminated in a loading dock on the site of the former goods shed.

Further changes were initiated at Redruth in the 1930s, as a result of which the 1852 station building was demolished, and the present red brick booking office and waiting room erected in its place; the earlier, downside waiting room was, however, retained. Both of these buildings are equipped with projecting platform canopies - the up side building having a gable roof canopy, while the canopy on the down side building is formed of an extension of the roof covering.

Redruth was an important traffic centre for both passenger and freight traffic, and in the 1920s and early 1930s its passenger bookings always exceeded 100,000 tickets per year. In 1923, for instance, the station issued 127,547 tickets and 889 seasons, while in 1935 101,059 tickets and 1,015 season tickets were issued. The amount of goods traffic handled over the same period declined from 45,009 tons in 1923 to 20,380 tons in 1935 - though the annual figure had increased to 27,193 tons by 1938.

The types of goods traffic handled during the 1930s were typically coal and general merchandise, the heyday of the Cornish mining industry having long passed by that time; in 1938 Redruth dealt with only 1,057 tons of 'other minerals' (i.e. non-coal traffic). Most of this was incoming road-making materials, and only 20 tons of mineral traffic was dispatched from the station in that year (a staggeringly-small quantity, when one considers that Redruth was once regarded as a centre of the mining industry).

In 1913, Redruth had employed 29 people, but this figure had risen to 34 by 1932 and 35 by 1938, most of the additional employees being motor drivers who carried out collection and delivery work within an area extending about 4½ miles in each direction from the station. The collection and delivery area was free within Redruth itself, but charges were made for consignments sent to or from more distant destinations such as Portreath (4 miles) or Porthtowan (4½ miles from Redruth).

As one might expect, a busy traffic centre such as Redruth employed a variety of people in the Traffic Department. In the late 1920s and early 1930s these typically included two booking clerks, four goods clerks, two parcels porters, one leading porter, four porters, one working foreman, two goods checkers, one goods carter, one leading carter, two motor drivers, one horse parcel vanman, four goods porters, one 'caller off', one goods shunter, four signalmen, one signal lampman and one charwoman. This relatively large labour force was controlled by a class one station master.

The passenger station has survived more or less intact since the 1930s, but the spacious goods yard at nearby Drump Lane has succumbed to rationalisation.

The train service provided in recent years has consisted of around 16-18 workings in each direction, most of these services being long distance main line workings between Penzance, London or other destinations. In June 1965, for example, local travellers had a choice of 16 up and 19 down trains on weekdays (with an enhanced service on Saturdays), while in September 1995 there were 18 up and 19 down workings on weekdays, and a modified service on Saturdays.

The main up side station building at Redruth, photographed on 12th March, 1996; this red brick 1930s structure replaced the original West Cornwall Railway station building. It still contains a privately-run refreshment room, in addition to the usual booking office and waiting room facilities.   *S.C. Jenkins*

The down side station building at Redruth on 12th March, 1996. This timber structure is considerably older than its counterpart on the up platform; at the time of writing it is in very poor condition.   *S.C. Jenkins*

In historical terms, Redruth was of particular interest in so far as it had been the eastern terminus of the Hayle Railway and, until its closure in 1936, the Hayle Railway's Tresavean branch had provided a tangible link with the early days of railway operation in West Cornwall. The branch had diverged south-eastwards from the West Cornwall main line at Redruth Junction (9 miles 45 chains), and this junction had also given access to the former Hayle Railway terminus, which remained in use as a coal yard after 1852.

Redruth was also notable in that it was the location of one of the former West Cornwall Railway timber viaducts - the structure in question being sited in a built-up area immediately to the west of the passenger station. These viaducts were thought by many local travellers to be less stable than their counterparts on the neighbouring Cornwall Railway. In March 1882, for example, *The West Briton* published a letter from a correspondent, who considered that the West Cornwall viaducts were 'inferior altogether to the not very desirable erections of the same kind on the Cornwall line'.

They had (suggested the letter writer) been designed to carry relatively light narrow gauge trains, but they were nevertheless expected to support 'the tremendous burden' of broad gauge trains, for which they were not intended 'and not calculated'. The Hayle and Redruth viaducts, continued the letter writer, were 'scandalously dangerous, and in no wise adequate to the strain of broad gauge traffic'; they should, he urged, be 'superseded forthwith by something less dangerous to the necks of the public'!

In similar vein, the paper itself suggested that the viaducts at Redruth and elsewhere were unsafe, and on 22nd September, 1881, local travellers may have been alarmed by the following report:

> It would be interesting to know how much of the timber used in building the Redruth viaduct about 30 years ago remains in its place to this day. Years ago rumour spoke of the shaky condition of this viaduct; yet by dint of continual attention, and frequent visits from gangs of navvies, with a new piece of timber here, another piece there and masonry rests at two or three places, it still stands, and bears up the heavy loads which daily go over it.
>
> Navvies have been, for the last week or two, engaged in repairing it, the scene of operations being, for the most part, at Penryn Street, where some 'legs' of old timber have been replaced by new ones, and whilst this has been doing, a temporary prop from the ground has done its part to share the burden, and keep the structure up. May we ever expect to have a new viaduct at Redruth, or must we still put up with the present one?

In fact, the remaining West Cornwall Railway timber viaducts were much safer than they looked - most were, nonetheless, replaced in the 1880s, and as we have seen, the very last example, at Penponds, had been rebuilt by 1899. At Redruth, the original 60 ft high timber viaduct was replaced by a solid masonry structure, which straddled Penryn Street area with a confidence which Brunel would surely have admired!

Leaving Redruth, down trains immediately cross Redruth viaduct, and then traverse a semi-urbanised mining area that is dominated by relics of the once-prosperous Cornish mining industry. This somewhat bleak landscape is dotted with the tall chimneys of stone-built engine houses while, nearer at hand, streets of terraced workers' houses and plain Nonconformist chapels recall the sombre

An unidentified GWR 4-4-0 heads westwards across Redruth viaduct during the early years of the 20th century. The siding on the left of the picture served the original WCR goods shed.

Lens of Sutton Collection

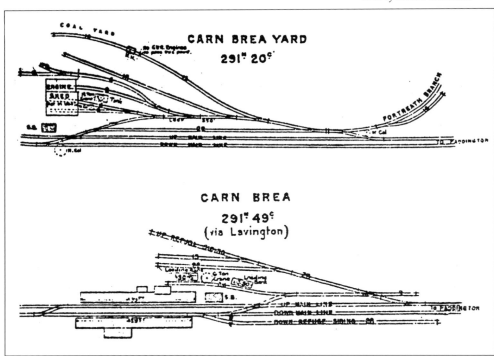

landscapes of the industrial North. This grim landscape was, in truth, the industrial heart of Cornwall, and although large numbers of mines had been abandoned by the 20th century, few modern visitors can doubt Cornwall's former importance as the centre of the world tin mining industry.

Carn Brea

Carn Brea, the next station (11 miles 8 chains) was situated roughly mid-way between Redruth and Camborne. Originally known as 'Pool',* this two-platform stopping place had once functioned as the junction for goods services to Portreath, which were worked northwards over the single track Portreath branch as recounted in Chapter One. A small station, Carn Brea was nevertheless provided with a range of facilities for both passenger and goods traffic; its two goods yards were equipped with the usual coal wharves, cattle pens and loading docks, together with weigh-houses and yard cranes.

The various facilities provided in and around Carn Brea were fairly complex, the station being the junction, not only for the Portreath goods branch, but also the North Crofty branch, which joined the main line just 31 chains to the west of the passenger station.

The station proper consisted of up and down platforms, linked by a Great Western style plate girder footbridge, with small buildings on each platform and a three-siding goods yard on the up side. There were, in addition, up and down relief sidings on each side of the running lines, the down siding being laid parallel to the running line while its counterpart on the up side extended along the rear of the goods yard. The yard itself was equipped with loading banks and a 6 ton fixed hand crane.

Carn Brea Yard, some 29 chains to the east of the passenger station, was situated on the up side of the running lines. It consisted of two loop lines from which a number of sidings diverged to serve coal wharves and the former West Cornwall Railway locomotive sheds and workshops. The Portreath branch converged with the loop line at the east end of the yard, the junction being effected by means of a simple turnout that was facing to up trains.

The Portreath branch was mentioned in connection with the Hayle Railway in Chapter One, but it may be worth mentioning here that this single line goods branch was worked by train staff without block telegraph on the 'one-engine-in-steam' system. The branch was closed to all traffic beyond North Pool on 1st January, 1936, and the remaining section between North Pool Siding and Carn Brea Yard was closed on 1st April, 1938.

The demise of this obscure Cornish goods line did not pass unrecorded, and in June 1938 *The Railway Magazine* printed the following obituary notice:

> On April 1st, 1938, the GWR Portreath branch was closed for traffic as between Carn Brea yard and North Pool siding, thus presumably writing finis to the career of yet another historic railway in West Cornwall.
>
> This line, of a little over three miles from Carn Brea yard to the small seaport of Portreath on the north coast of Cornwall, was one of several short branches promoted

---

* Carn Brea station was not sited *exactly* on the site of Pool station.

Carn Brea station looking west towards Penzance on a dull winter's day around the turn of the century. The goods yard can be glimpsed to the right, while an 0-6-0 saddle tank stands on the up main line.   *Lens of Sutton Collection*

Carn Brea, looking west towards Penzance. In its later years Carn Brea was under the control of the Redruth station master.   *Lens of Sutton Collection*

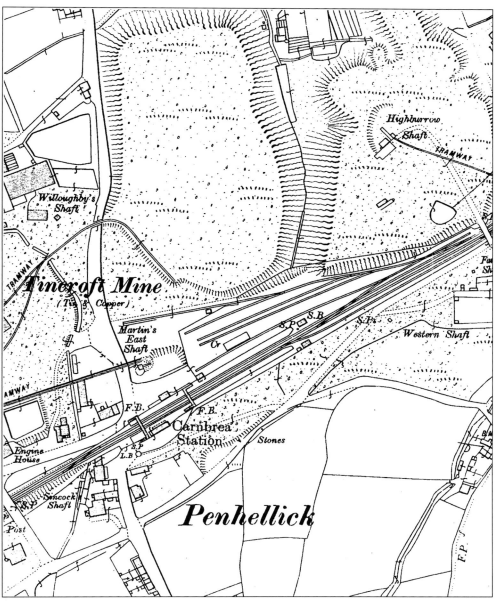

Carn Brea station.

Reproduced from the 25", 1907 Ordnance Survey Map

by the Hayle Railway in 1834 in connection with its main line from Hayle Foundry to Tresavean Mine near Redruth.

The purpose of the branch was the shipment of minerals; it was opened in 1838 or 1839; but was never used for public passenger traffic. Together with the rest of the Hayle Railway, the Portreath branch became part of the West Cornwall Railway in 1846.

The amount of passenger and freight traffic handled at Carn Brea decreased inexorably during the late 19th and early 20th centuries - particularly in terms of freight. In 1913, 56,211 tons of goods was handled, but this figure had dropped to around 25,000 tons per annum during the 1920s, and approximately 5,000 tons a year by the 1930s; in 1935, for instance, only 4,424 tons were dealt with, though this meagre figure had risen to 5,418 tons by the following year.

On the passenger side Carn Brea's bookings declined from 38,213 tickets in 1913, to 15,991 ordinary tickets (and 42 seasons) in 1923. In 1937, the station issued only 6,630 tickets, falling to just 5,425 passenger bookings (and 18 seasons) in the following year. In 1903, Carn Brea had a staff of 15, but its staffing establishment was progressively reduced over the next few years. In March 1925, the staffing establishment consisted of one general clerk, two porters, one goods porter, one goods shunter, four signalmen, one charwoman and a class three station master.

In the later Great Western period, Carn Brea employed seven people, while, for administrative purposes the station was placed under the control of the Redruth station master. Carn Brea was, by that time, the most lightly-used stopping place between Truro and Penzance, and under these circumstances it was an obvious candidate for early closure in the years following World War II. In the event, closure took place even before the publication of the Beeching Plan, and the last trains called in 1961.

Little now remains to mark the site of this abandoned Cornish station, the pace of rationalisation having quickened during the 1960s; the station goods yard and associated trackwork was taken out of use in 1965-67, while Carn Brea Yard was taken out of use in August 1967. The up refuge line was briefly reinstated in 1970, but it was finally abandoned in December 1972. The signal box at Carn Brea Yard lingered on for a few more months, but it was finally closed on 29th May, 1973.

G.W.R.

Redruth

Chapter Seven

The Stations and Route - Camborne to Penzance

From Carn Brea, the route continues for a little under two miles to Camborne. The view from the carriage windows is still predominantly industrial - indeed, the houses, abandoned mines and Nonconformist chapels of Redruth and Camborne form one virtually continuous settlement, with no real distinction between them.

In recent years a number of modern industrial units have grown up on land once occupied by relics of the mining industry while, elsewhere, nature has started to reclaim the ruined engine houses and spoil heaps which abound in this distinctive landscape, the result being a sort of semi-urban sprawl that is as grim and depressing as any part of the industrial North or Midlands.

Camborne

There was, at one time, a small stopping place at Dolcoath (on the eastern side of Camborne), but this diminutive halt had a life of only three years, having opened in 1905 and closed in 1908. Dolcoath Siding, at a point some 11 miles 40 chains from Truro, remained in use for coal and later milk traffic, while at nearby North Crofty Junction (11 miles 40 chains), the North Crofty goods branch diverged northwards from the main line. Both of these industrial sidings were entered via connections that were trailing to up trains. Dolcoath Siding was finally taken out of use in December 1983, while North Crofty goods siding was closed in 1948 and lifted in the following year.

Continuing westwards, trains soon pass Roskear Junction signal box, which formerly controlled the Roskear goods branch and an adjacent coal siding. Both of these goods facilities are now, however, closed and lifted. Roskear Junction box is a typical gable-roofed cabin of the middle 1890s, with dark, purple-blue brickwork and small-paned windows; it has remained in use in connection with an adjacent level crossing.

Nearing the important intermediate station at Camborne, down trains clatter past a large engineering factory on the north side of the line. This was once operated by Messrs Holman Brothers - a famous Cornish firm which, like their friendly rivals, Harvey's of Hayle, specialised in mining and engineering products both for home consumption and throughout the world.

The canyon-like wall of the factory runs parallel to the railway for a considerable distance while, to the south, an area of open ground was formerly occupied by a mine. Crossing Trevu Road on the level, the line immediately enters Camborne station, where trains come to a stand in the down platform.

Camborne, in many ways the 'capital' of the Cornish mining area, is 12 miles 54 chains from Truro. The main station building here is on the up side, in which position it is conveniently-sited in relation to the town centre. The usual booking office, waiting rooms and public toilets are provided, the building itself

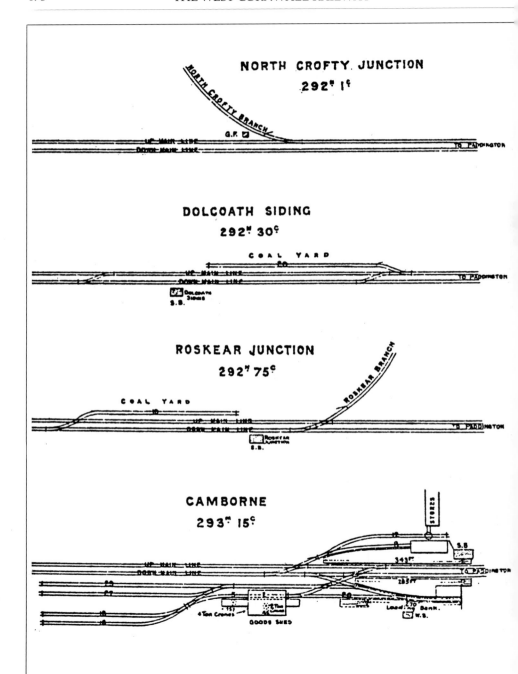

A postcard view of the up side station building at Camborne in the early years of the 20th century. An 0-6-0 approaches with a goods train from the Redruth direction.

Lens of Sutton Collection

A closer view of the up side building at Camborne; the wooden hut to the left of the main, red brick block appears to be of West Cornwall origin.   *Lens of Sutton Collection*

Camborne station, looking east towards Paddington around 1912. A steam railmotor can be glimpsed in the up platform, beside the main station building.   *Lens of Sutton Collection*

Camborne station, looking east towards Paddington, probably around 1920.
                                                    Lens of Sutton Collection

being a typical late Victorian standard GWR design. The nearby goods shed, in contrast, was a characteristic broad gauge style structure, similar to scores of others found throughout the Great Western system on lines engineered by Brunel (or his assistants).

The station building is a hip-roofed structure with tall, decorative chimneys; in its original guise, it featured a projecting platform canopy, but this has now been taken down. The building is constructed of a curious mixture of English and Flemish bonding - particularly in the centre part of the platform frontage, which exhibits an untidy pattern of headers (bricks laid crossways) and stretchers (bricks laid longitudinally). The main building material is red brick, but dark purple-blue bricks are employed for decorative effect at the corners and around the doors and windows. The building has a projecting extension at the rear, which was clearly a later addition to the main Victorian fabric.

Prior to rationalisation, the main up side building was flanked by two other structures, a small 'Brunelian' style wooden hut, and a standard gable-roofed signal cabin. The hut was constructed of horizontal timbers and, from its general appearance, it may have dated back to the West Cornwall period; the signal box, in contrast, was a late-Victorian structure of brick and timber construction dating from the mid-1890s.

Facilities on the down platform are now confined to a simple 'bus stop' type shelter, though in steam days a substantial waiting room had been provided. The up and down platforms are linked by a plate girder footbridge, which is dated 1940, and replaces the roofed bridge shown in the accompanying photographs.

The track layout at Camborne formerly provided goods sidings on both sides of the running lines, the main goods yard being on the down side while two further sidings were situated behind the platform on the opposite side of the line. These sidings were linked to the main lines by a system of crossovers, one of which left the up running line by a trailing connection and crossed the down line on the level, in order to reach the goods shed and adjoining sidings. The up side sidings here were removed in the 1930s, though the goods yard proper remained in use until May 1965.

The goods shed was used for the loading and unloading of general merchandise traffic, while the nearby sidings were available for the handling of coal, minerals and other forms of bulk traffic. The yard crane was of four tons capacity in the 1920s, but it was later increased to six tons.

The goods yard sidings have now been lifted, but this has enabled the up and down platforms to be considerably lengthened, and eight-car HST formations can now be accommodated with ample room to spare. The up platform was lengthened in 1937, but the down side was not extended until the British Railways era (1980).

Camborne has always handled a considerable passenger traffic; in 1913, for example, 150,288 tickets were issued, while in the early 1930s the station typically dealt with around 113,000 bookings per year, in addition to about 400-500 season ticket sales - the latter, of course being used by regular travellers.

Goods traffic over the same period fell from 76,348 tons in 1913, to an average of 19,000 tons during the 1930s. In 1932, for example, 18,326 tons of freight were

Camborne station, looking east towards Paddington on 11th March, 1996. Note that the platform canopy has been removed, while a 'bus stop'-style shelter has replaced the down side waiting room.   *S.C. Jenkins*

A closer view of the up side station building at Camborne on 11th March, 1996.   *S.C. Jenkins*

handled, whereas in 1937 the corresponding figure was 21,094 tons. As in the case of Redruth, most of this goods tonnage was accounted for by general merchandise traffic, the local mining industry having gone into a steep decline by that time. On the other hand, Camborne's long association with hard rock mining has not entirely ceased, and the town is still the home of the world-famous Camborne School of Mines.

Gwinear Road

Departing from Camborne, down trains continue south-westwards, and having passed beneath Pendarves Road, the route drops at 1 in 70 and 1 in 60 towards Gwinear Road. At Penponds, roughly mid-way between Camborne and Gwinear Road, the line crosses the 121 yd Penponds viaduct, which was one of the longest on the West Cornwall route prior to its reconstruction at the end of the 19th century.

In the case of Penponds, the replacement of the original timber viaduct was effected by means of a deviation line, which was built on a parallel alignment to the south of the old West Cornwall single line. The new bridge was wide enough to accommodate a double track, although when first used on 3rd September, 1899 it carried only one operational line, the new double track section between Camborne and Gwinear Road not being brought into use until the following January. The new masonry viaduct was 170 yards shorter than its timber predecessor, which had been no less than 291 yards long. Conversely, the deviated line that was brought into use in 1899-1900 incorporated a correspondingly greater proportion of embankment.

Continuing westwards, trains speed past the site of Sandy Lane signal box, which formerly controlled an isolated level crossing about half a mile beyond Penponds viaduct. The box is shown in the July 1883 working time table, but it had evidently been abolished by the end of the 19th century.

Gwinear Road, the junction for branch services to Helston, was 15 miles 14 chains from Truro. Three platform faces were provided, the down platform being an island with tracks on either side. Helston trains used the outer face of this island platform, but there were no run-round facilities for branch trains and for this reason it was necessary for incoming branch workings to run-round on the main line (wrong line operation being unavoidable in this situation).

The main station building was a timber structure on the down side, and there was a somewhat smaller waiting room on the up platform. The up and down sides were linked by a plate girder footbridge, and a public road crossed the running lines at an awkward angle at the east end of the passenger platforms. On a minor point of detail, it is interesting to find that the level crossing gates needed to protect this skew crossing were said to have been the longest in Cornwall!

The evolution of Gwinear Road station was a long, and somewhat complex process that started as far back as the 1840s, when regular passenger services commenced running on the Hayle Railway. In those days, however, the facilities provided for the travelling public would have been primitive in the extreme, and the only 'station building' available would have been no more than a simple hut or shack.

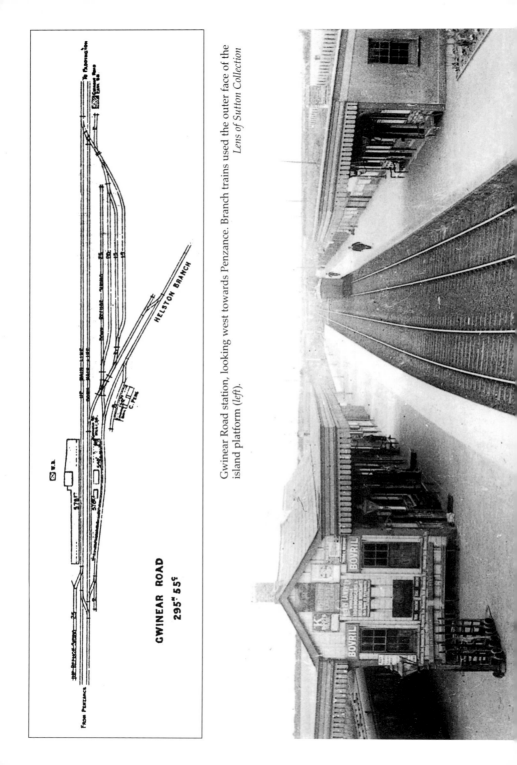

GWINEAR ROAD
295" 55°

Gwinear Road station, looking west towards Penzance. Branch trains used the outer face of the island platform (*left*).

Lens of Sutton Collection

Gwinear Road station, looking east towards Paddington in the Edwardian period, around 1912. The Helston branch diverged from the main line immediately beyond the level crossing, which was said to have had the largest gates in Cornwall! The main line platforms here were 578 ft long, and the branch platform had a length of 540 ft.   *Lens of Sutton Collection*

'Grange' class 4-6-0 No. 6808 *Beenham Grange* passes Gwinear Road East signal box with a broccoli special on 7th April, 1960.   *P.Q. Treloar*

A view of Gwinear Road, looking towards Penzance. An unidentified '45XX' class 2-6-2T locomotive stands in the branch platform with a Helston train.   *Lens of Sutton Collection*

The up platform at Gwinear Road, looking east towards Truro and London.
                                                                    Lens of Sutton Collection

In West Cornwall Railway days, Gwinear Road consisted of a single passenger platform on the down side of the line, together with a run-round loop for goods traffic, and a group of sidings on the down side. The station does not appear to have been used for crossing purposes at that time.

Important developments took place during the early 1860s, when the Helston Railway was promoted with Powers to construct a branch line commencing from 'A siding near the Gwinear Road station'. The siding in question would clearly have been one of the goods sidings on the down side, which would otherwise have obstructed the route of the proposed branch line. Indeed, the junction arrangements at Gwinear Road gave rise to several problems, but the layout of the new station was finally decided after consultations had taken place between Sylvanus W. Jenkin (1821-1911) the Helston Railway Engineer, and Peter J. Margary (1820-1896), the GWR Divisional Engineer at Plymouth.

In April 1886, Mr Jenkin attended a Helston Railway Directors' meeting and produced the plans of the new station, which were approved by the Helston Railway Board members. At a later meeting, Mr Jenkin read a letter from Peter Margary explaining the new signalling arrangements at the junction, and on Monday 9th May, 1887 the Helston branch was opened to traffic - the rebuilt station being brought into use at the same time.

The rebuilt station provided two main line platforms, each with a length of 578 ft, together with a 540 ft branch platform on the south side. The down side buildings featured projecting canopies on both sides, while the up side building boasted a single pitch roof that was continued over the platform as a canopy.

Both buildings sported decorative 'groove and hole' valancing, which did much to enliven structures that would otherwise have been of utilitarian weather-boarded construction. The up side building was subsequently extended at its eastern end, in order to provide a greater length of platform covering on the eastbound platform.

It is of interest to note that the contractors responsible for the new station buildings at Gwinear Road were Messrs Thomas Olver & Sons of Falmouth - a well-known local building firm which had been established in 1811. Olvers had erected numerous public buildings in Cornwall, and they had also built the Cornwall Railway stations at Lostwithiel, Falmouth, Penryn, Par, St Austell and elsewhere.

There was an array of sidings on the down side of the line which were employed primarily for storage and re-marshalling purposes, while a siding on the up side was used mainly for the loading of broccoli and other agricultural traffic. The station was controlled from two signal boxes, one of which (Gwinear Road West) was on the down platform, while the other (Gwinear Road East) was sited at the eastern extremity of the station complex. Both of these boxes were of the later, hipped-roof pattern, with five-paned windows. The West box was re-sited in 1916, the original West box having been situated at the east end of the up platform.

Gwinear Road was, on occasions, a busy place, and in addition to the regular arrival and departure of the Helston branch train, its goods sidings were often fully occupied by long rakes of wagons or vans. In addition, the track layout

An unidentified member of the 4-6-0 'Hall' class crosses the level crossing at Gwinear Road with an up evening postal train in May 1958.   *Joe Moss Collection*

A down train near Angarrack headed by 'Hall' class 4-6-0 No. 4953 *Dunley Hall* in May 1940.
                                                                          B.A. Butt

included lengthy up and down refuge sidings which were frequently used to berth slow moving freight trains that would otherwise have caused delay to more important passenger trains.

In staffing terms, Gwinear Road provided employment for a labour force of around 14 people. In 1929 these included six porters, three signalmen, two goods shunters, one clerk, one goods guard and a class three station master. Among those employed at this rural junction in the 1930s were booking clerk R.B. Williams, shunter A.J. Mewson and goods guard G. Stephens. Later, around 1960, the staff included goods guard D. Allen, leading porter R.C. Uren, and signalman I.V. Chatsworthy. The station master in the early 1960s was Mr W.D. Richards.

As the various goods facilities at Gwinear Road were employed mainly for storage or re-marshalling purposes, the amount of originating traffic dealt with here was relatively modest. Indeed, during the 1930s the station handled no more than 5,000 or 6,000 tons of freight a year. Passenger traffic was equally sparse, around 14,000 bookings per annum being fairly typical throughout the 1930s; in 1938, 13,288 tickets were issued, together with 98 seasons.

The closure of the Helston branch on Saturday 3rd November, 1962, deprived Gwinear Road of most of its passenger traffic, and Gwinear Road was itself closed to passengers in October 1964. The remaining goods service to Helston was withdrawn in that same month, and the branch was then lifted. Goods facilities remained in use at Gwinear Road for a few more months, but the end finally came in 1965, with the closure of Gwinear Road East and Gwinear Road West signal boxes.

All remaining sidings and connections at the former junction station were taken out of use in August 1965, and in the following October the gated level crossing was replaced by automatic lifting half-barriers. Today, very little remains of this once-busy junction station where, in days gone by, travellers had changed into a Great Western branch train for the 8¼ mile journey to Helston.

Angarrack

From Gwinear Road, the route continues its descent towards Marazion, the steepest gradient on this section being 1 in 59. Angarrack viaduct, about 3½ miles beyond Gwinear Road, is an impressive structure that towers 100 feet above local ground level; its length is 240 yards, some 26 yards shorter than the timber viaduct it replaced. There had once been, in the very early days, a small station at Angarrack, but this obscure stopping place was closed in February 1852.

As mentioned in connection with the viaduct at Redruth, the condition of the West Cornwall Railway timber viaducts was beginning to cause much disquiet during the 1880s when, by all accounts, they were regarded with suspicion by nervous travellers. The West Cornwall bridges were, from the very start, less substantially-built than their counterparts on the neighbouring Cornwall Railway, and with the introduction of heavier locomotives and rolling stock after the Great Western takeover, it became clear that the viaducts in question would need to be strengthened or replaced in their entirety.

'Manor' class 4-6-0 No. 7813 *Freshford Manor* is seen north of Angarrack with a down fitted freight in 1958. *P.Q. Treloar*

An unidentified 'Hall' class 4-6-0 crosses Angarrack viaduct with a down express for Penzance on 4th July, 1959. *P.Q. Treloar*

Much criticism had been levelled at the Angarrack viaduct which, by reason of its great height, had aroused the greatest comment. Accordingly, the foundations of a new viaduct built of stone were laid in 1881 alongside the original timber structure, and local rail users breathed a collective sigh of relief. One traveller even wrote to *The West Briton* to say that he was:

> Thankful to find that the Great Western Railway Company intends at once to rebuild the Angarrack Viaduct. Not a day too soon! It ought to have been condemned before. A poor man was on it the other day when a train went over, and he was quite horrified by what he felt and saw.

The rebuilding work took around four years to complete, but the new stone viaduct was finally completed and brought into use on 4th October, 1885. There had been several accidents and fatalities during the rebuilding, and in one incident a crane collapsed, throwing a group of unfortunate workmen on to the ground, far below.

There were also some troublesome labour problems during the rebuilding operations, and on one occasion the masons withdrew their labour as a protest against the exposed conditions in which they were expected to work. At first the employers refused to provide adequate shelter, but they eventually gave in - though by that time many of the men had left the district and moved to the North of England, where there was plenty of railway bridge-building work.

Despite the strike that had disrupted the Angarrack contract, the men who built the bridges and maintained them were highly skilled craftsmen, who were particularly noted, for having a 'pride in the job'. They were thought so highly of by the bridge engineers, that every effort was made to keep the gangs intact and for them to move, as a body, from one bridge contract to another.

Hayle

Continuing south-westwards , the railway falls towards Guildford viaduct which, like its neighbour at Angarrack, was formerly constructed of timber; the new Guildford viaduct is 123 yards long and 56 ft high. As their trains cross this lofty structure, travellers can, by glancing to the right, see the Copperhouse district of Hayle. Copperhouse was the site of a small halt, which had a life of only three years, having opened in 1905, and closed in 1908.

Hayle station (18 miles 48 chains), was a two platform stopping place, with a goods loop on the up (north) side, and a single dead-end siding on the down side. The main station building was at the western end of the down platform, and there was an additional waiting room on the up side. The two 440 ft platforms were linked by a girder footbridge, and there was a typical 'Brunel' style goods shed on the down side. Other facilities included an engine shed, a water tower and a standard Great Western signal box - the latter structure being distinguished by its cantilevered upper storey.

The busy goods branch to Hayle Wharves left the main line at the western end of the aforementioned goods loop. Like the other industrial sidings *en route* to Penzance, the wharves line originated in the days of the Hayle Railway -

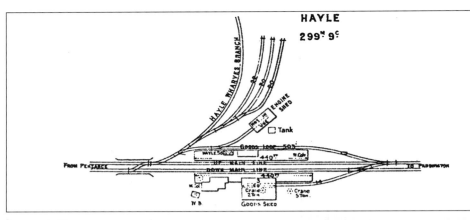

Hayle station, looking west towards Penzance, probably *circa* 1920. The goods shed can be seen to the left of the down platform, while a small engine shed is visible to the right.

Lens of Sutton Collection

A useful view of Hayle station, looking east towards Paddington around 1912, and showing the West Cornwall station building and goods shed.

Lens of Sutton Collection

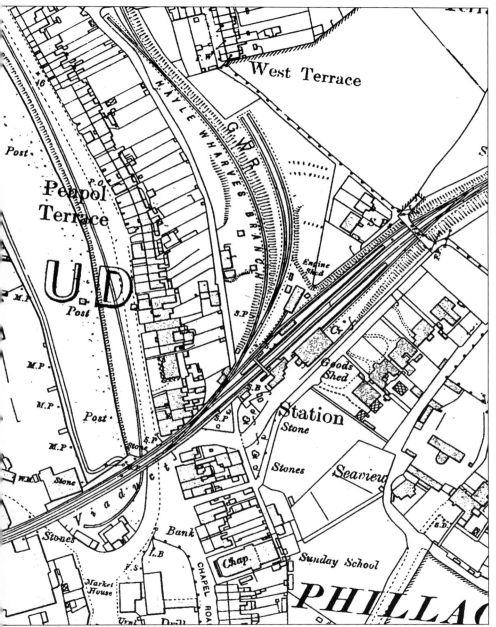

Hayle station. Note the Hayle Wharves branch diverging northwards on the up side, and the single-road engine shed in the 'V' of the junction.

Reproduced from the 25", 1907 Ordnance Survey Map

Hayle station, looking west towards Penzance around 1980. Note the signal box, with its jetted-out upper storey; the small BR-built station building was subsequently demolished.

Lens of Sutton Collection

A detailed view of the road overbridge at the east end of Hayle station, on 21st September, 1996. A privately-owned camping coach has recently been installed at the rear of the down platform, this converted BR Mk I vehicle being available for holiday lets.   *S.C. Jenkins*

indeed, the wharves branch incorporated part of the original 'main line' between Hayle and Gwinear Road.

Unlike many of the other stations between Truro and Penzance, Hayle retained its original West Cornwall buildings throughout the Great Western period, and for this reason it provided an interesting comparison with the rebuilt stations found elsewhere on the former West Cornwall route. The up and down station buildings were both simple, timber-framed structures clad in horizontal boarding, with low pitched gable roofs; the main down side building was equipped with a small canopy.

The signal cabin was, on the other hand, a much later addition. When resignalled by the GWR during the mid-1890s, Hayle had been given two signal boxes known as Hayle East Box and Hayle West Box. In the event these two cabins were destined to have relatively short lives, and they were replaced in the early years of the 20th century by an entirely new box on the up platform.

The new box was, in most respects, a typical GWR hip-roofed cabin with five-pane window frames, but as a result of the relatively narrow width of the platform it was given an unusually narrow brick locking room, the glass and timber upper floor being jetted-out over the platform on supporting brackets (cabins of similar design were erected at Dawlish, on the South Devon line, and at Yarnton Junction on the Oxford, Worcester & Wolverhampton route).

Hayle was, for many years, an industrial area, and it formerly handled a relatively large quantity of goods traffic. In 1903, for instance, 75,443 tons of goods were dealt with, while in 1913 this figure had risen to 83,950 tons. Thereafter, the published traffic statistics show a marked decline, though around 22,000 tons of freight a year were still being handled throughout the 1930s.

The passenger traffic dealt with at Hayle remained surprisingly healthy over a period of many years, with approximately 52,000 tickets being issued each year together with about 300 season ticket sales; in 1903 some 56,862 tickets were issued, while in 1938 55,006 tickets were issued, plus 367 seasons. The staff complement at Hayle around 1930 comprised two clerks, five porters, two signalmen, one porter-signalman, one checker, one signal lampman, one motor driver, one van guard and a horse shunter, under a class three station master.

Like other rural stations throughout the county, Hayle suffered a period of rationalisation during the 1960s, most of its sidings and connections being removed in 1964 and 1967. This reduction in facilities left the Hayle Wharves branch *in situ*, though the connection to this historic line was reduced to a single turnout from the up line that was facing to up trains.

The Hayle Wharves branch remained in use until the early 1980s, fuel oil and chemicals being the last forms of traffic handled on this relatively little-known industrial branch. Sadly, in 1981, Esso decided to close the oil storage depot on the North Quay, and this brought about the final closure of the branch in 1983. Hayle was then developed as a holiday resort, and most traces of its industrial past were quickly obliterated.

In its declining years, the wharves branch was operated as simply as possible. Trains reversed down the 1 in 30 incline to reach the Esso oil depot on North

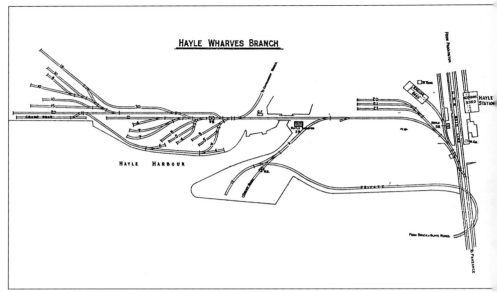

A 1959 view of the Hayle Wharves branch. A pair of horses haul two vans to Harvey's. A '45XX' class 2-6-2T can be seen in the distance on Hayle viaduct.   *P.Q. Treloar*

A pannier tank passes a Bedford 'O' lorry as it works along the Hayle Wharves branch on 10th April, 1959.   *Hugh Davies*

'45XX' class 2-6-2T No. 4571 shunts on the level crossing at Hayle harbour on 4th July, 1959.
P.Q. Treloar

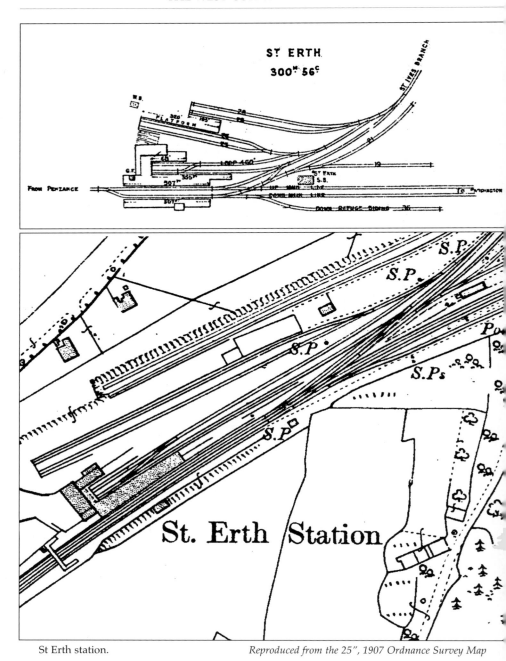

St Erth station.   *Reproduced from the 25", 1907 Ordnance Survey Map*

Quay, and having shunted incoming tank wagons for collection by the wharves tractor, the locomotive accelerated back up the steep gradient with the empty oil tank wagons. Having re-gained the main line the train - which was normally headed by a class '22' or class '25' Bo-Bo diesel locomotive - proceeded westwards to St Erth or Ponsandane, crossing from the up main to the down main line by means of a crossover at the west end of Hayle viaduct (since lifted); on reaching St Erth or Ponsandane, the locomotive ran-round its train prior to working the tank wagons back along the West Cornwall line towards Plymouth.

Hayle has remained open as part of the present day passenger system, and in September 1995 it was served by nine up and 10 down services, most of these workings being Regional Railways services worked by class '158' two-car multiple units.

Hayle viaduct, to the west of the station, carries the West Cornwall line above Foundry Square and the site of the former Hayle Railway terminus; the viaduct is an arched stone structure with a total length of 277 yards; it is 34 feet high, and was built in 1886 in place of the earlier wooden viaduct.

St Erth

Having crossed Hayle viaduct, westbound trains pass through a shallow cutting, and then emerge onto a low embankment; to the right, the Hayle Estuary can be clearly seen, with the St Ives branch discernible on the far shore. Reaching a brief section of 1 in 70 rising gradient, the railway curves leftward to enter St Erth station, and with the St Ives line converging from the right, trains come to a stand in the gently-curving platforms at this attractive country junction, which is 20 miles 15 chains from Truro.

Until 1877, St Erth had been known as St Ives Road but, on the opening of the St Ives branch, the station was re-named. The junction has three platforms, the main up and down lines being used by through trains, while terminating St Ives branch workings use a dead-end bay on the up side. The branch bay formerly had its own run-round loop, and there were, in addition, four dead-end goods sidings on the up side of the line, together with two further sidings in the 'V' of the junction, and two long refuge sidings on the down side. The two main line platforms are about 500 ft long, while the branch bay is a little over 400 ft in length.

Architecturally, St Erth is quite unlike the neighbouring stations at Redruth and Camborne. The main buildings, on the up side, are solidly built of dressed granite, with arched window and door apertures and extensive wooden canopies. As the branch platform is at a lower level than the main line, the canopy is angled in such a way that it can provide protection for both levels.

Prior to rationalisation, the main station building on the up side contained a full range of facilities for the travelling public, including a booking office, general waiting room, ladies waiting room, parcels office, station master's office and public toilets for male and female passengers. In addition, a projecting wing of the 'L'-shaped main building also contained a refreshment room which was popular with local farmers and traders, who gathered there when bringing items to the station for dispatch by train.

St Erth station, looking west towards Penzance on 30th May, 1920. The palm trees and sub-tropical flower gardens were planted by the GWR to underline the 'Riviera' atmosphere of the far west. The angled roof of the up side canopy can be clearly seen.   *Lens of Sutton Collection*

A general view of St Erth station looking west along the branch bay platform around 1920. The stone station buildings can be seen in the background. This station was originally known as 'St Ives Road', but its name was changed following the opening of the St Ives branch in 1877.

Lens of Sutton Collection

A further view of St Erth station, looking west towards Penzance during the British Railways era. Platform 1, the main down platform, is visible to the left, while platform 2 is to the right of the picture.   *Lens of Sutton Collection*

A view of St Erth station from the road, showing part of the solid stone-built station buildings and the wooden canopy.   *Lens of Sutton Collection*

'Modified Hall' class 4-6-0 No. 6988 *Swithland Hall* enters the down platform at St Erth, while an unidentified '45XX' prairie tank waits in the bay platform (*extreme left*). The standard Great Western signal box can be glimpsed in the distance.   *N. Stead Collection*

'45XX' class 2-6-2T No. 4563 stands in the down platform at St Erth.   *Lens of Sutton Collection*

Facilities on the down platform consist of a small, gable-roofed waiting room which is built of dressed granite, and once sported a small canopy. There is also a large timber-built waiting shelter. The up and down platforms are linked by a standard Great Western type covered footbridge, and the station is signalled from a brick-and-timber signal box on the up side of the running lines. The signal cabin is a typical gable-roofed box dating from the mid-1890s, and exhibiting the small-paned windows and other architectural features common to Great Western signal boxes built at that time; internally it contains a 69-lever frame.

St Erth typically handled around 30,000 passenger bookings a year in the years before World War I, and this level of traffic remained constant during the 1920s and 1930s. In 1932, for example, 28,851 tickets were issued, while season ticket sales totalled 158. On the freight side, the station was one of the less busy stations on the West Cornwall line. In 1903 it handled only 5,208 tons of freight, though by 1930 this modest figure had increased to 9,934 tons.

Attempts to establish a bulk traffic in china clay failed to make much headway, and although a china clay siding was installed at St Erth for use by the Porthia China Clay Company in the 1920s, this facility produced very little revenue for the railway. Later, however, a private siding agreement was signed with Unigate, and by the 1930s the station was sending large amounts of milk to London for consumption in the capital; the 1938 Railway Clearing House *Handbook of Stations* shows that the creamery was then being operated by United Dairies.

The Great Western had traditionally carried vast quantities of milk from the West Country to London, metal churns being used for many years. The introduction of glass-lined bulk milk tank wagons from 1927 onwards enabled milk traffic to be handed more efficiently in the face of growing road competition, and by the later 1930s centralised milk depots such as the one at St Erth had become of particular importance to the GWR. In addition to milk traffic, St Erth also forwarded large amounts of broccoli and other locally-grown agricultural produce, and this brought much extra freight traffic to the railway at certain times of the year.

The station employed about a dozen people, among them booking clerks D. Hodge and W. Harvey, both of whom left St Erth in 1928 to take up new positions at St Ives and Falmouth respectively, and parcels porters C.J. Anthony and F. Kent; Mr Anthony retired in 1934 after 35 years' service. At that time the staff complement was one booking clerk, six porters, two shunters, two signalmen and a class three station master.

Successive station masters at this Cornish junction station included R.J. May, W.C. Wooders and R.P. Grenfell, all of whom worked at the station in the 1920s and 1930s. Mr May, who retired in 1928, had worked on the railway for 44 years. Another long-serving station master was A.E. Hawker, who retired in 1923 having worked at St Erth for a period of 25 years.

St Erth has managed to escaped the down-grading of facilities that has taken place at so many other stations, and at the time of writing its well-built granite station buildings remain intact. There is no regular goods traffic, but much of the trackwork in the goods yard area has remained in place, and in February

A general view of Marazion station, looking east towards Paddington around 1912.
Lens of Sutton Collection

Marazion station looking towards Truro with Collett 0-6-0 pannier tank No. 9748 running through light engine on 11th September, 1959.   *R.S. Carpenter*

1996, it was reported that the former milk siding at St Erth was being overhauled, with the aim of introducing regular containerised bulk milk traffic between Cornwall and West Drayton - from where road vehicles would collect the containers for final delivery.

The introduction of multiple unit operation on the St Ives branch has resulted in the lifting of the run-round loop in the branch bay at St Erth, though in recent years many St Ives branch trains have in fact run to and from Penzance rather than terminating in the branch platform. This mode of operation means that many branch workings use the up main line platform at St Erth, 'wrong line' working being necessary when St Ives trains work through to Penzance as there is no direct connection from the branch to the down main line at St Erth; instead, westbound branch trains cross from the up main to the down main lines at the western end of St Erth station after calling at the main up platform to pick-up or set-down passengers.

Marazion

From St Erth, the West Cornwall line sweeps south-westwards towards the south coast of Cornwall, the now-closed station at Marazion (23 miles 72 chains) being situated virtually on the sea shore. As trains approach Marazion, travellers are rewarded with a breathtaking view of St Michael's Mount - a fairy tale castle rising majestically from an enchanted Celtic sea. For holidaymakers (many of whom have journeyed from distant London or the Midlands) the sudden and dramatic appearance of the Mount heralds the end of the long-journey westwards, and the start of summer holidays in and around Mount's Bay, or in the remote peninsulas of West Penwith or the Lizard.

When opened by the West Cornwall Railway in 1852, Marazion had been a very small stopping place, with a typical Brunel-designed timber station building. Like other small West Cornwall buildings, it had a low-pitched roof and a projecting canopy - these simple structures being very similar to the wayside station buildings found on other Great Western subsidiary lines such as the South Wales Railway and the Oxford, Worcester & Wolverhampton line. Marazion was known, for many years, as 'Marazion Road', the name being shortened to Marazion on 1st October, 1896. The original station had, by that time, been completely reconstructed, the earlier West Cornwall infrastructure having been replaced in its entirety.

The station was situated in a low-lying marshy area, and in earlier years train services were frequently disrupted by inclement weather. There were particular problems on the western side of the station, where the West Cornwall line was carried along the beach on a somewhat skimpy wooden viaduct. As mentioned above, this structure suffered severe storm damage on several occasions, notably on 26th December, 1852, when 200 feet of the supporting wooden structure was destroyed. A similar incident occurred on 20th August, 1856 when a down excursion train was unable to reach Penzance during a storm. In fact, the excursionists had survived a particularly eventful day, as recorded by *The West Briton*:

On the 20th instant, the children of the Penzance Wesleyan Association Sunday School, accompanied by friends, went by excursion train to Truro, but unfortunately had a very rainy day. They were joined at the St Erth station by children from St Ives and, unhappily, Mr Andrew Noall, one of the friends who accompanied them, died of apoplexy in the van. On their return, a mistake was made in the points at St Erth station, in consequence of which the engine took one line and the carriages another; the carriages went off the rails, and caused some alarm, but nothing worse.

On nearing Penzance, the sea was so violently assaulting the viaduct that it was thought advisable to stop the train on the other side, and the children to walk home. The ground swell along the margin of the bay was so great that the waves came breaking in, twenty, thirty, and forty feet high; they came with tremendous concussion against the wall which protects the terminus, and they swept over the railway viaduct, upon which they lifted large pieces of stone, so that it was considered unsafe to allow the train with the excursionists to pass over.

Further storm incidents interrupted services between Marazion and Penzance at various times during the 1850s and 1860s, and on these occasions trains were normally terminated at Marazion. On Sunday 24th January, 1869 the vulnerable timber viaduct was washed away at the Penzance end, but in 1871 a much stronger viaduct was brought into use - albeit still constructed of timber. This structure survived until 1921, when it was finally replaced by an embankment, carrying a double track line all the way to Penzance.

The rebuilt Marazion station was, like St Erth, something of a showpiece of Great Western architecture, its solid granite buildings being specially-designed to enhance the 'Cornish Riviera' atmosphere. The main station building was situated on the down side, and there was a much smaller waiting room on the opposite platform - both of these buildings being constructed of dressed granite blocks. These substantial, hipped roof buildings were erected by the GWR during the 1880s, and they reflected the company's standardised approach to architectural design.

The roofed, plate girder footbridge resembled that at St Erth, and there was a standard Great Western signal box to the west of the station building on the down platform. The latter structure was a gable-roofed brick and timber structure with ornate finials and a tall brick chimney. The platforms were fenced with traditional pale-and-space fencing while, until the late 1920s, the road from Marazion to Penzance had been carried across the line by means of a level crossing at the eastern end of the platforms. When the line was doubled between Hayle and Marazion in June 1929 the opportunity was taken to replace the crossing with the skew girder bridge which remains in use to this day.

Marazion's goods facilities were extensive. The main yard was on the up side, access from the running lines being by means of a goods loop that left the down main line via a trailing connection, and then crossed the up line on the level before re-joining the running lines at the east end of the platforms. Sidings diverging on the down side of the line provided further storage capacity at this well-appointed Cornish station. The up side yard was equipped with a spacious loading bank, and there was a small goods lock-up to the east of the station building on the down platform.

In common with St Erth and other stations in the far west of Cornwall, Marazion handled large amounts of broccoli and other perishable traffic, most of which was dispatched to the London markets. On 19th March, 1896, *The West Briton* recorded that:

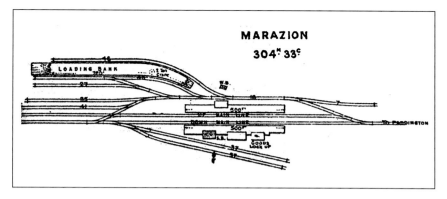

MARAZION

304ᴹ 33ᶜ

The returns of broccoli traffic from West Cornwall during the past week show that on Tuesday there were dispatched from the four stations of Penzance, Marazion, St Ives and St Erth, 163 truck Loads. This was beaten on Wednesday when the total was 174 trucks; and on Thursday about 100 trucks were sent off. Taking these to average two and a half tons to the truck, it will give a total of 1,092.5 tons loaded and dispatched.

The crates usually average thirteen to the ton, so that the total number of crates would be 14,202; and carrying the calculation a little further, and estimating the crates to contain five dozen broccoli each, which is a very fair average, it will give a total of 852,120 broccoli. On Wednesday, the heaviest day, the number of crates was about 5,605, containing something like 336,300 broccoli.

Broccoli traffic remained heavy for many years. In 1936, for instance, *The Great Western Railway Magazine* reported that no less than 30,000 tons had recently been sent from Marazion, Helston, Penzance and other stations in West Cornwall. It is interesting to note that broccoli consignments were usually dispatched in standard Great Western 'Mex' cattle wagons, and at the height of the broccoli season, long rakes of these vehicles could be seen standing in the sidings at Marazion.

When not needed for agricultural traffic, Marazion's commodious sidings were also employed as carriage storage roads, incoming trains being worked empty from Penzance to Marazion on summer Saturdays or at other times of heavy demand. When down workings were doubled-headed, it became usual practice for the trains concerned to be stopped at Marazion, so that the assisting engine could be detached. The train engine would then continue along the level stretch of track to Penzance, while the pilot engine waited at Marazion until the line was clear for it to proceed light to nearby Long Rock motive power depot.

In 1903 Marazion had a staff of 14, though this relatively large staffing establishment was reduced to 12 by the 1920s and to 11 in the following decade. A Great Western staffing list compiled in December 1922 showed that the staffing establishment comprised one goods clerk, one ticket collector, three porters, one goods shunter and five signalmen, three of whom were employed at nearby Long Rock. The station was controlled by a class three station master, this being the usual grade for station masters in charge of wayside stations on a Great Western main line.

Minor changes ensued during the next few years, and by 1930 one of Marazion's signalmen had been replaced by a porter-signalman, while the ticket collector had been replaced by a parcels porter and the goods shunter had been replaced by a goods porter. These staffing changes were presumably carried out as part of a cost-cutting exercise that enabled the Great Western to reduce its paybill expenses during the period of economic difficulties that took place during the 1920s and 1930s.

Two views at Marazion on 11th May, 1959. At around 2.30 pm '45XX' class 2-6-2T No. 4566 is seen shunting wagons loaded with vegetables (*above*). Subsequently 'Grange' class 4-6-0 No. 6824 *Ashley Grange* arrived from Long Rock engine shed to take the assembled train onwards. At 3.00 pm No. 6824 left Marazion with the up perishables train (*below*).

(Both) Michael Mensing

It is interesting to note that, during the hectic 'vegetable season', many West Cornwall stations were given extra staff to help with the loading of broccoli and other seasonal traffic. In the case of Marazion, the authorised staffing establishment in 1929 included provision for three additional grade two porters, one class three shunter and one class two yard foreman during the vegetable season. In that year, Marazion's paybill expenses were £2,138, whereas the station's total receipts were £34,060. Staffing costs were thus about six per cent of the station's income, which was regarded as a very healthy state of affairs.

It may also be worth mentioning that Marazion was provided with a camping coach. Such coaches had first been introduced by the London & North Eastern Railway during the mid-1930s, but the Great Western was quick to follow suit, and in 1934 *The Railway Magazine* announced that redundant four- or six-wheeled GWR vehicles had been adapted for use as 'railway caravans for the holiday camper'. Bogie stock, was later introduced, and, for many years, one of these specially-adapted vehicles could be seen parked in the sidings at Marazion.

The coach could be hired throughout the summer from April to October by holidaymakers who purchased ordinary return tickets in advance of their stay, and it could be booked for periods of one or two weeks. Towels, bed linen, cutlery and other essentials were provided, but people staying in the coach had to use the nearby station building for toilet and washing facilities.

Marazion was, at one time, a place of some importance, being a market centre and small port in its own right. The town was granted a charter of incorporation by Elizabeth I on 13th June, 1595, and it thereby became the first chartered town in the Hundred of Penwith. In the 18th and early 19th centuries it was favoured as a place of residence by local gentlemen and professional people, who built many picturesque Georgian-style houses in the long main street.

The town had become a holiday destination by the early years of the 20th century and the 1903 *Little Guide to Cornwall* described it as a place enjoying a 'quiet and respectable prosperity, from the beauty of its position and the interest of the neighbourhood'. On the other hand, this small, but very attractive resort never became as popular as nearby Penzance, and the station was rarely busy. In the Edwardian period, Marazion issued around 30,000 tickets per year, but this very respectable figure had declined to 8,070 tickets (and 76 seasons) by 1930. In 1938, the station issued only 6,734 ordinary tickets, although it is interesting to note that sales of season tickets had reached 111.

Freight traffic remained relatively healthy throughout the 1920s and early 1930s. In general, the station handled around 19,000 tons of freight per annum, including about 2,000 tons of inwards coal traffic, 6,000 tons of inwards general merchandise, and between 9,000 and 13,000 tons of outwards general merchandise traffic. In 1934, for instance, the station dispatched 13,543 tons of general merchandise, most of this being broccoli or other vegetables. Just three years later, Marazion's goods traffic was included with that from Penzance, and in accounting terms the station 'lost' its most lucrative source of revenue.

There was, moreover, a move towards greater concentration of goods traffic at larger stations, with increasing use of road vehicles for local collection and delivery work. As we have seen, Penzance was one of the first Great Western 'Country Lorry Centres', and although this centralisation of traffic clearly led to greater operational efficiency, it resulted in the progressive elimination of many smaller stations. This process was greatly accelerated by the rapid development of road transport after World War II, which hastened the demise of many wayside stations.

Inevitably, Marazion station became one of the obvious candidates for closure during the Beeching years of the early 1960s, and in October 1964 this former West Cornwall stopping place was closed to passengers. Rationalisation proceeded apace throughout that decade, the down side sidings being removed in December 1962, followed by the closure of the extensive up sidings in September 1966. The signal box was closed on 18th September, 1966, and most of the remaining trackwork was lifted in the following year.

Perhaps surprisingly, the popular camping coaches that had for so long been a feature at Marazion survived the closure of the station by many years. There were, at the end, no less than six camping coaches at this location, all of these being former SR Pullman cars used by the British Railways Staff Association. The vehicles in question were Nos. W9869 *Mimosa*, W9870 *Calais*, W9871 *Flora*, W9872 *Juno*, W9875 *Aurora* and W9874 *Alicante*. They all dated from the pre-Grouping period, the oldest having been built in 1912. Four of the coaches were eight-wheeled guard and parlour cars, though *Calais* was a 12-wheeled parlour vehicle; *Mimosa* and *Alicante* were eight-wheeled kitchen cars.

The Marazion Pullmans were all withdrawn from service on the Southern Region in 1962, but at the end of that year they were sent to the Western Region for employment as camping coaches, Nos. 9869, 9870, 9871 and 9872 being stationed at Marazion in the 1963 summer season, while the remaining vehicles were sent to Fowey. Sadly, in 1964 it was decided that there would be no more camping coaches but a number, including those at Marazion, were retained for use by the British Railways (Western Region) Staff Association. The two coaches at Fowey were moved to Marazion, while similar vehicles were stationed at Dawlish Warren and Tenby.

The Marazion Pullmans remained in use throughout the 1960s and 1970s, though in later years the practice of sending them to Swindon every Autumn and returning them in the following Spring was abandoned. The six veteran coaches were, as a result, exposed to the elements without respite for 12 months every year. The siding upon which they were stationed was disconnected from the running lines, and grass began to grow between the rails and sleepers.

In 1985 the six Pullman cars were sold to a local hotel owner who hoped to maintain them as holiday accommodation. There was some attempt to refurbish the vehicles, but in 1997 they were broken into by vandals. Valuable marquetery panels were stolen by the intruders and, following this setback, the owner offered five of the cars for sale. No. 9871 *Flora* was moved to a place of safety in the London area, but at the time of writing *Calais* and two of the other coaches remain in a derelict condition on their severed length of weed-grown track. The adjacent station building now functions as a cycle hire centre, while present-day trains rush through the long-closed station without stopping.

By the beginning of January 2002, one of the remaining Marazion Pullman cars had been destroyed by arsonists, and the two survivors had suffered continuing vandalism since their abandonment.

Penzance

With journey's end now virtually in sight, down trains proceed along the shore line towards their destination passing, on the right, the site of the once-important steam locomotive depot at Long Rock (24 miles 30 chains). Opened in 1914, the shed replaced an earlier motive power depot that had been sited further along the line towards Penzance station. The new shed was a four-road, brick-built structure with an additional bay on the north side for repair work.

The depot was equipped with the usual facilities for coaling, watering and day-to-day maintenance; the shed proper measured approximately 210 ft by 66 ft at ground level, and the turntable was large enough to accommodate 'Castle' class 4-6-0s, or other Great Western main line locomotives. Access to and from the shed was controlled from a standard GWR hip-roofed signal cabin known as Long Rock signal box, which stood on the down side of the running lines within yards of the sea. The box was brought into use in 1912, and its frame was renewed in 1958. This box was finally closed in June 1974.

Locomotives allocated to Penzance and based at Long Rock included the familiar GWR pannier, Prairie and 4-6-0 types. In 1947, for example, the locally-based engines included 'Castle' class 4-6-0 No. 4097 *Kenilworth Castle*; 'Hall' class 4-6-0s Nos. 4946 *Moseley Hall*, 4947 *Nanhoran Hall* and 4949 *Packwood Hall*; 'Grange' class 4-6-0s Nos. 6801 *Aylburton Grange*, 6808 *Beenham Grange* and 6825 *Llanvair Grange*; and several '43XX' class 2-6-0s, '45XX' class 2-6-2Ts and '2021' class 0-6-0 pannier tanks.

Long Rock was adapted for use as a diesel depot in the late 1950s, and closed to steam in 1962. Further changes followed in 1974 when the line was singled between mile post 325 and Penzance station, the former down line being adapted for bi-directional working, while the up line was, in effect, turned into a siding for empty stock movements to and from Long Rock and the adjacent carriage sidings.

From Long Rock, the now singled main line continues westwards, with the sea close at hand on the left-hand side and extensive empty stock sidings to the right. Ponsandane signal box, between Long Rock and Penzance station, was once notable in that, although in all other respects a standard Great Western signal cabin, it sported an unusual flat-roof, which was said to have been provided to appease local landowners who would otherwise have been denied an unobstructed view of St Michael's Mount! The box closed on 24th June, 1974, when the line was singled.

Running westwards along the long embankment that replaced the damage-prone Penzance viaduct in 1921, trains soon reach Penzance station, where the Great Western Railway main line ends with some formality, in a four-platform terminus with attractive stone buildings and a lightweight overall roof.

Situated some 25 miles 67 chains from Truro, and 305 miles 20 chains from Paddington (via Bristol is 20¼ miles longer), Penzance was, in many ways an appropriate 'ending' for the Great Western main line. In steam days it was a comparatively small, but nevertheless busy terminus with an air of importance out of all proportion to its modest size. When first opened, however, the

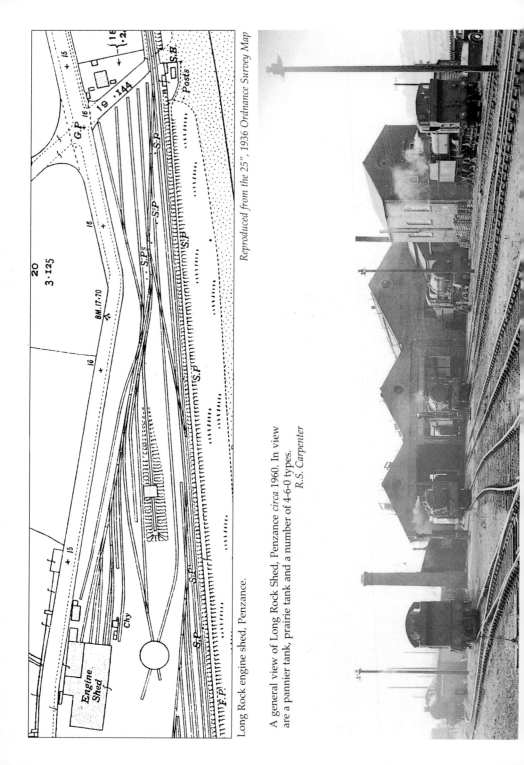

Long Rock engine shed, Penzance.

Reproduced from the 25", 1936 Ordnance Survey Map

A general view of Long Rock Shed, Penzance *circa* 1960. In view are a pannier tank, prairie tank and a number of 4-6-0 types.

R.S. Carpenter

original West Cornwall station had been little more than a branch line terminus with cramped platform facilities, ramshackle buildings and a minimal track layout.

This original West Cornwall terminus was clearly inadequate, and at a time of increasing traffic requirements, the station was extensively rebuilt, with much improved accommodation for both passenger and freight traffic. The rebuilding operations were completed in 1879-80, and as a result Penzance gained new terminal buildings and a larger overall roof. Further changes were put into effect after the abolition of the broad gauge in 1892, while in 1937 the Great Western again remodelled the platforms and track layout in order to provide sufficient accommodation for holiday traffic.

In its final form, the terminus had four long terminal platforms, with a number of additional bays for parcels and sundries traffic. The westernmost extremity of the station was covered by the 1879-80 overall roof, and the main terminal buildings were situated at right angles to the buffer stops. Interestingly, these buildings, which were solidly and substantially constructed of regularly-coursed stonework, were situated at a higher level than the platforms, the station being in effect a split-level design, with its waiting rooms at platform level and the booking office at street level.

Access from the booking hall area to the platforms was via stairways and a raised balcony - the latter feature providing an ideal vantage point from which to view the constant activity on the platforms below. The platforms were numbered in sequence from one to four, platforms one to three being protected at their westernmost ends by the overall roof, while platform four terminated in the open, on the south side of the train shed.

The terminus was signalled from a standard Great Western brick and timber signal box. This characteristic hip-roofed structure was sited to the east of the platforms, on the up side of the running lines. It remains in use at the time of writing.

In West Cornwall days, the goods facilities at Penzance had been concentrated on a cramped site between the passenger station and Albert Quay, but additional loading facilities were subsequently installed at Ponsandane, and these were much enlarged and expanded during the 1930s, when Ponsandane was developed as the town's principal goods yard.

The old West Cornwall goods yard had contained a typical Brunelian timber goods shed with two covered sidings, one of which extended beyond the shed to serve Albert Quay. The original engine shed had been sited beside the goods shed, and this structure was later adapted for use as a goods loading facility. The two sheds then formed an enlarged goods shed containing three covered sidings, while two additional goods sidings terminated in end-loading docks, the longest of which had a length of 270 ft. The main goods shed contained a central loading platform with a length of 140 ft.

The original West Cornwall goods yard was radically altered during the 1930s alterations and, thereafter, the site of the old yard became a loading area for parcels and perishables. The latter form of traffic was of particular importance at Penzance, large quantities of broccoli, potatoes and fish being handled every year, together with large consignments of flowers from the Isles

Ponsandane Sidings at Penzance, where much of the perishable traffic was loaded, particularly broccoli. Note the use of 'Mex' cattle wagons for broccoli traffic.   *R.C. Riley*

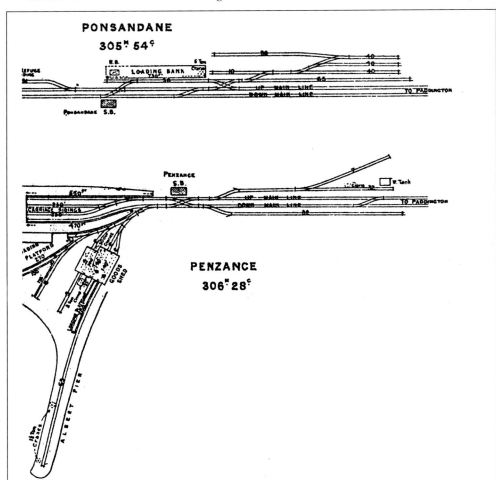

PONSANDANE

305ᴹ 54ᶜ

PENZANCE

306ᴹ 28ᶜ

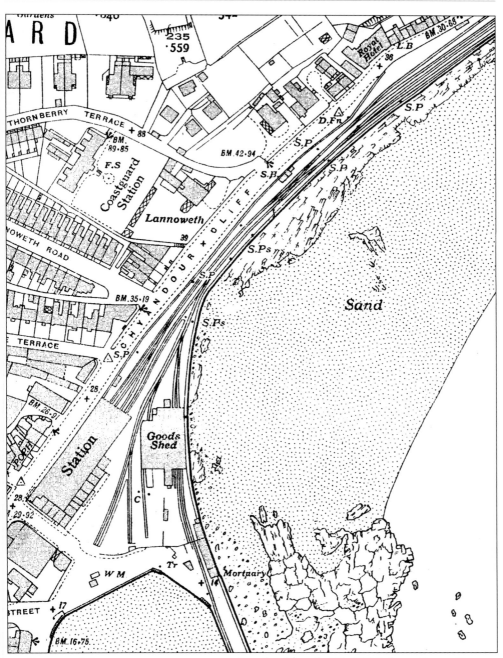

Penzance station.

Reproduced from the 25", 1936 Ordnance Survey Map

A useful view of Penzance station from the adjacent Chyandour Cliff Road. This *circa* 1930 view shows the layout at the terminus prior to the 1937 reconstruction, with the goods shed to the left and the 1879 train shed to the right.   *Lens of Sutton Collection*

A platform view of the rebuilt station, looking east towards the terminal buffer stops, probably around 1939. The widened platforms can be clearly seen, although the 1879-80 train shed is more or less unchanged. It will be seen, however, that the platform layout has been altered, giving three covered platform roads in place of the earlier two; to facilitate this alteration, part of the screen at the end of the train shed has been cut away.   *Lens of Sutton Collection*

of Scilly. At the end of the Victorian period, the demand for flowers was almost insatiable, and by 1910 no less than 450 tons of flowers were being sent to London each year. In the 1930s, the station dispatched well over 300,000 consignments of fish, flowers, vegetables and parcels each year.

On the passenger side, Penzance was by any definition a very busy station, over 140,000 tickets being issued in 1913, while by 1931 - by which time the Great Depression had started to eat into railway traffic receipts throughout the country - there were still 82,224 bookings a year, together with no less than 1,130 season ticket sales. The number of season tickets issued continued to rise for several years thereafter until, by the later 1930s, there were well over 2,500 season ticket sales per annum. In 1937, Penzance issued 2,622 season tickets, while ordinary ticket sales totalled 75,218; in that same year, the station dealt with no less than 325,812 parcels and miscellaneous consignments.

In terms of freight traffic, Penzance station handled about 45,000 tons a year during the early years of the 20th century, most of this traffic being in the form of general merchandise. There was very little coal traffic, although about 1,500 tons of coal were forwarded from the station each year; one assumes that these consignments were delivered by sea to Penzance Harbour and moved to inland destinations by rail. The station was dealing with about 45,000-50,000 tons of freight per annum by the 1930s, rising to 71,451 tons in 1938. This apparent increase can be explained by the fact that Marazion's goods traffic was included with that of Penzance after 1937.

The authorised staff establishment at Penzance station during the late 1920s and early 1930s generally comprised two booking clerks, three parcels clerks, two telegraph clerks, one general clerk, two station inspectors, one parcels foreman, one train ticket collector, one travelling parcels porter, two leading parcels porters, three parcels porters, 10 porters, one motor parcels vanman, one horse parcels vanman, seven goods shunters, five signalmen, five passenger guards, 10 goods guards, and one charwoman.

As we have seen, most of the intermediate stations on the West Cornwall line were controlled by class three station masters, but Penzance was sufficiently important to have a 'special grade' station master.

The basic staffing establishment of around 60 people was swelled during the busy vegetable, flower and fish season, when various additional staff were needed to help deal with the vast influx of extra traffic. In 1929, these included one class five clerk, six porters, one parcels porter, one working foreman, one yard foreman, three goods shunters, and four goods guards. In addition to these 17 extra staff, it was usual for one class five clerk, and two or three grade two porters to be employed for the duration of the summer season.

The number of non-seasonal staff at Penzance was increased from 60 to 70 in 1935, while in 1938 the staffing establishment had reached 78, most of these extra staff being employed in the goods department as road delivery drivers.

Penzance station has changed very little over the years though, following the demise of parcels, sundries and fish traffic, the loading bays and goods-handling facilities that had formerly been situated to the south of the platforms have been taken out of use and partially lifted. Additional car parking spaces have appeared on the land once occupied by these goods and parcels facilities,

'Hall' class 4-6-0 No. 4955 *Plaspower Hall* has just arrived at Penzance with the 7.35 am from Newton Abbot on 11th May, 1959.   *Michael Mensing*

An exterior view of Penzance station, photographed around 1950, and showing the substantial granite buildings erected as part of the 1879-80 reconstruction scheme.

Lens of Sutton Collection

while the nearby terminal building has been refurbished to provide modernised booking, waiting room and passenger enquiry facilities. Other parts of the granite building have been rented-out to private commercial tenants.

The basic track layout now comprises the four main terminal roads, together with a group of three former parcels and sundries bays on the south side which are now used to stable parcels vehicles and mail vans; two additional dead-end sidings extend eastwards on the down side of the running line, and these are also used to store spare or redundant parcels vans. The adjacent platform four is used mainly (though not exclusively) by EWS as a mail platform, a class '08' diesel shunter being used to propel the empty mail trains to and from their stabling point at Long Rock.

In general, Penzance has remained a thriving railway centre, with more or less constant activity as High Speed Trains, class '158s' and local dmu sets arrive and depart throughout the day. In the summer of 1996, for example, there were 23 arrivals and 22 departures from the station, together with an evening Travelling Post Office (TPO) working which ran as far as Bristol on the outward journey and returned in the early hours of the morning. This interesting working was usually formed of seven Penzance (Long Rock) allocated coaches, including two TPO vehicles, one TPO stowage coach, and four 'BG' type full-brake stowage vans.

Neighbouring Long Rock has, similarly, remained a hive of railway activity. Although the former steam motive power depot has now been demolished the present-day locomotive, carriage and maintenance depot is a relatively large establishment; work began on the new depot on 30th March, 1976, when the first sod was ceremonially cut by the Chairman of Penwith District Council. Rapid progress was made during the summer of 1977 when the old steam shed was swept away and in its place a 750 ft-long HST depot appeared alongside the main line. The remodelled facilities included a carriage cleaning plant, a fueling depot, staff accommodation, workshops, stores and a boiler house. This new depot was brought into use in October 1977, its overall cost being about £1,500,000.

The revised track layout at Long Rock incorporates six lengthy berthing sidings at the east end of the complex near the former site of Long Rock signal box, together with five additional sidings at the west (Ponsandane) end. The HST shed is a single-track structure with a continuous maintenance pit throughout its length, and the entire depot area is linked to the nearby passenger station by means of the former up line, which enables empty stock movements to take place independently of the running line.

The depot usually houses one or more HST units, together with the above-mentioned EWS mail vehicles. It also serves as a 'sub shed' for Wessex diesel multiple units, which are serviced there in between turns on the St Ives branch or on long distance services to Plymouth or beyond.

Since its opening for public traffic almost a century and a half ago this westernmost extremity of the British railway system has exerted an inexorable fascination out of all proportion to its modest size. It is, after all, 'the end of *the* line' - the Great Western Railway - and there is nothing beyond it but the desolate landscapes of West Penwith, and the vast emptiness of the Atlantic Ocean.

Two commercial period postcards of Penzance. In the view above we see a general view of Penzance. The train shed of Penzance station can be seen slightly to the left in the middle distance. This postcard carries a 1906 postmark. The scene below is of the Promenade and is from a card produced by R. Williams of Penzance. *(Both) S.C. Jenkins Collection*

The Promenade, Penzance.

Chapter Eight

Penzance and the Railway

Penzance, through its harbour the commercial focus of the Land's End peninsula, stood to gain considerably from a rail connection to the rest of England. Its relatively meagre participation in Cornwall's staple industries was compensated by a strategic location - the largest fishing fleet in the West of England was based at Newlyn, barely a mile westwards along the coast, market gardens almost surrounded the town and the mines of St Just and Pendeen were thriving. Penzance also had some industries, principally tin smelting, tanning and leatherworking and it was expected that the railway would bring about a large increase in the number of visitors to the town, drawn by the promise of a mild, healthy climate and the historical and scenic attractions of the Land's End peninsula.

Penzance was, and is, a small town in a thinly populated county. At the time of the 1851 census, a year before the West Cornwall Railway arrived, the population of the Borough was 9,168. Forty years later the count had risen by 35 per cent to a still modest 12,432 but in the area covered by Penzance Union, basically the Land's End peninsula, including St Just and St Ives, the population fell over the 40 years from 53,316 to 48,276. For this the collapse of the mining industry, around St Just, was largely to blame.

In the 19th century the principal breadwinners in Penzance were the menfolk and the opportunities open to women were few and largely restricted to domestic or similar work. As always, there were exceptions, either out of necessity or by inclination. Outside Penzance the position was less clearcut. In the fishing industry women had a distinct land-based part to play in the preparation of the catch for market. They also sold fish in the neighbourhood and 'jousters', with their baskets of fish, were familiar sights in the streets of Penzance. In the mining industry, women also had a role as surface workers or 'bal maidens'.

It was generally the menfolk who made the decisions concerning such matters as jobs and job locations and this chapter is therefore based on the 1851 and 1891 statistics for working men, summarised below. It will be seen that Penzance had little direct involvement in fishing, or mining, industries that prospered or sank according to factors beyond the power of any railway to influence.

Borough of Penzance: Extracts from the censuses of 1851 and 1891

	1851	%	1891	%
Occupied houses	1,875		2,564	
Occupants – Males – working	2,262	24.7	3,023	24.3
Other	1,608	17.5	2,257	18.2
Females	5,298	57.8	7,152	57.5
Total	*9,168*	*100.0*	*12,432*	*100.0*

221

Male occupations	1851	%	1891	%
Butchers, slaughterers, curriers	115	5.1	112	3.7
Boot and shoe makers, cordwainers	296	13.1	105	3.5
Saddlers	12	0.5	63	2.1
Mariners	91	4.0	108	3.6
Fishermen	19	0.8	26	0.9
Other maritime, dockworkers	101	4.5	93	3.1
Basket makers, coopers	28	1.2	47	1.6
Engineering, smiths etc.	101	4.5	142	4.7
Carpenters, cabinet makers, masons	390	17.2	522	17.2
Serpentine workers	8	0.4	21	0.7
Agriculture, market gardening	105	4.6	96	3.2
Mining	16	0.7	28	0.9
Labourers	135	6.0	192	6.3
Inn, hotel proprietors / employees	49	2.2	96	3.2
Musicians, theatre performers	17	0.8	34	1.1
Carriers, cabmen, errand boys	102	4.5	253	8.4
Railway	4	0.2	106	3.5
Post Office, Telegraph	6	0.2	70	2.3
Shopkeepers	430	19.0	508	16.8
Professional, banking, church etc	203	9.0	372	12.3
Servants	34	1.5	29	0.9
Total	2,262	100.0	3,023	100.0

Emigration and Immigration

Victorian Cornwall, like Ireland, lost many of its ablest men in waves of emigration. Out-of-work miners were enticed to the gold fields of South Africa - indeed to any country where there was mineral to be won - and the West Cornwall stations witnessed many sad departures overseas. Some miners returned with greater or lesser fortunes and not all had to dig for them. George Bellringer said goodbye to his friends at Penzance and departed for the mines of Johannesburg. On arrival there he was met by some Penzance men who persuaded him to enter a Kruger Lottery. He did so, won £3,000 and returned immediately to Penzance, announcing there that the streets of Johannesburg were indeed paved with gold!

It was not only the miners who left Cornwall. Penzance was not large enough to sustain an increasingly highly educated population and often those looking for work in the professions, the civil service, post office and telegraph companies had to go elsewhere. For example, of the four sons of the postmaster of Penzance, J.G. Uren, two joined the Eastern Extension Telegraph Company and made their careers in the Far East, one emigrated to Australia and the fourth, seeing all his friends leave Penzance, joined the Post Office in Birmingham.

While some of the young men of Penzance were leaving the town others, not always young, were migrating to it. The following figures summarise the origins of the town's working male population, in 1851 and 1891.

Penzance: birthplaces (working males)

	1851	%	1891	%
Penzance	1,009	44.6	1,422	47.0
Madron, Newlyn, Gulval, Marazion	252	11.1	249	8.2
Rest of Land's End peninsula	265	11.7	273	9.0
Other Cornwall	416	18.4	495	16.4
Devon	73	3.2	130	4.3
Other England	139	6.2	332	11.0
Scotland, Ireland, Wales, Overseas	90	4.0	112	3.8
Not given	18	0.8	10	0.3
Total	2,262	100.0	3,023	100.0

The table does not include retired and convalescent men. Their numbers were relatively small - 156 men gave their occupations as 'retired' in 1851 and 250 in 1891. A high proportion of these came from outside Penzance.

The percentage increase for Penzance and the reduction for Madron, etc. should be viewed with caution. Penzance included within its rateable area a portion of Madron (at Alverton and Treneere) - known as Madron in Penzance - and Madron included a portion of Penzance (at Wherrytown, Nancealverne and Lescudjack) - known as Penzance in Madron!

Excluding Penzance and Madron, the most striking changes between 1851 and 1891 are the reductions in working men hailing from the rest of the Land's End peninsula (due to the mining collapse) and from 'Other Cornwall', and the 4.8 per cent increase in those coming from 'Other England'.

The principal industries, trades and professions directly or indirectly affected by the coming of the railway to Penzance are considered below. One of the most important local industries, tin smelting, was not greatly affected by the railway. The smelting process used 14 cwts of culm (basically coal dust) from South Wales to 28 cwts of tin ore and took place in a Brunton furnace (another product of the fertile mind of William Brunton, senior). The culm was brought to Penzance by ship, the ore by road from the local mines.

Leatherworking

Typical of the established businessmen who spoke in favour of the West Cornwall at the House of Commons Committee enquiry, was John Charles Lanyon, of Redruth. He was a man with widespread interests in West Cornwall businesses, an ironmonger, currier, seedsman, gas and coke manufacturer and holder of shares in mines and ships at and 'around' Penzance. Lanyon told the Committee that 'one of the largest tanneries in England' was at Penzance and that it supplied Liverpool, London and towns throughout the United Kingdom. He added, for good measure, that tannery waggons also went up from

Penzance to St Austell and St Columb, but gave no indication as to why he felt that ranked alongside trade with the rest of the United Kingdom.

Leatherworking was one of the most important industries in Penzance in 1851 in terms of numbers employed and there is little doubt that responsibility for the collapse of that industry by 1891 (and subsequently) could be laid at the door of steam power. Hides were imported to Penzance from overseas by sailing ship in 1851 for an industry based in small workshops employing traditional methods of production. Steam power enabled larger ships to sail with ease to ports nearer to major centres of population, where steam powered factories using local coal could capitalise on economies of scale. Steam power then brought cheaper goods down to West Cornwall by rail to undercut the local products. The workshops of Penzance could not compete on level terms in mass markets but a few bespoke boot and shoemakers survived the initial onslaught. Even so, by 1891 few young men were following in their fathers' footsteps, to join a declining business.

Against the trend, one branch of leatherworking not only survived but expanded. In a generally more prosperous Penzance the numbers of horse-drawn cabs, omnibuses and carts had increased dramatically (causing the postmaster to complain to the council about the smell of ordure drifting into the Post Office from a nearby cab-stand). Where there were horses, saddlery was required.

By association, it might have been expected that the number of butchers and slaughterers in Penzance would have fallen over the 40 years but this did not happen. Penzance supplied meat over a wide area - there had been a large pork market at Redruth, and in Penzance the pork market had been deemed able to accommodate quite a throng if the day of the West Cornwall Railway's opening dawned wet.

The Harbour

The importance of the harbour to Penzance was mainly due to inward trade, serving the town and its hinterland. There was little local industry to use the harbour as a springboard for exports.

Richard Pearse, Lloyds Agent at Penzance, Consul for various nations, ship-owner and general merchant, stated in evidence before the House of Commons Committee that incoming trade amounted to 45,000 tons annually. This was a considerable volume of trade considering the small size of sailing merchantmen in those early Victorian days. Of that total, timber for the mines and the building trade was the single largest import, accounting for 14-15,000 tons annually, half coming from Norway and half from Canada. The balance was made up of coal from South Wales, flour from Ireland, hides from Buenos Aires (some 200 shiploads) and lesser tonnages of corn, tallow, hemp and other goods. Fish was also landed at Penzance - 4,000 tons in the year before the enquiry - but this trade was almost entirely due to adverse weather conditions. When easterly winds prevailed, the fish were landed at Penzance, to fetch what they could. When the winds were westerly, fish were taken direct to Southampton or Bristol.

Before the broad gauge link to London the only outward trade that might have provided a steady source of trade from Penzance harbour, market-garden produce, instead left via Hayle. From Hayle the produce was taken by steamer to Bristol, on Mondays and Thursdays, for onward carriage to London by the Great Western.

The numbers employed in the docks changed little between 1851 and 1891 and, apart from a falling off in the import of hides, the business conducted there also changed little. Because the railway into Cornwall was broad gauge, and the South Wales railways had been narrowed in the 1870s, it was always cheaper to bring coal to Cornwall by sea. Coal for the mines, domestic consumers, the Penzance gasworks (2,000 tons per annum) and the railway itself was therefore still brought in by ship and landed at Albert Pier, where the railway had laid down a siding, with cranage. Even after 1892, when broad gauge was abandoned, it was customary for coal for the mines and gasworks to be brought to Penzance by ship. The Great Western changed over to rail delivery, as one might expect, to supply its own needs.

Before the introduction of a dedicated service the up Mail train took modest quantities of fish. If the landings warranted it the railway would provide a special train and, in April 1868, 5,000 baskets of fish were dispatched from Penzance in three such trains. Swimming in the waters off Land's End on Friday morning and sold at Billingsgate early the following morning, the fish were eaten within 36 hours of being caught.

Penzance became an increasingly convenient harbour at which to land fish. The Great Western introduced a weekday 'Express Fish, Meat and Perishable' goods train to cater for the growing trade. In 1890 this train left Penzance at 12.30 pm, arriving at Paddington at 3.22 am, in time for the early market. Six-, and later eight-wheeled wagons were purpose-built for the carriage of fish, such was the importance of the trade. Seeing the better service available, steam trawlers from East Coast ports were quick to use Penzance as a landing stage for their catches. Local fishermen, dependent on sail and missing the best prices for early fish, responded by hiring a steam ship to pick up their catches at sea and collect fish from the Scillies. Their ship, the *Rover* could bring 100 tons of catches into harbour.

The Great Western exacted a considerable price for their monopoly service and, with the dealers and middlemen, shared the greatest part of the housewives' purchase price - and at no risk to themselves. Writing in the Post Office magazine J.G. Uren, Postmaster of Penzance, fulminated at length on the iniquity of a fisherman receiving only one-sixth of the final price for his work. His main target was the railway, which charged £4 per ton for carriage to London - 'Silk or tea can be brought from China, ton for ton, cheaper than fish can be carried from here [Penzance] to London'. Uren championed a narrow gauge connection between Penzance and the rest of the country, firing off a typical broadside in 1880:

> The evils resulting from the want of uniformity of gauge can hardly be estimated. Not only is the cost of making the line broad instead of narrow enhanced . . . at every point where the competing gauges converge [sic] there is serious interruption to the traffic. To say nothing of the passengers and their belongings which, to a certain extent, may

transfer themselves, it is calculated that the removal of 'goods' from one train to another is equal to a money tax of from 1s. 6d. to 2s. 6d. per ton. Take for instance the transfer of livestock. How it must weary and deteriorate the poor brutes to be bundled out of one truck into another when, but for the break, they might go straight through to their destination. Or, to come nearer home, who can say how many markets our fish and garden produce are shut out of simply owing to the break of gauge?

It was a legitimate grumble. London could be supplied by broad gauge, but the markets of Birmingham and the North had to await the conversion of the line to narrow gauge, in May 1892.

Post and Telegraph

Penzance had subsisted for centuries on locally based and managed employment but a change in business culture came in the latter decades of the 19th century with the dramatic increase in the number of working men who were answerable to distant employers, wore uniforms and were subject to well-codified disciplines.

When John George Uren became Postmaster of Penzance in 1864, after service in Falmouth, Devonport and Constantinople, he inherited an office staffed by a postmistress and just one assistant. The Post Office had been situated in various houses in Penzance occupied by the postmistress, chiefly in Chapel Street.

Uren was not only Postmaster, he also managed the Telegraph Office and as both services expanded the need for new premises became urgent. Uren procured a suitable site at the top of Market Jew Street, and, in the rather curious way such matters were then conducted by the Post Office, took out a long lease of it in his own name. At the time of the official opening of the new office, on 2nd November, 1883, the Penzance office staff numbered 40, including two superintendents and 30 clerks and carriers. In the year before moving to the new office, they had dealt with 60,000 telegrams and 2½ million letters, and took £100,000 in money orders and deposits in the savings bank. A far cry from 1864.

The railway regulated the postman's day. Mail arrived in Penzance just after 8 am and was sorted and on its delivery round by mid-morning. As Penzance served most of the Land's End peninsula a postman's round could be quite extensive and for some time letters between Penzance and Land's End were delivered by one postman, Bullock. For 18 shillings a week Bullock would walk 26 miles daily with a load that might weigh up to 30 lb. As he could neither read nor write the mail was placed in order for him before he set out and he was reputed never to have made a mistake. When he retired, at 70, his doctor advised him to leave off gradually - which advice he took by running errands for the farmer's wives! Between the railway and men such as Bullock a letter posted in London would reach its St Just destination the next day - a far cry from the mail coach days, when a letter might take three days to reach Penzance from London, and quite probably a speedier service than we can depend upon in the 21st century!

The Railway

The census of 1851 records that there were then four railway employees in Penzance. The West Cornwall was still over a year away from opening its terminus there and it is not surprising that all four were labourers. By 1891 Penzance had become the busy terminus of a broad gauge line extending to London and 106 staff were counted in the census that year. They included several lodgers, possibly caught by the ennumerator before returning to Plymouth or further afield, and it may be fair to suppose that a similar number of Penzance-based staff were counted elsewhere.

The growth of the railway population between the early, isolated West Cornwall days and the inclusion of Penzance in the national network is demonstrated by a comparison between the occupations of railway staffs in 1864, when a town directory was published, and 1891. Both sets of figures relate to men living within the Borough.

As early as 1864 skilled employees came to Penzance from elsewhere, the town having no skills base from which to provide staff such as drivers and firemen, and in 1891 only 11 staff out of 106 were born in Penzance. The Great Western encouraged mobility of staff, which was the way promotion was gained, and only local men close to retirement could be reckoned to make Penzance their permanent home.

	1864	1891
Railway officers	4	5
Drivers	3	17
Firemen	3	11
Fitters		6
Cleaners		10
Guards	6	20
Signalmen		3
Porters	8	14
Carriage examiner		1
Policemen		1
Lamp trimmers		1
Shunters		1
Labourers	2	3
Clerks	—	13
	26	106

Such was the ingrained sense of rank among staff in the railway that, in 1891, one of the Great Western staff lodging in Penzance insisted on being described in the census as a 'Rover' driver. And who would not have been proud of that?

The impact of the railway staff on Penzance was almost entirely in numerical terms only. While Mr Uren had his say on most amenity developments in the town, and fought to persuade the Elder Brethren of Trinity House to link their lighthouses to the mainland by telegraph, following the loss of the *Schiller* on the Isles of Scilly in 1875, the railway officers fought shy of wielding any influence in local matters. In Great Western days, where local matters were of concern to the railway it was generally from Paddington that any involvement came. In defence of the local railway staff, few owed any allegiance to the towns they lived in, for they were seldom in one spot for long. The local Postmaster, on the other hand, had a virtual freehold on his office.

The train services to and from Penzance had expanded considerably since the first years of the West Cornwall. By 1890, for example, the penultimate year of the broad gauge, there were 10 trains in to and out of Penzance each weekday, including seven up and six down passenger trains. The fastest train up to London was the 'Cornish Express' which departed from Penzance at 11.15 am and arrived at Paddington 8 hrs 35 mins later. The down 'Cornish Express' arrived at Penzance at 6.57 pm, having departed from Paddington at 10.15 am.

Train services from and to Penzance - 1890

Up trains

6.25 *am*	Fast passenger	arr. Paddington	6.00 *pm*
8.15	Express passenger	arr. Paddington	6.30
10.00	'North Mail'	arr. Paddington	10.20
11.15	'Cornish Express'	arr. Paddington	7.50
12.30 *pm*	Express fish etc.	arr. Paddington	3.22 *am*
1.45	Fast passenger	arr. Bristol	9.30 *pm*
3.20	Goods	arr. Bristol	4.20 *am*
5.00	'Night Mail'	arr. Paddington	4.00
6.25	Passenger	arr. Plymouth	10.26 *pm*
8.05	Passenger	arr. Truro	9.24

Down trains (arr.)

7.35 *am*	'Night Mail'	from Paddington	(dep.	9.00) *pm*
10.45	Passenger	from Plymouth	(dep.	6.50) *am*
12.42 *pm*	Passenger	from Plympton	(dep.	8.45)
1.40	Goods	from Bristol	(dep.	1.00)
2.50	Passenger	from Bristol	(dep.	6.15)
4.15	Newspaper	from Paddington	(dep.	5.30)
4.25	Goods	from Newham	(dep.	10.07)
6.57	'Cornish Express'	from Paddington	(dep.	10.15)
8.45	Passenger	from Paddington	(dep.	9.00)
9.00	Fast Express	from Paddington	(dep.	11.45)

Tourism

The later growth of the tourist industry is dealt with more fully in Chapter Five and here only the years up to 1891 will be considered.

In 1849, three years before the railway came to Penzance, a report on the town's condition was prepared by George T. Clark, Superintending Inspector of Public Health. He did not mince his words, as the following extracts make clear:

Public nuisances are tolerably numerous. The most considerable are the slaughter houses, of which there are 14 in the town and nine in one street. In several of the larger squares and courts are open dungheaps and cesspools . . . Dysentry prevails in the lowest part of the town . . . it is impossible in words to convey an adequate idea of the filth of the older and more densely peopled quarter of the town near the quay . . . There are eight low lodging-houses in various parts of the town; the persons frequenting them are dirty and objectionable, requiring the surveillance of the police . . . There are no sewers in Penzance, and no house drainage.

There was little in the report to encourage the notion of Penzance as a holiday resort and, as matters stood, the attractions of the neighbouring countryside would hardly make up for the discomforts of using the town as a holiday base.

Fortunately, matters were not allowed to stand. In the year following the report the provision of a decent sewage system was put in hand and the building of the railway station in 1851/52 also necessitated the sweeping away of some of the worst housing in the town.

Where might a tourist stay in Penzance? Clark identified 23 licensed public houses in 1849. Fifteen years later a directory of Penzance listed 20 Hotels and Inns. There was no indication in the list of the quality of each establishment but three inns and a like number of hotels took advertising space to proclaim their facilities for visitors. By the time an *Official Guide to Penzance* was published, *circa* 1876, the position had improved still further. Seven hotels are shown on the map accompanying the guide and the visitor had a 'Cricket and archery ground', three museums and a Billiard Club to cater for his amusement and edification. The historic and scenic sights of the Land's End peninsula are described in detail, villages such as Newlyn hardly at all.

The advertisements for the hotels show that the town was intent on attracting a discerning class of visitor. The Queens Hotel, on the Promenade, proclaimed 'This magnificent Hotel has recently been greatly enlarged, entirely re-arranged, and handsomely furnished' and made great play of having been patronised by HM the Queen of Holland. The principal staff came from outside Penzance - the chef was French and the waiters German. Mounts Bay House, on the Esplanade, was '. . . furnished in the most modern style . . . well supplied with Hot and Cold Baths and replete with every accommodation suitable for Tourists to West Cornwall'. All the hotels made a point of sending cabs to meet incoming trains.

Horse omnibuses ran regularly, and for hire, to the main tourist highlights and more sophisticated pleasures could be sampled in Penzance. Among those caught up in the census in 1891 were opera singers, touring thespians and music hall entertainers. By the time the Great Western came to promote the 'Cornish Riviera' a well-developed infrastructure was in place for the more discerning visitor.

The Artists

The spread of art schools after the Great Exhibition of 1851 gave rise to a surge in the number of young men and women who saw painting as a possible occupation. The better breeched among them found it a congenial way in which to spend, or eke out, their private means while others, less fortunate, hoped they might earn a decent living through their art. These young artists were gregarious by inclination and 'artists colonies' sprang up where there was good subject matter and, no less important, abundant and cheap accommodation. In the 1870s France, especially Brittany, was a prime destination for young artists from this country, from mainland Europe and as far afield as the United States.

By 1880 a 'colony' of artists was well established at Pont Aven, in Brittany and among the artists there, albeit briefly, was Walter Langley. He depended upon his art for a living and, with a wife and growing family in Birmingham, could not afford to stay long in Brittany. His more usual sketching ground had been the villages of the Warwickshire and Worcestershire Avon, where there was an abundance of picturesque subjects within an hour or so of home, but his visit to Brittany gave him a taste for travelling further afield.

In exhibitions in Birmingham, Langley had seen the work of other artists who had visited Cornwall and as the railway gave the Duchy the advantage of being readily accessible to home he, with a fellow Birmingham artist, Henry Pope, decided to go down there for a painting holiday in the early Summer of 1880. Langley's sketches that year show a preference for Newlyn and the nearby countryside and ready sales of his Newlyn work prompted him to return there in 1881 with another Birmingham artist, Edwin Harris. With a commission for a year's work, Langley finally settled in Newlyn with his family, early in 1882, the first artist to make the fishing village his home. He found in Newlyn subject matter he could respond to in his art, in the lives of the fishermen and women of the village and, in 1883, his first major paintings from Newlyn secured his recognition in London and brought the fishing village to the notice of other artists. Accessibility, by rail, good subject matter and cheap accommodation were all assured and artists came to settle in Newlyn and the surrounding area in increasing numbers - over 100 at one stage - and the 'Newlyn Colony' became the foremost colony of artists in the land.

Penzance had not been without home-grown art and the year Langley first came to the town, 1880, saw the building there of a new Art School. It was a somewhat bewildering experience for the local students to find so many professional artists in their midst, particularly as the latter were not over-ready at first to yield their trade secrets! Some artists, however, saw there was a further string to be added to their financial bow and established their own 'art schools' to cater for the amateur keen to follow in their footsteps. Elizabeth and Stanhope Forbes were particularly successful teachers and attracted many students to their classes.

In all this artistic development the railway played its part. Not only had it brought artists to the area, it catered for them in other ways. The great event of the artistic year was the sending up of paintings to the Royal Academy each Spring and the number of large canvasses dispatched from Penzance (and St Ives, where another colony was growing apace) was sufficient for a dedicated luggage van to be attached to the 'Flying Dutchman' express to take them to London. Where the paintings led, the artists followed, to see whether their work was well hung, to visit dealers and patrons, and meet relatives and friends.

The railway played an important part in the practical side of the artists' lives but it hardly featured at all in their work. One of Newlyn's foremost artists, Stanhope Forbes, had strong railway connections through his father and uncle, yet it was not until the 20th century that he turned to the railway for subject matter with posters for the London, Midland & Scottish Railway.

Bricks and Mortar

Penzance experienced a boom in private and public building in the last decades of the 19th century. The housing stock in 1851 was 1,875, by 1881 had risen to 2,303 and 10 years later stood at 2,564. The number of persons engaged in building and allied trades remained at a constant 17.2 per cent of the male working population.

Speculative building accounted for much of the increase in the housing stock and a considerable proportion of the new housing was for rent. This suited many incomers who, like the artists, could not be certain of the length of their stay. Needless to say, it also suited those who had no capital, or no desire to sink what capital they had in a home.

It was not only on house-building that the tradesmen were employed. As the town's prosperity increased a progressive Corporation engaged in improving the civic amenities. In 1867, public buildings were opened with great pomp and ceremony on lands north of Alverton. These housed the County Court, police station, cells, Guildhall and Council Chamber. Of more interest to the townspeople and visitors, perhaps, the building at Alverton also housed St John's Hall, where concerts and other entertainment could be held, and the renowned Geological Society had its home.

The original source of the town's prosperity, its harbour, was not neglected. The advent of steamships meant that there was no longer an urgent need to create at Penzance a harbour of refuge but rather a floating harbour at which ships could discharge their cargoes whatever the state of the tide. The work was put in hand, and completed by November 1884.

Conclusion

This has been but the briefest introduction to a subject that would bear further examination, and not only as regards Penzance. The railway link to Penzance from the rest of England could hardly have been expected to change radically the nature of a town so far from the main centres of population and, indeed, it has not. What it did achieve for Penzance was a sense of connection with the capital, and larger cities, through its express services.

It was inevitable, perhaps, that some industries would be affected by newly facilitated competition from 'up-country' but what was less certain in the early years was the extent to which local industry could use the railway to its advantage. The staple industries of fishing and market gardening benefited from swifter transport but there was little else in Penzance and the Land's End peninsula that stood to gain much from the coming of the railway.

An exception to the rule was the tourist industry, an industry barely in existence in 1852. From the outset the mass tourist market was eschewed in favour of a more thoughtful and genteel market. The character of Penzance has remained intact but the general prosperity of the townsfolk may have suffered as a result.

Penzance station, looking west on 16th August, 2001. A class '153' unit stands in platform 3 with a St Ives branch working. The overall roof had recently been repaired by Railtrack, but as there was no provision for smoke emission, HST units were not allowed to enter the covered parts of platforms 1, 2 and 3. Perhaps for that reason, platform 4 was frequently used by HST sets.

S.C. Jenkins

A detailed view of Penzance signal box on 16th August, 2001.   *S.C. Jenkins*

Chapter Nine

Into the Millennium

The end of the war in Europe was followed by the election of a Labour Government which had promised to bring the railway system into state ownership. Accordingly, on 1st January, 1948 a nationwide fanfare of locomotive whistles heralded the demise of the 'Big Four' railway companies and the creation of a new organisation known as British Railways. As we have seen, this radical change of ownership had little immediate effect, and the West Cornwall line and its branches was painlessly transformed into part of the Western Region of British Railways.

Privatisation

The British Railways era lasted for half a century between 1948 and the completion of a controversial privatisation process in 2000. During that time, the railway system was subjected to continual political interference, much of which was hostile if not downright vindictive. In the 1990s the Conservative party, having successfully privatised many other nationalised industries, decided to return the railways to private ownership.

As a first step towards this goal, the Government created a number of distinct train operating companies, several of which have already been mentioned in connection with train services on the West Cornwall line. As far as the West Cornwall route and its branches are concerned, the train operating companies involved were known as 'Great Western', 'Inter-City Cross Country', 'Regional Railways South Wales & West' and 'Rail Express Systems'. In the meantime, the locomotives and rolling stock that would be used by these and other companies on the privatised railway were allocated to three rolling stock leasing companies.

The rolling stock leasing companies were sold to private owners in November 1995, while in the next few weeks the American-based Wisconsin Central Transportation Corporation successfully bid for Rail Express Systems (RES) and BR's three main freight operating companies. On 4th February, 1996 the Great Western train operating company was sold to a management buy-out team, and Railtrack was itself sold in the following May. These developments left Cross Country Trains and the South Wales & West train operating company under state ownership, but a few months later it was announced that the latter company had been sold to a bus company.

The most important result of this policy was the creation of Railtrack as an infrastructure company, and the consequent fragmentation of the British railway network. The method of denationalisation adopted was extraordinary, in that it entailed a complete divorce between the railway network and the trains that were to run upon it. Moreover, the Tory theorists who concocted this unusual scheme envisaged that myriad train operators would compete with each other to run commercial services over the same stretches of line, the 'commercial' nature of these operations being heavily-subsidised by vast amounts of taxpayers' money.

In effect, this system harked back, not to the highly successful Victorian era, but to the Georgian period, when canal companies and tramways had allowed a diversity of different operators access to their systems in return for the payment of tolls. The 'last great privatisation' therefore turned the clock back 200 years, and destroyed the essential unity of a system that had been carefully built-up successively by the Hayle Railway, the West Cornwall Railway, the Associated Companies, the Great Western Railway, and finally BR. Political commentators wondered if the Tories were trying to privatise BR in such a way that the next Labour Government would be unable to unravel the resulting mess.

In the event, the private owners of Railtrack failed to provide investment - although the company continued to pay out dividends to its shareholders. This situation became unacceptable to the Labour Government which had inherited the situation from its predecessors, and in 2001 the company was placed in receivership. Despite these appalling problems, the privatised train operating companies managed to provide a viable service on the West of England main line.

There has been little change in terms of train services over the West Cornwall route, the principal trains between Paddington and Penzance being operated by First Great Western while the important long-distance express services between Cornwall and the Midlands, North and Scotland are handled by Virgin Cross-Country Trains. The 'Cornish Riviera Express' now leaves Paddington at 10.45 am in the down direction and 9.42 am in the up direction, while the 'Cornishman' leaves Penzance at 9.22 am in the up direction *en route* to Scotland; the return service arriving in Penzance at 9.24 pm. Wessex class '158' two-car units continue to provide useful secondary services over the West Cornwall line, while the same train operating company provides branch line services to Falmouth and St Ives.

Freight Traffic

Much interest surrounded the activities of the Wisconsin Central Transportation Corporation following its acquisition of a large part of the former British Railways freight operation. In its native North America, Wisconsin Central had successfully won back a significant proportion of freight traffic from rival road transport operators, much of this new traffic being in the form of wagon load consignments. It was suggested that similar business strategies could, be applied in Britain - with obvious ramifications for lines such as the West Cornwall route, which does not at the present time carry any freight traffic west of Truro.

It was, in general, much easier for freight traffic to be carried when suitable sidings and other infrastructure have regained *in situ*, and in this context the West Cornwall line is more fortunate than many other lines in that at least some residual trackwork has been retained at Penzance, St Erth, Truro and on the Falmouth branch. As we have seen, Truro has recently handled military and fertilizer traffic in its remaining bulk load sidings, while St Erth is being considered once again as a terminal for containerised milk traffic. Similarly, the neighbouring Falmouth branch has recently carried occasional consignments of containerised coal for local domestic consumption.

These modest traffic flows were the sort of business that Wisconsin Central - trading under its 'English Welsh & Scottish Railway' brand name, was expected to cultivate, and it is to be hoped that similar traffic can be brought back to the West Cornwall main line in the years to come.

The Role of the West Cornwall Railway

The West Cornwall Railway from Penzance to Truro, and the Cornwall Railway from there to Plymouth have, between them, served Cornwall well. Together, they form a vital economic lifeline that is as important today as it was in the Victorian era. The Cornish peninsula is, by English standards, a very long way from London and other large centres of population, and for this reason the railway has retained many advantages over rival forms of transport - this is certainly the case in terms of longer-distance journeys to or from London, Birmingham and other destinations in the Midlands or North.

Historically, the railway has etched itself into local folk memories and traditions in a way that is quite remarkable; so much so that Cornish people still speak of going 'up the line' when they travel up country. The term 'up the line' is also used as a euphemism for 'gone' or 'gone away' - a tangible legacy of the dark days of the 19th century mining depression, when thousands upon thousands of people left Cornwall in emigrant specials that took them to the ports on the first stage of their one-way journeys to new homes beyond the sea.

The late running or non-arrival of an important main line train such as the 'Cornishman' is sufficiently 'news worthy' for the information to be broadcast on local Cornish radio - and such late running can cause considerable disruption on connecting branch lines, with the consequent need to run fleets of taxis for travellers who would otherwise be stranded at junction stations such as Truro and St Erth. (More recently, this practice has ceased, but habitual travellers now claim significant refunds from the train operating companies if their connections are missed.)

There have, from time to time, been suggestions, that the West of England main line should, be cut back to Plymouth, leaving no more than a local service on the westernmost section from Plymouth to Penzance. Such a development would be a disaster, both for the railway and for Cornwall itself, which would thereby, become isolated from the main railway system. There is, fortunately, no suggestion that further contractions of the railway system are being planned at the present time. On the contrary, there are even one or two pieces of good news - notably the introduction of improved long distance provincial services under the Wessex and Wales & Borders 'Alphaline' banner, and the above-mentioned freight revivals. Hopefully, there will be more of these welcome developments in the years to come, as the privatised train operating companies introduce new initiatives in response to the needs of the travelling public. In this respect there might even be cause for cautious optimism, not just for the West Cornwall route, but for the railway network as a whole.

Acknowledgements

Research over a number of years inevitably brings one into contact with many people and if any who have helped us gather information about the West Cornwall Railway are not mentioned below it is an omission we regret and apologise for - we owe them thanks in equal measure to those named.

Documents relating to the West Cornwall and the Associated Companies are to be found in the Public Record Office at Kew, principally under RAIL, the Cornwall County Record Office, Truro, the House of Lords Library, and in private collections. Contemporary newspapers have been consulted at the Cornish Studies Library, Redruth, the Morrab Library, Penzance, the University of Leicester Library and Falmouth Public Library. Our thanks are due to the ever-helpful staff of all those bodies.

We would like to thank the following for the help, always willingly given, that they extended to us and for many constructive suggestions along the way:

Alan Garner, Sam Bee, Mike Jolly, Peter Totman, Pat English and
  Russell McCoy of the Broad Gauge Society
Dr Michael R. Bailey, Stephenson Locomotive Society
Tom Richards of the Firefly Trust
Ken Surman, Great Western Society
Jonathan Holmes, Penlee House Gallery & Museum, Penzance
Ted Thoday, Western Australia
Peter Treloar
Chris Turner
John M. Strange
The late John L. Smith of Lens of Sutton
John Cummings
John Alsop

We hope that publication will result in more information coming to the surface and the uncovering of any errors in this account (which are down to us).

Stanley C. Jenkins & Roger Langley
2002

Bibliography and Further Reading

MacDermot's *History of the Great Western Railway* and the relevant volumes of *The Locomotives of the Great Western Railway*, published by The Railway Correspondence and Travel Society, have been invaluable sources of information.

At first glance, the following list would appear to contain ample material on the West Cornwall Railway, but on closer examination it will be seen that many of the listed books and articles relate to locomotives, rather than railway history. In fact, very little has ever been written on the railway history of Cornwall, the West Cornwall company being a particularly neglected subject. Happily, considerable work has been undertaken at various times on Cornish local history, and some of the many books available on this interesting county have been included in the bibliography.

Angove, Richard, Penzance Reassured, *The Railway Magazine*, March 1977

Anthony, G.H., *The Hayle, West Cornwall & Helston Railways* (1968), Oakwood Press

Bailey, H.T.S., Over the Wall: Reminiscences of Penzance, *Railway World* May 1968

Barton, D.B., *A History of Copper Mining in Cornwall* (1961), Truro Bookshop

Barton, D.B., *The Cornish Beam Engine: Its History & Development* (1965)

Bennett, A., The Making of the Cornish Riviera, *Railway World*, April 1984

Broad Gauge Society publications (Broadsheets and Newsletters)

Carter, Clive, *The Port of Penzance* (1998)

Copsey, John, Cornish Halls in the 1930s, *Great Western Railway Journal*, Cornish Special Issue, 1992

Copsey, John, Granges at Work, *Great Western Railway Journal*, Nos. 27 & 28, 1998

Copsey, John, The Aberdare 2-6-0s, *Great Western Railway Journal* No. 21, 1997

The Cornishman, passim

The Cornish Telegraph, passim

Croucher, Andrew, Brunel's Grandeur in Wood, *The Railway Magazine,* January 1994

Cummings, John, *Railway Motor Buses & Bus Services* (1980), Oxford Publishing Co.

Curnow, W. H., *Industrial Archaeology of Cornwall*

English, Pat, Gwinear Road Station, *Model Railway News*, February 1967

Fairclough, A., *The Story of Cornwall's Railways* (1970), Tor Mark Press

The Falmouth Packet, passim

Farr, K.S., Seventy-five Years of the Cornish Riviera, *The Railway Magazine,* July 1979

Farr, Keith, The County Set, *The Railway Magazine*, February 1967

Fenton, D., Brunel Viaduct in N Gauge, *Railway Modeller*, October 1969

Freezer, Cyril J., Locomotives of the GWR: Bulldog & Dukedog, *Railway Modeller*, December 1967

Freezer, Cyril J., Locomotives of the GWR: The Moguls, *Railway Modeller*, August 1968

Freezer, Cyril J., Locomotives of the GWR: The Halls, *Railway Modeller, June* 1969

Freezer, Cyril J., Locomotives of the GWR: The Last of the 4-6-0s, *Railway Modeller*, November 1968

Freezer, Cyril J., Locomotives of the GWR: The Smallest Prairies, *Railway Modeller*, December 1968

Freezer, Cyril J., Locomotives of the GWR: The 45XXs, *Railway Modeller,* January 1969

Freezer, Cyril J., Locomotives of the GWR: Granges & Manors, *Railway Modeller*, June 1968

Freezer, Cyril J., Locomotives of the GWR: The Aberdares, *Railway Modeller,*
   July 1969
Freezer, Cyril J., Locomotives of the GWR: No. 34, *Railway Modeller,* March 1968
Great Western Railway, *Traffic Dealt with at Stations & Goods Depots, passim* (PRO
   RAIL 253/45)
Great Western Railway, *Holiday Haunts, passim*
Great Western Railway, *Towns, Villages, Outlying Works etc* (1938)
Great Western Railway, *Working & Public Timetables, passim*
Guy, Andy, *Early English Railways*
Hamilton Jenkin, A.K., *Cornish Seafarers* (1932)
Hamilton Jenkin, A.K., *Cornwall & the Cornish* (1933)
Hamilton Jenkin, A.K., *Cornish Homes & Customs* (1934)
Hamilton Jenkin, A.K., *The Cornish Miner* (1927)
Heaps, Chris, The Helston Railway 1887-1964, *Railway World* November 1964
Holmes, Jonathan, *Penzance & Newlyn* (1992)
Institute of Civil Engineers Minutes (1851-1852)
Jenkins, Stanley C., *The Helston Branch Railway* (1992), Oakwood Press
Jenkins, Stanley C., Steam Days at Truro, *Steam Days* No. 125, January 2000
Jenkins, Stanley C., Steam Days at Penzance, *Steam Days* No. 152, April 2002
Jenkins, Stanley C., The St Ives Branch, *Great Western Railway Journal,* Cornish
   Special Issue, 1992
Jenkins, Stanley C., The Helston Branch, *Back Track,* November-December 1989
Jenkins, Stanley C., The Falmouth Branch, *British Railway Journal* No. 27 1989
Langley, Roger, *Walter Langley: Pioneer of the Newlyn Art Colony* (1997)
Lowe, A.C.M., The West Cornwall Railway, *The Locomotive Magazine,* December
   1938 & January 1939
MacDermot, E.T., *History of the Great Western Railway, Vol. II* (1927), GWR
Noah, Cyril, *A History of Cornish Mail & Stage Coaches*
Noah, Cyril, *Cornish Seines & Seiners (1972)*
Nock, O.S., The Cornish Riviera Express, *The Railway Magazine,* June 1970
Nock, O.S., *History of the Great Western Railway, Vol. III* (1967), Ian Allan
Palin, Michael, *Happy Holidays: The Golden Age of Railway Posters* (1987), Pavillion
Pitt, Rodney, Hall of Fame, *The Railway Magazine,* January 1973
Pool, P. A., *The History of the Town & Borough of Penzance* (1974)
The Railway Times, passim
The Royal Cornwall Gazette, passim
Salmon, Arthur L, *The Little Guide to Cornwall* (1903)
Semmens, P.W.B., *The Heyday of GWR Train Services* (1990), David & Charles
St John Thomas, David, *A Regional History of the Railways of Great Britain: Vol. 1
   The West Country (1960)*, David & Charles
Tangye, Michael, *Portreath* (1968)
Tangye, Peter, The West Cornwall Railway and the Broad Gauge, *HMRS Vol. 14*
Thomas, Charles, *Views and Likenesses* (1988)
Thorne, Graham, *The Portreath Branch* (1991)
Uren, John G., Published letters and articles.
Uren, Thomas A., Dr Dadgers (unpublished biography)
The West Briton, passim
Woodfin, R.L, *The Cornwall Railway* (1972), W. Jefferson & Son
Young, Robert, *Timothy Hackworth and the Locomotive* (1923)

Index

Abolition of broad gauge, 105-7
Accidents, 17, 18, 58 ff., 85, 95, 97, 102, 121
Acts of Parliament, 26, 28, 34, 39, 42, 63, 67
Adams, W.B., 57
Angarrack, 7, 10, 12, 15, 16, 17, 18, 22 ff., 35, 37, 103, 104, 189, 191
Apollo, locomotive, 83, 87
Appleby, Henry, 50, 53, 61, 83, 97
Associated Companies, the, 4, 41, 53, 60, 61, 62 ff., 104, 234
Atmospheric traction, 22, 24, 25
Avonside, Messrs, 83, 85, 87, 91
Baldhu, 104
Barlow rails, 28-9, 39, 47, 51, 62
Barlow, W.H., 28-9
Blackwater Jn, 159, 163
Blackwater viaduct, 37, 102, 103, 159
Bodmin & Wadebridge Railway, 9, 43
Bone, John, 61
Borrie, Peter & Co., 48, 49
Bristol & Exeter Railway, 22, 41, 43, 46, 57, 62, 67, 79, 85, 94, 99
British Railways, 4, 119, 131 ff., 137 ff., 151 ff., 164, 181, 210, 233, 234
Broad gauge rails laid, 42, 63
Brunel, Isambard K., 23 ff., 29, 34 ff., 47, 48, 60, 171, 181, 205
Brunton, William, 27, 49, 51, 60, 223
Bush, H., 62, 63
Camborne, 7 ff., 23, 31, 33, 35, 45 ff., 65, 97, 100, 103, 104, 118, 173, 177 ff., 199
Camborne, locomotive, 49, 50
Camping coaches, 209, 210
Carn Brea, 11, 12, 15, 31, 35, 46 ff., 69, 73, 77, 85 ff., 97, 105, 118, 173, 176
Carn Brea, locomotive, 48 ff., 77, 83, 85
Ceres, locomotive, 83, 85, 87
Chacewater, 35, 37, 95, 102, 104, 118, 158 ff.
Chacewater viaduct, 37, 103, 159
Chanter, J., 48
Chanter, locomotive, 48, 49, 50
Charlton, C.P., 60, 61
Copperhouse, 10, 11, 12, 16, 49, 58, 191
Cornishman, the, 109, 111, 154, 234, 235
Cornish Riviera Express, 107-111, 119, 129, 131, 135, 137, 139, 234
Cornubia, locomotive, 12, 48, 49, 50
Cornwall Minerals Railway, 57, 87
Cornwall Railway, 22, ff., 33, 34, 41, 42, 45, 46, 47, 62, 97, 99, 100, 145, 155, 189, 235
Coryndon, locomotive, 48, 49, 50
Country Lorry Centres, introduction of, 117
Cyclops, locomotive, 83, 85, 87
Davy, Sir Humphry, 6, 33
Denbigh, G.S., 62, 97
Dieselisation, 137 ff.
Directors' names, 26, 61

Dolcoath, 177, 178
Doubling of the line (list), 104
Drump Lane goods depot, 104, 165, 169
Dublin & Kingstown Railway, 24
Electrification scheme, proposed GWR, 135, 137
Falmouth, 6, 13, 19, 22 ff., 42, 101 ff., 109, 121 ff., 135, 145 ff., 154, 155, 203, 234, 235
Falmouth, locomotive, 50, 51, 53, 83, 85, 87
Ferguson, H.T., 67, 98
Fiennes, Celia, 6
Fishing industry, 21, 33, 99, 219, 221, 225, 231
Flying Dutchman, the, 100, 109, 111, 230
Fox, locomotive, 83, 85, 87
Fulton, Robert, 6
Gooch, Sir Daniel, 118-9
Great Blizzard (1891), 100-2
Guildford viaduct, 103, 191
Gwinear Road, 4, 18, 35, 38, 59, 100 ff., 183 ff., 195
GWR, 4, 12, 22, 24, 26, 35, 43, 46, 49, 57, 61, 62 ff., 99 ff., 145 ff., 181 ff., 225, 227, 229, 234
GWR bus services, 111-6
Harvey & Co., 10, 26, 37, 48, 58, 177
Harvey, Henry, 11
Hayle, 7 ff., 16, 23 ff., 35, 45, 46, 48, 58, 60, 61, 69, 77, 85, 95, 102, 103, 104, 118, 171, 191 ff., 199, 206, 225
Hayle Foundry, 10, 11, 37, 176
Hayle Harbour, 10, 55, 58
Hayle, locomotive, 50, 51, 53, 77, 83
Hayle Railway, 4, 10 ff., 22 ff., 38, 45 ff., 61, 63, 69, 104, 171, 173, 176, 183, 192, 199, 234
Hayle Railway locomotives (list), 50
Hayle viaduct, 36, 37, 58, 103, 199
Hayle Wharves, 11, 12, 17, 38, 85, 191, 192, 195, 196, 197, 199
Helston, 6, 9, 10, 62, 67, 100 ff., 183, 207
Helston, locomotive, 50, 51, 53, 83, 88
Helston Railway (Branch), 4, 100, 102, 109, 125, 135, 183 ff., 189
Ironsides, locomotive, 49, 50, 51
James, William, 9
Jenkin, S.W., 187
Johnson, W., 25
Kirtley, Matthew, 53, 63
Laffan, Captain, 31, 47
Lance, locomotive, 89, 91
Langley, Walter, 230
Ley, Edwin (promoter), 60
Liveries, 57, 88, 135, 143
Llynvi & Ogmore Railway, 83, 85, 88, 93
LNWR, 49, 53, 83, 85, 123, 127
Locomotive list, Hayle Railway, 50
Locomotive list, WCR, 50, 53, 83
London & Croydon railway, 48, 49

Long Rock, 207, 211, 212, 219
LSWR, 22, 42, 43, 67
Manchester, Sheffield & Lincolnshire
   Railway, 61, 97
Marazion (Road), 23, 31, 35, 37, 47, 65, 91,
   103, 104, 113, 117 ff., 189, 205 ff., 217
Margary, Peter, 187
Mars, locomotive, 83, 85, 87
Merz & McLellan, 135, 137
Midland Railway, 28, 53, 63, 67
Mining industry, 5 ff., 38, 163, 169, 173, 176,
   177, 183, 203, 219, 221, 222, 223
Moorsom, Capt. W.S., 23-24, 27, 28, 29, 60
Motive power, 48 ff., 77 ff., 119 ff., 151, 211
Mounts Bay, locomotive, 50, 51, 53, 83, 88
Murdoch, William, 7
Nationalisation, 131, 233
Nestor, locomotive, 83, 87
Newcomen, Thomas, 7
Newham (Truro), 33-5, 37, 38, 41, 51, 63, 69,
   73, 77, 95, 145, 151, 153 ff.
North Crofty, 12, 38, 173, 177
Official opening (WCR), 31-3
Olver, Thomas & Son, 187
Oxford, Worcester & Wolverhampton
   Railway, 37, 195, 205
Pendarves, locomotive, 48, 49
Penponds, 10, 12, 15, 16, 17, 21, 22, 25, 28, 29,
   37, 58, 103, 171, 183
Penryn, 22, 25, 31, 34
Penwith, locomotive, 50, 51, 53, 83, 85, 89
Penwithers Jn, 34, 37, 42, 58, 59, 85, 95, 103,
   104, 154, 155, 159
Penwithers viaduct, 37, 102, 159
Penydarren Tramroad, 8
Penzance, 6, 13, 16, 20 ff., 28, 35, 40, 45 ff., 55,
   59, 60, 61, 62 ff., 82, 99 ff., 103, 105, 108,
   145 ff., 191, 195, 205 ff., 221 ff., 234, 235
Penzance, locomotive, 29, 49, 50, 51, 53, 83, 88
Penzance viaduct, 37-9, 47, 65, 102, 108, 205,
   206
Permanent way, 28, 29, 39, 47, 66
Perranporth branch, 145, 147, 151, 159 ff.
Pike, R.H., 60
Poldice, 8, 21, 163
Ponsandane, 103, 104, 199, 211, 213 ff.
Ponsonooth, 26
Pool, 10, 11, 12, 16, 19, 35, 173
Portreath, 7 ff., 10 ff., 18 ff., 36, 38, 42, 45, 55,
   61, 77, 85 ff., 91, 118, 163, 169, 173, 176
Privatisation, effects of, 233 ff.
Redruth, 8, 10, 11, 12, 13, 15, 16, 18, 21 ff., 29,
   31, 35, 37 ff., 42, 43, 45, 46, 47, 55, 57, 61,
   63, 69 ff., 85, 88, 91, 94, 102, 104, 117, 164
   ff., 173, 176, 177, 183, 189, 199, 224
Redruth & Chasewater Railway, 9, 10, 12, 21
Redruth, locomotive, 50, 51, 53, 57, 83, 85, 89
Redruth viaduct, 36, 37, 68, 103, 171, 172

Ritson (contractor), 28, 29, 39
Road motor services, 111 ff.
Rolling stock, 55, 57, 88, 91 ff., 135
Roman occupation, 5
Roskear, 10, 12, 38, 118, 177
Roskear Junction, 177, 178
St Erth (St Ives Road), 6, 10, 31, 35, 38, 67, 99,
   103, 104, 109, 111, 197 ff., 234, 235
St Ives, 22, 26, 60, 67, 69, 99, 105, 107, 109,
   111, 113, 116, 118, 119, 125, 135, 139, 199,
   203, 205 ff., 219, 221, 234
St Ives, locomotive, 50, 51, 53, 83, 88
St Just, locomotive, 50, 53, 85, 83, 87, 95
St Michael's Mount, 205
Sandhills, 10, 11
Sandys, Carne & Vivian, 49, 50
Scorrier, 8, 35, 38, 104, 162 ff.
Sedley, locomotive, 91
Sheriff, J.D., 61, 62, 97
Slater, Mr, 61
Slaughter, Gruning, 50, 53, 83, 89
Somerset & Dorset Railway, 67, 85
South Devon Railway, 22, 24, 41, 43, 46, 53,
   62, 67, 69, 73, 83, 88 ff., 97, 98, 99, 195
South Wales Railway, 37, 205
Stephenson, R. & Co., 50, 51, 53, 59, 75, 83,
   85, 87
Stockton & Darlington Railway, 49, 52
Stothert & Slaughter, 49, 50, 51, 53, 83, 89, 91
Tourism, 118, 119, 228, 229
Tregenna Castle Hotel, 118, 119
Tremenheere, Seymour, 22, 27, 43
Tresavean, 10, 12, 17, 19, 21, 38, 171, 176
Trevithick, Francis, 53, 57
Trevithick, Richard, 8, 51, 53
Truro, 6, 13, 16, 22 ff., 34, 41, 45 ff., 55, 59, 63
   ff., 99 ff., 106, 144 ff., 177, 183, 195, 199,
   206, 234, 235
Truro, locomotive, 50, 51, 53, 59, 60, 83, 85
Truro Road (Higher Town), 33 ff., 61
Truro viaduct (Cornwall Railway), 145
Uniforms, West Cornwall, 61, 97
Uren, J.G., 222, 225-226
Vignoles rail, 47
Vigurs, Louis (WCR Chairman), 26, 60
Vulcan Foundry, 53, 83, 87
Watt, James, 7
WCR goods stock (list), 55, 87, 93
WCR locomotives (list), 50, 53, 83
WCR stations (list), 35
WCR viaducts (list), 37
Western National Omnibus Co., 113 ff.
Wheal Buller, 9, 21, 38
Wheal Crofty, 10
Wills, H.O., 28, 60, 107
World War II, 119, 129, 137, 153
Yolland, Colonel, 42, 65